Forever New

Forever New

The Speeches of

JAMES WRIGHT,

President of

Dartmouth College,

1998–2009

Edited by SHEILA CULBERT

DARTMOUTH COLLEGE PRESS

Hanover, New Hampshire

Dartmouth College Press

An imprint of University Press of New England

www.upne.com

© 2012 Trustees of Dartmouth College

All rights reserved

Manufactured in the United States of America

Designed by Richard Hendel

Typeset in Arnhem and Quadraat Sans types

by Tseng Information Systems, Inc.

For permission to reproduce any of the material in this book,
contact Permissions, University Press of New England, One Court Street,
Suite 250, Lebanon NH 03766; or visit www.upne.com

Page 244 constitutes a continuation of the copyright page.

Library of Congress Cataloging-in-Publication Data

Wright, James Edward, 1939– author.
Forever new: the speeches of James Wright, President of Dartmouth
College, 1998–2009 / Edited by Sheila Culbert.
    pages cm
ISBN 978-1-61168-332-5 (cloth: alk. paper)—
ISBN 978-1-61168-333-2 (ebook) (print)
1. Dartmouth College—Presidents. 2. College orations—Dartmouth
College. I. Culbert, Sheila, editor of compilation. II. Title.
LD1443.W75 2012
378.742´3—dc23   2012014972

5 4 3 2 1

In memory of

Edward Connery Lathem

Librarian of the College

and

Editor Extraordinaire

CONTENTS

Acknowledgments / ix

Introduction by Sheila Culbert / xi

1. APPOINTMENT AS PRESIDENT OF DARTMOUTH COLLEGE

Remarks following the Announcement by the Board of Trustees,
    April 6, 1998 / 3

Dartmouth: Forever New, September 23, 1998 / 10

2. CONVOCATION ADDRESSES, 1999–2008

September 21, 1999 / 24

September 19, 2000 / 31

September 24, 2001 / 35

September 24, 2002 / 40

September 23, 2003 / 46

September 21, 2004 / 54

September 20, 2005 / 60

September 19, 2006 / 65

September 25, 2007 / 70

September 23, 2008 / 74

3. SELECTED SPEECHES ON VARIOUS TOPICS, 1999–2009

Address to First-Year Students, September 15, 1999 / 81

Report to the General Faculty, October 18, 1999 / 86

Class of 1950 Reunion Luncheon, June 10, 2000 / 94

Libraries in the Cyber Age, July 12, 2000 / 98

Growing and Preserving: A Mutual Challenge, November 26, 2000 / 106

Remarks to the Alumni Council, May 18, 2001 / 109

Address Delivered at Beijing Normal University, October 10, 2002 / 114

Remarks to the Alumni Council, May 2, 2003 / 121

Unleashed: Mobile Computing Conference, October 8, 2003 / 129

Remarks to Class Officers, September 16, 2004 / 133

Remarks in Memory of David T. McLaughlin '54 Tu '55,
    President Emeritus of the College, October 4, 2004 / 140
The Leslie Conference on the Future of the Liberal Arts,
    November 6, 2004 / 144
Dartmouth Lawyers Association, October 11, 2003 / 152
Remarks at the Memorial Service for James O. Freedman,
    Fifteenth President of Dartmouth College, May 15, 2006 / 159
Athletics and Life: Essay for the Class of 1964, on Its
    Fiftieth Reunion, 2007 / 164
Honoring Veterans, October 6, 2007 / 170
Eleventh Annual Report to the General Faculty,
    October 27, 2008 / 172
The Yellow Ribbon Program and Private Colleges,
    February 2, 2009 / 185
Veterans Day at the Vietnam Memorial Wall, Washington, D.C.,
    November 11, 2009 / 196

4. COMMENCEMENT ADDRESSES, 1999–2009
    June 13, 1999 / 202
    June 11, 2000 / 205
    June 10, 2001 / 208
    June 9, 2002 / 211
    June 8, 2003 / 214
    June 13, 2004 / 217
    June 12, 2005 / 220
    June 11, 2006 / 222
    June 10, 2007 / 224
    June 8, 2008 / 227
    June 14, 2009 / 230

5. FAREWELL
    Letter to the Dartmouth Community, June 29, 2009 / 235
    A Welcome to the Wheelock Succession, September 22, 2009 / 242

ACKNOWLEDGMENTS

I had the great privilege of working with President Wright as his chief of staff during most of his presidency. These were years of enormous professional satisfaction and growth for me as I learned so much from Jim, and so this undertaking—the compilation of some of his speeches—was a true pleasure. Throughout his presidency Jim Wright saw himself first and foremost as a teacher-scholar, and this identity comes through clearly in his speeches. The selections included in this volume should provide readers with a sense of the depth of his commitment to Dartmouth College, to the education of young people, and to the creation of new knowledge.

A number of people deserve my sincere thanks in bringing this collection to publication. Steve Roth '64, trustee and friend of Dartmouth and of Jim Wright, who made the publication of this collection of speeches possible. Louise Moon, assistant to the president emeritus, who helped to compile and locate many of the speeches included; Cheryl Reynolds, the secretary to the Board of Trustees for both Jim Wright and his predecessor James O. Freedman, who helped in multiple ways with the selection and editing. I would also like to acknowledge former provost and Mandel Family Professor of Russian, Barry Scherr, for his advice and help in coordinating this publication. Finally, I would like to thank my husband Richard Wright for his ongoing support and encouragement.

INTRODUCTION

Jim Wright is an unabashed optimist. As his speeches reveal, he believes in the fundamental values that shaped the American republic—opportunity and accessibility, individuality and a shared sense of community. He carried this idealism into his presidency of Dartmouth College and, indeed, throughout his career as teacher and historian. As you will see in the speeches included here, as president he returned to these themes over and over again.

Wright—president of Dartmouth from 1998 to 2009, and before that provost, acting president, dean of faculty, associate dean, and respected member of the history department—grew up in decidedly modest circumstances in Galena, Illinois. While his father was serving in the army and his mother working in a defense plant, Jim Wright spent a considerable part of his childhood with his grandparents. His grandfather worked in the mines and, during the Great Depression, when work was hard to find, his grandmother took in laundry. His parents never owned their own house, and they didn't get a car until Wright was in his teens. Modest though it was, it was also a childhood that he looks back on fondly. In that close-knit working-class community, children grew up expecting to work in the mines, on their family farms, or at the local factories. Few if any went on to college. True to form, as soon as he finished high school, the seventeen-year old Wright, along with four of his best friends, joined the U.S. Marine Corps, where he served for three years. As luck would have it, he served between the Korean and Vietnam Wars, so never saw combat, but he made a lot of friends and saw the world.

The military opened up his horizons, including the idea of a college education. At the end of his service, he applied to Wisconsin State University-Platteville. He paid his way through college by working various jobs, including as a powder man in the mines setting dynamite charges, and also as a bartender, night watchman, and janitor. Ever present, on his desk—during his years as a professor, later as president, and now in retirement—is the small powder man's knife, with its hilt wrapped in black electrician's tape, that he used in the mines to split the paraffin on dynamite sticks. He would tell students who asked about it that it reminded him of where he had come from, and he would urge them to never forget where they came from either.

His time at college was exciting. This was the 1960s, and he was intellectually challenged by the work and encouraged by the opportunities now available to him. He loved reading and history and talking with faculty and his fellow students about ideas. After his undergraduate career, Jim received a fellowship from the Danforth Foundation that made it possible for him to pursue graduate study at the University of Wisconsin at Madison, where he earned master's and doctoral degrees in history and where he studied with the distinguished American historian Allan G. Bogue. On completion of his graduate work, Dartmouth's History Department offered him an appointment as assistant professor of American History beginning in July 1969. Against all the odds he had landed a position at an Ivy League institution. Jim and his family, now including three small children, drove from Wisconsin to New Hampshire that summer, through upstate New York, amid the traffic and hitchhikers returning from Woodstock.

At Dartmouth, he quickly became one of the most popular faculty members in the department with his courses on the American West, American politics, and the US survey course. He was promoted to associate professor in 1974 and to professor of history in 1980. David Shribman, a member of the Class of 1976 and one of Jim Wright's students, described him this way:

> He stood there in front of the lectern at 105 Dartmouth Hall and told the most remarkable stories. About cattlemen and ranchers. About the role barbed wire played in the building of the West. About fights over water, and land, and (Native American) souls. About how Hollywood created its own West. About how the West was not so much a place as an idea. . . . He told them in such a marvelous way. . . . I remember how I was hooked on Jim Wright's voice and on the man and on the way he looked at the world. I was so hooked that I called up my father, himself a Dartmouth '47, and told him he had to get in the car and drive up here and listen to this man lecture. Just how often has a Dartmouth student demanded that his father drive to college to hear a history lecture? In the dead of a New Hampshire winter?

First students—and then alumni and alumnae—became hooked on Jim Wright's lectures, and he became especially popular on the alumni circuit. The Class of 1964 adopted him as a member, while the Class of 1969 adopted Susan Wright, who was equally beloved of Dartmouth alumni. His first alumni trip was to the Rocky Mountain Club in Denver, Colorado in 1970. John Kemeny had just recently been elected president, and there was a great deal of buzz among alumni about the college becoming co-educational as well as about the antiwar protests on campus. Not surprisingly, the conversation in Denver was lively, but Wright loved these discussions with alumni around the important issues facing the college. He participated in numerous alumni seminars, and his lectures with English Professor Jim Epperson in the 1978 Alumni College on the topic "Where Have All the Heroes Gone?" became a classic of the alumni circuit.

He was not only a popular professor; he was also a distinguished historian. A specialist in American political history with a focus on the history of the American West, he is the author or editor of five books: *The Galena Lead District: Federal Policy and Practices, 1824–1847* (1966); *The West of the American People* (1970); *The Politics of Populism: Dissent in Colorado* (1974); *The Great Plains Experience: Readings in the History of a Region* (1978); and *The Progressive Yankees: Republican Reformers in New Hampshire* (1987). He received a Social Science Research Council Grant, a Guggenheim Fellowship, and a Charles Warren Fellowship at Harvard.

As a graduate student Jim Wright had been among the pioneers in using statistical analysis in his research. As a young faculty member in the 1970s, he early recognized the power of film in teaching history and was involved in a number of television projects. In the late 1970s he was the senior historian for a six-film series on the history of the Great Plains that received eight awards. Later, he was appointed chair of the Organization of American Historians Committee on Television, Film, and Media. He not only wanted to excite a passion for history in his students; he also wanted to expand their understanding of what was history and who should be included. And he wanted to share this understanding with a broader public.

Wright was actively involved in creating the Native American Studies Program in 1972, having chaired the faculty committee that recommended the program's establishment. He was equally supportive of the Women's Studies and African and African American Studies Programs. In a 1997 speech to the Black Alumni of Dartmouth, then Dean of Faculty James Wright explained his approach to diversity in the curriculum. He told the assembled alumni that while the critics said there was a political agenda surrounding the work to diversify the curriculum,

> it is a political agenda that is rooted in the founding values of this Republic. . . . Students and faculty gain intellectually from a more diverse campus. Diversity among students and faculty helps us all to understand the complicated richness of the world in which we live. A campus that values difference and that supports diversity is a campus that encourages its members to explore the complexities that are central to the intellectual life. . . . We need to educate our students to understand and appreciate difference while at the same time encouraging them to be inclusive and pluralistic. This is not social engineering as some critics have claimed. It is fundamentally a matter of education.

It was not surprising that in 1978 President John Kemeny and Dean of Faculty Leonard Rieser asked Jim Wright to chair a comprehensive review of the curriculum and of the recently introduced year-round calendar—probably his first introduction to academic politics on a grand scale. It was a significant assignment for an associate professor. The committee took on the politically delicate issue of whether to require certain common courses of undergraduates, and apparently the faculty could agree on very little. At times he felt frustrated and defeated. Indeed, on one occasion he ran into former President John Dickey in the library, who asked him how things were going. Jim explained that they were not going particularly well and that it looked as if the faculty would vote down many of the committee's recommendations. President Dickey responded by saying that changing an academic institution was a slow business that took many years. Mr. Dickey went on to tell him that he could think of no single instance in his own presidency that had fundamentally changed the college. Rather, the changes that he had accomplished had been the result of a slow accretion of smaller changes and of processes that engaged a wide range of people. He urged Jim Wright not to give up.

Mr. Dickey's encouragement was a lesson that Wright would remember throughout his own administrative career, culminating in his presidency: to accomplish your vision you need patience, the political skill to bring along others, and an unwavering belief in what you are doing.

Eventually, following the recommendations of another curriculum review committee that President James Freedman asked then Dean of Faculty Wright to chair, in 1990–91, the faculty adopted all of that committee's proposals. Many were the same as or similar to those the Wright Committee had recommended in the 1970s. After the faculty vote in support of the new curriculum, Wright said that he immediately thought of Mr. Dickey's advice.

In 1981, Dean of the Faculty of Arts and Sciences Hans Penner asked Wright to serve as the associate dean of faculty for the social sciences (1981–85), his first administrative appointment. He went on to serve two terms as dean of the Faculty of Arts and Sciences (1989–97), a six-month stint as acting president (1995), and a year as provost (1997–98). In 1998 the Board of Trustees elected Jim Wright as the sixteenth president of Dartmouth College. In his ten-year report, prepared in 2008, Wright reflected on his forty years at the college:

> The Dartmouth that I came to in 1969 was a different school in so many ways from Dartmouth today. It was a school with 3,200 undergraduates, all men of course, and probably less than 10 percent students of color and fewer than one hundred international students. We were on a conventional nine-month calendar, with Saturday classes. There were only a few off-campus programs—essentially language instruction programs conducted in Western Europe. The three professional schools were still called "affiliated" schools. Most faculty lived in Hanover and largely spent their days in their offices or laboratories and were avuncular advisers to students on all matters, academic and personal. . . .
>
> Today Dartmouth is a far richer, less homogeneous place, one that operates around the year and around the world, and our affiliated schools have become exceptional professional schools. Dartmouth functions in an environment that is more laden with governmental regulations and demands, with a range of compliance restrictions, with governmental oversight defining some basic relationships between the college and its students. We are part of a global society and subject to the patterns of a global economy.

Jim Wright was very much a part of those changes; he had spent his career making Dartmouth an academically stronger, more diverse, and more fully integrated school. He insisted that diversity supported the strong teaching culture and sense of community that defined the Dartmouth he had joined in 1969. When he assumed the presidency, he had been at Dartmouth for almost thirty years and had long acknowledged his love for this College on the Hill. He had served under Presidents John Sloan Dickey (although for less than a year), John Kemeny, David McLaughlin, and James Freedman, and he had worked with each of them closely in some capacity. He had sought out John Dickey's advice when he chaired the 1979 curriculum review committee; John Kemeny had asked him to chair this committee, and the two met regularly to discuss it; David McLaughlin had appointed him chair of a trustee-level committee to look at student life; and Jim Freedman had made him dean of the Faculty of Arts and Sciences and had asked him to take another look at the curriculum. A student of Dartmouth history, Jim also had a great admiration for Presidents William Jewett Tucker and Ernest Martin Hopkins. Each of these presidents had had a significant impact on the college that they loved—they were ambitious for the future of Dartmouth and were unafraid of change.

Wright was always respectful of the legacy of the previous members of the Wheelock succession—of their attempts to build its academic reputation, to recognize the importance of a student's moral development, to be a more inclusive place—and he wanted to build on their accomplishments. He also recognized that Dartmouth was, to use a phrase that he employed often, "a work in progress." Indeed, in his speech following his announcement as president, he quoted from President William Jewett Tucker, who said that the "risks of inertia are far greater than the risks of innovation." President Wright would return to Tucker—as well as to his other predecessors—often, as he balanced his respect for the legacy of Dartmouth with his own ambitions for the school.

Those ambitions included five key areas of emphasis: (1) the unique strength of the undergraduate college with a professionally strong faculty committed to teaching; (2) a shared and inclusive community where all students and faculty were welcomed; (3) a need to broaden Dartmouth's accessibility to students from an even wider range of experiences; (4) a desire to enhance the quality and reputation of the faculty; and (5) an attempt to fold the professional and graduate programs more fully into the life of the college. Taken together, these priorities defined an academic community that was collaborative and that encouraged students and faculty to play a leadership role in making the world a better place. When Jim Wright retired at the end of eleven years as president, it would be these accomplishments that he would look back on most proudly. Other issues would intrude on the Wright presidency, to be sure, including two significant economic downturns, the impact of 9/11, the community grief following the tragic murders of two faculty members, Suzanne and Half Zantop, and a divisive and disappointing fight with a group of alumni, but he returned to his core goals every year. They sustained him.

He wanted Dartmouth to provide the best undergraduate experience of any school anywhere. He saw the college as very much the jewel in the crown of Dartmouth and the undergraduate experience as distinctive from those offered by its Ivy League peers. He was particularly proud that *U.S. News & World Report* recognized Dartmouth as having the best undergraduate teaching program in the country and with the recognition in 2004 by Booz Allen Hamilton, a strategy consulting firm, of Dartmouth as an enduring institution—one of only two academic institutions in the world so cited, the other being Oxford University. While he was reluctant to put too much credence in these types of journalistic ventures, these particular surveys recognized the essential elements of Dartmouth.

Jim and Susan Wright were particularly close to undergraduate students and spent a considerable amount of time attending athletic events and arts performances, having lunches and dinners with student groups, and going to other student events. They truly enjoyed Dartmouth students and recognized in them a capacity for leadership. The Wrights were always upbeat about students' potential to do good in the world. Wright often quipped that with young people like these, his generation did not need to worry about the future of the Republic. Consistent with their view of Dartmouth as an inclusive community, the Wrights respected and embraced not only the students, but also everyone who lived and worked at Dartmouth, including staff and faculty, as being part of a team.

Jim Wright would be quick to say that he could not have accomplished as much as he did without the support, collaboration, and continuous encouragement of his wife, Susan DeBevoise Wright, whose love for the college equaled his own. Susan had been a member of the Dean of the College area since 1979, and even though she stepped down when her husband became president, she remained involved in student life—

indeed, generations of students would look Susan up when they returned to campus each spring for reunions, and she was at least as popular as he was on the alumni circuit. Susan Wright served as class dean, the first director of the Mellon Mays Undergraduate Fellowship Program, international student adviser, coordinator of the Presidential Scholars Program, graduate fellowship adviser, associate director of Career Services, and from 2003 through 2008, director of the Montgomery Endowment. She knew everyone at the college and was equally active in civic affairs. In 2008 the Hanover Chamber of Commerce recognized the Wrights with its first "Community Spirit" award, and in 2009 the Dartmouth Board of Trustees awarded each of them an honorary doctorate. Their relationship was very much an equal partnership, and Susan remained Jim Wright's closest adviser on all matters to do with the college throughout his tenure.

Jim Wright wanted Dartmouth to be as accessible as possible to as broad a range of students and faculty as possible. He also wanted to make it possible for all students to participate in the full experience and to make Dartmouth a place where everyone could feel at home. With the support of the Board of Trustees, the college significantly expanded financial aid under Jim Wright's leadership, and the percentage of students receiving aid increased from 42 percent to 48 percent. He eliminated tuition for undergraduates from families with incomes below $75,000, extended need-blind admissions to international students, and eliminated loans for all students so that they would not leave Dartmouth with their opportunities shadowed by debt. His work to help veterans from Iraq and Afghanistan gain access not only to Dartmouth but also to other colleges and universities was a direct outgrowth of his work to broaden student access to Dartmouth.

As a scholar and teacher first and foremost, President Wright recognized the centrality of faculty to the quality of the education that students receive. He made it one of his top priorities to hire the best faculty members and to provide them with all the support they needed to be successful. For Jim Wright, the faculty was key to maintaining and enhancing the undergraduate academic program, and for almost twenty years he oversaw all tenure decisions—whether as dean of the Faculty of Arts and Sciences or as president—for the arts and sciences as well as all reappointments, promotions to full professor, faculty fellowships, and appointments to endowed professorships. He insisted that faculty members needed to be both scholars, with the potential to distinguish themselves in their discipline, *and* outstanding teachers. As dean of faculty he began a program of reviews for every academic department, and he continued this work as president. Under his watch, the Faculty of Arts and Sciences grew significantly, with the addition of new faculty and new programs. He sought to reduce both undergraduate class size and the student-faculty ratio, and to raise faculty compensation to be competitive with that at other Ivy League and top private colleges and universities.

Finally, he wanted to build closer ties between the undergraduate college and the graduate and professional programs. Wright saw the professional schools (Geisel School of Medicine, Thayer School of Engineering, and the Tuck School of Business Administration), as well as the graduate programs in the arts and sciences, as more than appendages; they were integral to the richness of the institution. Each part of the college was stronger because of its association with the others. As president, Jim Wright encouraged these connections wherever he could, and his administration saw the development of the joint Master's of Engineering Management degree in the Thayer and Tuck Schools, interdisciplinary work between Thayer and the medical school, the Bridge Program at Tuck for undergraduates, and much closer ties between all the professional schools and the undergraduate college.

There were other accomplishments. The arts flourished, as student interest in the arts departments increased and student performance groups multiplied. Under the leadership of their dynamic directors, the Hopkins Center and the Hood Museum offered exciting programs and collaborated ever more effectively with the academic departments. It may have been symptomatic of the time that the most popular minor for engineering science majors became studio art. As one of his last presidential actions, he secured funding and trustee approval for a new arts center on Lebanon Street, which is scheduled to open in 2012. Wright also invested in and encouraged the development of athletic programs and a strong outdoors program. He believed that these were part of the culture that defined Dartmouth. He supported coaches and players and was a frequent and enthusiastic spectator at athletic practices and games. He and Susan Wright tried to see every team compete.

Facilities opened during the eleven years of the Jim Wright presidency included new academic buildings; new residence halls and housing for undergraduates, graduate students, and faculty; new athletic facilities; plus major projects at each of the professional schools. When a large block of property in downtown Hanover came on the market, the trustees accepted his recommendation that the school buy it, both as a financial investment and as an investment in the quality of downtown Hanover. Wright knew that a strong and vibrant local community was a critical element in Dartmouth's strength. All in all, the Wright administration invested over one billion dollars in the Dartmouth campus, to ensure the very best facilities for faculty and students.

While the majority of Wright's work focused on issues internal to Dartmouth, he was also willing to take on outside projects. His work to increase educational access for injured veterans won him, and the college, national recognition, and he was honored by the US Marine Corps, by the Veterans of Foreign Wars, by ABC-TV News, by the New England Council, and by the New England Board of Higher Education. He served too on a task force convened by the College Board to examine the decline in American postsecondary completion rates that recommended new guidelines and goals, and he participated as a board member with the NCAA Division 1 group of presidents, serving on the task force that recommended significant academic standards for student athletes.

During his tenure as president, the Dartmouth endowment grew from $1.6 billion in 1998 to $3.7 billion in June 2007, while the Dartmouth College Fund grew from $20 million to $42 million in 2008 and to $38 million in 2009. A phenomenal fundraiser, Wright headed the Campaign for the Dartmouth Experience, raising $1.3 billion dollars. These additional monies certainly helped to pay for much of the new building on campus, as well as for the financial aid expansions and other initiatives. The years of the Wright administration encompassed both the highs of the bull market and the deepest lows of the bear market during the international global crisis of late 2008. The administration was thus not without its budgetary problems, particularly in 2000–2001 and again in 2008–2009. In June 2009 the endowment stood at $2.8 billion, down about $1 billion from its peak.

At both these junctures, the college had to cut budgets and face difficult choices. President Wright and his senior team established a set of guidelines to help determine the choices they made: the quality of the student experience; financial aid and need-blind admissions; and the hiring and retention of the best faculty needed to be protected. The priorities meant that the administration and auxiliaries needed to bear the brunt of the cuts. Jim Wright brought in the management consulting firm McKinsey & Co., to review the administrative practices of the college and to recommend ways in which the college could not only be more effective but also save money.

The budget cuts of 2008 and 2009 were particularly painful because of the scale of the international crisis. In the months immediately following October 2008, the Dartmouth endowment dropped by 18 percent—or $700 million. The college relied on the endowment for approximately 35 percent of its annual operating budget; hence, Dartmouth, like peer schools across the country along with other not-for-profit organizations, found itself facing a significant shortfall. Jim Wright charged Provost Barry Scherr and Executive Vice President Adam Keller with cutting approximately 10 percent of the budget over two years, while continuing to adhere to the key institutional priorities. This they did, and the Board of Trustees approved the plan in the spring of 2009, shortly before the conclusion of his presidency.

Of the other issues that would mark the Wright presidency, the Student Life Initiative and the fight over alumni representation on the Board of Trustees were the two most prominent. In many ways these intertwined issues formed a backdrop to the entire Wright presidency. The Student Life Initiative grew out of the trustees' decision in 1998 to ask the new president to review student life at the college. The president and the trustees wanted to ensure that the student experience included all students and supported and enhanced the academic life of the college. Concern had grown through the 1980s and 1990s about the role of the fraternity system and alcohol on campus. Not surprisingly, the campus-wide discussion about what student life should look like at Dartmouth encouraged a broader debate about the role of fraternities and sororities, alcohol, diversity, and who should control social life. Jim Wright told the faculty in September of 1999 that the initiative "is about addressing long-deferred capital needs, it is about making fully available the special strengths of Dartmouth, it is about ensuring that the residential and social system supports and enhances the academic mission of Dartmouth. It is about affirming the importance of community, the importance of inclusiveness, the importance of alternatives and options, and the necessity of addressing issues to do with the abuse of alcohol and other drugs." And on another occasion he explained, "It is about our values and our purposes, our traditions and our aspirations."

Lines were quickly drawn in the sand around those "values and purposes, traditions and aspirations," around what was acceptable or not acceptable for different factions within the community, and the rhetoric used by all sides made constructive conversation difficult. The debate became part of a broader national conversation around political correctness and social engineering. Although the committee members who made the final recommendations on student life as well as the trustees who approved the final plan came from across the political spectrum, the debate at times took on a conservative-liberal dynamic. Wright regretted the way that the SLI, as it became known, played out and the ways in which it divided rather than united the community. Regrets aside, however, the initiative ultimately accomplished many of its goals. Dartmouth constructed new dormitories, allowing more students to live on campus, and enhanced the social space in those dormitories, so that students had alternatives to fraternity basements. The Dean's Office encouraged fraternities and sororities to aspire to higher rather than minimal standards of behavior. And the initiative provided more support and resources to the various diversity groups on campus and expanded support for athletics and physical recreation.

The Student Life Initiative not only created a stir on campus; it also awakened a just-below-the-surface discontent with the ways in which the college had evolved since the early 1970s and the advent of coeducation. In the intervening years, alumni, students, and faculty had debated coeducation, fraternities (and eventually sororities), the Indian symbol, President Kemeny's recommitment to diversity, President McLaughlin's concern over student life, the *Dartmouth Review*, divestment, and President Freedman's perceived attempt to "Harvardize" the college. And running through all these debates was a more persistent concern regarding alumni participation in the governance of the college — or perhaps, rather, these issues raised the question of who controlled the governance of the college. Dartmouth at that time, unusual among colleges and universities, allowed the alumni to nominate 50 percent of the trustees. With every controversy came a corresponding attempt by various alumni groups to control the trustee election process, starting with the election of a "dissident" trustee in 1980 and the filing of multiple lawsuits against the college. When Jim Wright became president in 1998, he had been part of these conversations and controversies for thirty years and was closely identified with many of them. He had served as Jim Freedman's dean of faculty and provost and made no secret of his deep and continuing admiration for Freedman and his vision for the college, or for the commitment of all three of his predecessors to diversity and coeducation.

In a speech to the Alumni Council in December 2006, he told the assembled alumni that Dartmouth needed to look beyond its divisions to its shared values. He was confident that these would help unify the community, for surely

> we are not split down the middle on providing here the strongest comprehensive student learning experience in the country; we are not split down the middle on the need to recruit, retain, and enable faculty who are leaders in their fields and share in a passion for teaching and mentoring Dartmouth students; we are not split down the middle on the need to protect need-blind admissions and make Dartmouth truly welcoming to all students, regardless of their background or their family's means. We are not split down the middle because these values and this sense of purpose are the center of our legacy and are at the core of our shared responsibility.

The divisions within the alumni body disappointed President Wright. While he applauded the Dartmouth propensity to debate and dispute energetically, he regretted the way the debate often became personal or mean-spirited, and he tried hard to heal the rifts. He knew that Dartmouth alumni shared a passion for their school, and it was this passion that he tried to encourage.

In 2009 the chair of the Dartmouth Board of Trustees, Charles E. Haldeman Jr., '70, summarized Jim Wright's career at Dartmouth in this way:

> In the forty years since you came to Hanover, Jim, you have served as teacher, scholar, dean, acting president, provost, and president. Your leadership has led to stronger academic programs, remarkable improvements to the physical campus, an expanded financial aid program, enhanced student life, and increased diversity across the community. You have honored our traditions while ensuring that the

education provided here remains relevant to the world in which we live and to the future we face. You advocated for educational access on the national stage, particularly for veterans and those less privileged.

At heart, Jim Wright was always a teacher. His election to the presidency of Dartmouth College gave him not only the opportunity to lead the college he loved, but also the opportunity to use the presidency as a bully pulpit to encourage his students to make a positive difference in the world.

The speeches gathered in this collection, particularly the annual convocation and commencement addresses, illustrate that calling. It is in these addresses that he was most intentional about his goals and his aspirations for Dartmouth, for the Dartmouth faculty, and ultimately for Dartmouth students. His complete speeches also contain a great deal of Dartmouth history, and I have tried throughout the collection to include as many such pieces as possible. I hope that readers of this book will derive the same enjoyment and enlightenment from the speeches as the original listeners did.

Forever New

1

APPOINTMENT AS PRESIDENT OF
DARTMOUTH COLLEGE

REMARKS FOLLOWING THE ANNOUNCEMENT
BY THE BOARD OF TRUSTEES, APRIL 6, 1998

James Wright delivered these remarks to the Dartmouth community from
Alumni Hall following the announcement of his appointment as president.

As Yogi Berra, one of the sages to whom I regularly turn, said, "When you come to a fork in the road, take it." I take it with pleasure. Following my discussion with the trustees this weekend and now being here, at this place, this afternoon, with friends and colleagues, and reflecting upon the exciting opportunities we have ahead of us, gives me a great sense of anticipation. I am grateful for this singular opportunity to lead Dartmouth into a new century. I thank the trustees for their confidence.

I would also like to add my thanks to those of Mr. King in recognizing the contributions of President Freedman and Mrs. Freedman. They have been great and supportive friends of Susan and of me. The Freedman presidency has been marked by a growth in the intellectual distinction of Dartmouth and by the recognition that this is now a place more open to difference and less defined by contention. Even as the institution is richer because of their contributions, so too all of us are enriched who have come to know them personally. Jim's and Sheba's personal grace and quiet courage, their intellectual warmth, their good humor and good will, these are qualities that leave their indelible marks on our individual spirits just as they have upon our college. Jim, we are delighted that you and Sheba will be remaining here at Dartmouth; we value and treasure your continuing presence.

Thirty years ago this coming fall, I made my first visit to Dartmouth, indeed, my first visit to New England for a job interview in the History Department. I was very pleased to accept their offer and thought I would be here for a few years. I was encouraged from the very beginning by a group of colleagues who were supportive of each other, colleagues who took both teaching and scholarship seriously. And I was captured by an environment in which faculty, students, and staff cared about each other, and cared about the broader world of which this campus was only a small part. It is important to know that I still today consider myself—and always will

3

James Wright as a new faculty member in 1969. Photo by Adrian N. Bouchard.

consider myself—first and foremost a faculty member, a teacher, and a historian. Dartmouth is a far more complicated place than it was when I came here, but I believe the basic themes and values remain. This is a place where all members of the community take seriously their responsibilities to each other and are committed to the values of this institution.

I have asked three special friends to join Susan and me today, three people who have worked closely with me and who personify that commitment: Gail Vernazza, June Sweeney, and Jeannine McPherson. They have supported me over many years and are colleagues deeply committed to the purposes of Dartmouth. Even the most complicated organizations finally come down to people, and I would salute all of the people, from faculty to those who take care of our superb facilities, who make this place true to its principles and give me great confidence in the assignment I will assume.

There will be ample time over the next several months for me to share with you in detail my vision for Dartmouth and the objectives of my presidency. I expect to engage in a wide discussion of who we are and what we aspire to be, sharing with you my perspectives and learning from yours. For now, let me outline some of the important principles that will inform my presidency. President William Jewett Tucker said that the "risks of inertia are far greater than the risks of innovation." I have no interest in inertia. We end the twentieth century in a position of real strength, thanks to the commitment and efforts and vision of my predecessors. John Dickey raised our aspirations and reminded us of our common obligations to our world and to others. John Kemeny moved us through a period of significant change and enlarged in every way our sense of who defined this community. David McLaughlin enabled us to rededicate the residential experience and secured our financial strength. Jim Freedman reminded us that our primary commitment and obligation is to the life of the mind. And it has been the very special support of Dartmouth's alumni for this place and its values that has enabled our college to thrive and excel.

Our legacy is wonderful but our task is unfinished—it will always be unfinished. Now we must focus upon the next century and prepare ourselves for the challenges that it will surely bring. We need to affirm the importance of the liberal arts in this world of change. My vision of Dartmouth is of a research community that is committed to attracting and retaining the very best faculty and recruiting and engaging the very best students. A place marked by learning rather than teaching, learning in which students are full participants rather than passive observers. A place where the out-of-classroom experience fully complements the formal classroom learning. A place where students enjoy the freedom and independence to shape their own lives. Freedom and independence entail responsibility. Being a member of a community involves necessary negotiations between our personal interests and the values that bind us together. I expect to participate fully with the Board of Trustees, with faculty and administrators—and especially with students—in a full discussion of what membership in this community means.

Our shared responsibility is to assure a place that attaches the highest priority upon learning, to assure a community that is open to everyone, a community that does not demean women—indeed that does not demean anyone—a community that does not tolerate the harming of others and that tries to prevent the harming of oneself. Let us celebrate all of our members and understand our obligation to the world in which we live. As we discuss the way to secure these things, understand that I think we can do no less. My sense of this community is that we need to come together to discuss our common purposes, and I intend to be an active participant in this discussion.

I also told the Board of Trustees that I fully intend to participate in debates that have a national resonance. One has to do with the value of research. Research in the academy is not a pastime that competes with teaching but a critical activity that informs the best teaching. It is too easy to dismiss research by focusing on things that have failed or projects that critics deem foolish. The American research university is the most successful in the world, and we should never forget the importance of this to our national well being—not simply in those critical research fields that we hope make our lives safer and our world more familiar, but in the arts and the humanities that make our lives fuller and richer.

Dartmouth is a research university in all but name, and we are not going to be deflected from our purposes. This is a place that is marked by flexibility, by a sense of community, and by full opportunities for interdisciplinary work bridging not only arts and sciences departments but also including the strong programs we have developed in the professional schools. I hope to work with the deans and with the faculties to strengthen these ties. For, finally, it is the strength of the faculty and their work that makes Dartmouth such an attractive place for the very best students. And the very best students attract an even stronger faculty.

I have particularly enjoyed over the last fifteen months my involvement with the three professional schools. I am impressed by their strength and by their sense of excellence. I am excited about the prospect of looking for new ways to build upon their accomplishments and to expand even more their ambitions. We have the potential here to develop new models of academic medicine and of health-care delivery, to strengthen engineering as a professional field while enriching its ties to the liberal arts, and to build upon Tuck's position as a residential business school committed to new models of business research and education. Dartmouth's venerable professional schools and her impressive graduate programs are fundamental to the special character of this college.

I strongly reaffirm our commitment to affirmative action and to diversity. This is not simply due to some sense of long-standing obligation, although this is important. This is not simply due to our need to provide opportunities to minority students, although it is hard to imagine our society if we neglect this responsibility. Most importantly, our commitment to diversity is rooted in the fact that we are an educational institution. It is hard for me to imagine education going on without a richly diverse student body and faculty. The world is diverse, and so must we be. I will see that we do not let up in our recruitment efforts. But recruitment is only the first step. This community needs to do still more to welcome and salute difference.

A personal note may underline my commitment to this principle. My path to Dartmouth was not a direct one—I didn't commence my college education until I was twenty-one years old because post-secondary education was not something that was part of my community or its values. One of my grandfathers was a miner and the other was a farm worker. Neither finished eighth grade. My father was a bartender. He dropped out of college during his first semester because the depression blunted his aspirations. I worked for a time myself as a miner—a powder man in three-hundred-foot-deep hard rock mines.

I know well the distance from there to this spot for this occasion. Once I began to study, I found a world of excitement and of opportunity. I have been fortunate, and I have benefited from the support and encourage-

Wright lecturing in 1985. Personal photo (presented to Wright by an unknown person).

ment of teachers, mentors, friends, and family over the years. I recognize personally the power of education and the capacity of institutions like Dartmouth, at their best, to enable full opportunities and rich lives. The postwar democratization of American higher education has been a wonderful story, and I have been pleased in my time at Dartmouth to see this extended to be fully inclusive. I can assure you that on my watch there will be no letting up in this college's commitment to a diverse and rich student body, faculty, and administration and to a financial aid program that will sustain this.

Some of you will know that Emily Dickinson has a special and personal importance to Susan and to me. We were married in her house. She wrote in one of her poems:

> "Hope" is the thing with feathers
> That perches in the soul
> And sings the tune without the words
> And never stops—at all . . .

I am privileged to be at a place whose soul is indeed filled with hope, and I will be honored to be the president of an institution so richly endowed with people who share in that sense of optimism and promise. Thank you.

DARTMOUTH: FOREVER NEW,
SEPTEMBER 23, 1998

*James Wright gave this speech on the occasion of his inauguration
as the sixteenth president of Dartmouth College.*

President McLaughlin and President Freedman, my fellow Dartmouth Trustees, Professor [John Hope] Franklin, Assembly President [Josh] Green, colleagues from the faculty, staff, and administration, graduates, honored guests, Dartmouth students, good friends and neighbors: It is with a sense of awe and with keen anticipation that I embrace this new responsibility at the institution I have loved and served for twenty-nine years, under four presidents. I am grateful for the confidence placed in me, and I ask for your help and support in the time ahead.

I have been blessed by the exceptional people who have been part of my life. Provost Brinckerhoff has already acknowledged the presence on this occasion of members of my family. Many of us have been fortunate to have special teachers who have had a profound influence on who we are. Two of my undergraduate teachers are here today, professors Roger Daniels and Tom Lundeen. Your presence means so much to me. I have been privileged at Dartmouth these many years to have colleagues and friends within the faculty and administration who have taught me much and have encouraged me often—and who now sustain me as I assume this new assignment. Thank you.

I am also fortunate to share this platform with and to inherit the legacies of my predecessors in the Wheelock Succession. James O. Freedman and David T. McLaughlin are not only my friends; they have also been sources of enormous support and invaluable counsel to me over the years. Much of what Dartmouth is today derives from their work. And Jean Kemeny and Sukie Dickey, who are in the audience, we honor you and through you Presidents John Kemeny and John Sloan Dickey, men with whom I was privileged to serve and who did much to enhance and enrich this college.

This ceremony affords a rare opportunity—and for a historian it constitutes an obligation—to consider the values that, ingrained in Dartmouth's past, define the institution today, and to ask how that past informs our future. We all know that Dartmouth is a place marked by strong traditions. But Dartmouth's history is one that resonates and lives, not one that encapsulates and confines. I will share with you my understanding of what those traditions are and what they mean with regard to the tasks ahead of us.

Our traditions embody Dartmouth's core values—they have enriched us as an institution. Here at Dartmouth the sound of feet crunching on snow, the look and feel of soft September sunsets, the horizons marked by granite hills and large vistas, and a campus filled with secluded places, here these are not simply poetic abstractions. They are things that shape memories that mark lifetimes, and they continue to bind generations of Dartmouth's sons and daughters to each other and to this special place.

Dartmouth is part of a system of higher education that is the envy of the world. Like so much in this country, this system derives its strength from its richness and diversity. But this range of colleges and universities masks fundamental tensions within the academy—tensions between the individual and the community, between elite and democratic values, and between teaching and scholarship. These tensions, of course, play themselves out within this college as well.

Few institutions value more—or indeed, require more—independence of thought than do colleges and universities. Yet there are also few institutions that depend more on shared values. Here we are responsible for ourselves and free to pursue our interests. But this cannot be where our responsibility ends. This implicit tension between self and community is inherent within the academy; it is a tension that results in tremendous fragility, on the one hand, and tremendous strength, on the other. Through acknowledging the tension between our personal freedom and our responsibilities to each other, we are more likely to appreciate the former and to acknowledge and embrace the latter.

Since World War II, American higher education has established a stunning record in democratizing access for students who, in the past, would not have continued their education. But Dartmouth, in fact, had much earlier taken on this responsibility. While Dartmouth is an elite institution, to the extent that it is highly selective in admitting its students and recruiting its faculty, this was also the college that historically empowered the hill country farm boys of New Hampshire and Vermont. And our mission is even more explicit than that. Dartmouth's tradition means the recognition that from the very founding of the college our charter dedicated us to educating a diverse population of students. In 1921 Dartmouth's Board of Trustees affirmed this by adopting the policy of selective admissions to assure a more diverse student body. We were one of the first institutions in the country to take such a significant step.

Our charter purpose—"the education of American Indians and others"—has over time included not only Native Americans, but also African Americans, Asian Americans, and Latino and Hispanic students. It encompasses international students, as well as American citizens, and since 1972, women as well as men. Although many women came to Dartmouth before that date—faculty pioneers like Elizabeth Reynolds Hapgood in the Russian Department and Hannah T. Croasdale in Biological Sciences, and the first women exchange students—few things in our rich history have so positively shaped the quality of this community as did the decision to become coeducational.

Dartmouth is enriched by its diversity. We will not turn our back on our history. It resonates with our purposes and provides examples of their success. Remember that it was because of the efforts of Samson Occom, a Mohegan, that Eleazar Wheelock's vision found success here. It was here that Kan'ichi Asakawa, the son of a samurai, studied a century ago and then, as a professor, initiated in the United States the field of Asian Studies—even if we later permitted him to remove to New Haven. It was here that E. E. Just, the son of a slave, both studied and taught, a pioneer in the field of developmental biology.

As in the past, Dartmouth must be a place of opportunity for students of all backgrounds. It is hard to imagine education taking place in an environment that is fully like-minded and homogeneous. And so, Dartmouth seeks to attract a student body that reflects the richness of the world in which we live, and to offer an education that enables and empowers. To this end we must continue to enrich our financial aid and scholarship programs to ensure that we can do this. I pledge myself to this purpose.

We are prepared now to build upon our heritage of providing a comprehensive experience outside of the classroom. The diversity of our social options needs to reflect the diversity of the community. Students have a vision of what this might be, and I am excited to be able to work with them to pursue this. While the undergraduate student body should not be larger, we need to expand our social and residential choices and opportunities. We will attend to these things for this is a special place, and our mandate is to protect it and to enrich it.

The privilege of education also entails obligation to others. Dartmouth's tradition includes a dedication to the greater society to which we belong. It was here that Paul Tsongas and Nelson A. Rockefeller and Daniel Webster studied and began lifetimes of public service to our nation. We know that the purpose of a Dartmouth education is not merely the enhancement of the self. This is not a sufficient consequence of privilege. At Dartmouth and elsewhere education needs to engage and sustain a life of broader responsibility.

Thirty-five years ago, on the centenary of the emancipation proclamation, Dartmouth's President Dickey reflected upon the fact that the United States—and Dartmouth—had failed to meet the promise of Abraham Lincoln's action. He wondered how to explain such a thing in a society and at an institution that had been marked by good people. He concluded that the failure did not represent the triumph of human evil but rather the apathy of the good. President Dickey said, "In communities such as this, it is not so much that bad things were done, as that good things were not." President Dickey was right; our obligation is greater than to be self-indulgently successful or passively good.

While the tensions between the individual and the community and between elite and democratic values play themselves out in many institutions of higher education, it is the tension between teaching and scholarship that has particular meaning for Dartmouth. When I spoke to the Dartmouth community upon the announcement of my election as president, I reiterated what my predecessors in the Wheelock Succession had earlier acknowledged: that Dartmouth College is a university in all but name. What was true in President Dickey's day is even more true today. If neither of the descriptive labels—college or university—fits us easily, that is eminently acceptable, because we are comfortable with what we are and with what we aspire to be. Typically colleges are primarily concerned with undergraduate education and teaching. Universities are primarily engaged in graduate education and also place a greater emphasis on faculty research. We are proud to call ourselves a college, recognizing that Dartmouth is a college that has many of the best characteristics of a university. We are a university in terms of our activities and our programs, but one that remains a college in name and in its basic values and purposes. In this paradox, this tension, lies our identity and our strength.

Dartmouth was a pioneer in the establishment of professional schools: the fourth medical school in the country and the first in a rural area, the nation's first school of engineering, its first graduate school of business administration. From this heritage comes our enduring commitment to support the valuable work of these schools, and to ensure, in turn, that Dartmouth as a whole is enriched by their presence. Interdisciplinary work is strong here, in part because of our size, and we can make it stronger. The professional schools can serve as a greater resource to the college, even as the college can be a greater resource for them. I shall work with these schools, as well as with the graduate and undergraduate programs in the arts and sciences, encouraging them in particular to pursue ever more their fertile intersections.

Our support for the graduate and professional programs does not diminish our commitment to undergraduate education or our emphasis on excellence in teaching. Nor does taking seriously our obligation to pursue excellence as teachers in any way blunt our commitment to cutting-edge research and scholarship. Indeed each strengthens the other. Our direction is clear. We seek to build upon and to expand our dual commitment. We will work to continue to attract the very best faculty possible and to support them in their scholarship and research endeavors. And, in turn, we are equally committed to excellence in teaching, at all levels of this institution. We can enjoy the best of being a college and a university.

Dartmouth is a diverse residential college marked by faculty and students who are sustained by curiosity and who are never quite satisfied with answers. Our faculty know full well the privilege of teaching the exceptional students drawn to Dartmouth. I intend to return to the classroom this winter. In addition to the personal satisfaction I will derive from this, I hope by this action to emphasize my commitment to teaching even as we enhance our research activities.

There are many examples of our research heritage. It was here at Dartmouth that the first medical x-ray in the nation was taken. It was here that George Stibitz ran the first digital computer, that John Kemeny and Tom Kurtz developed both the BASIC computing language and timesharing. It was here that Ted Geisel and Robert Frost and Louise Erdrich played with the magic of language and shared with us their creative genius. Dart-

Passing of the Wentworth Bowl from President Freedman to James Wright at Wright's inauguration as Dartmouth's sixteenth president, in September 1998. Photo by Joe Mehling.

mouth is a place that has brought together accomplished scholars and talented students — scholars and students sustained by a shared love of learning. This is not only what calls us here, it is also the purpose that binds us together.

Our goal, then, remains the pursuit of our own historic mission. Our commitment is to learning and scholarship, within a talented and diverse community. We seek nothing less than to meet our own aspirations and purposes. And we will settle for nothing less. This requires that Dartmouth continue to evolve and to change, just as our society evolves and changes. Today, I say to you, that Dartmouth, while proud of its heritage, must be forever new. However deeply rooted in its rich history, Dartmouth is a dynamic, living community. We are free to set our own course. We welcome today students who will live their lives out in the twenty-first century. Our purposes are about their future and not our past. The Koran teaches that every soul should "look upon the morrow for the deed it has performed." Dartmouth is focused upon the morrow, the next century.

This is a community whose best hopes and aspirations can become a model for others to emulate. As we articulate and pursue our own niche, one that synthesizes the best of the college and the university, one that builds upon our rich past, we need to be comfortable with what we are. But we must never be complacent. We should recognize that Dartmouth remains a work in progress.

What does it mean for us as faculty members that Dartmouth is both a college and a university? It means that we share institutional obligations, even as we remain active participants in the worldwide community of scholars within our disciplines. It means that our small size can be an advantage, because of the flexibility it affords. Cooperative endeavors and shared ambitions often bear more and better fruit than can result from individuals working alone. Cross-disciplinary collaborations in many fields not only enhance the teaching and research enterprises, but they also contribute to personal and professional satisfaction. Being a faculty member at Dartmouth provides the opportunity to teach and to work closely with some of the finest undergraduate students in the country, in a residential community that encourages and supports research.

What does it mean for you as undergraduate students that Dartmouth is both a college and a university? It means a size and scale and aspiration sufficient to afford a rich curriculum, but within a community that one can stroll across in ten minutes and meet friends along the way. It means an unsurpassed range of off-campus opportunities and arts programs that are incredibly rich and accessible. It means the opportunity to study with faculty who are committed both to teaching and to scholarship. Perhaps most important, being a student at Dartmouth means being encouraged to take one's self seriously as a young scholar—a person of promise who has a rare and valuable opportunity to learn and grow. It means that here students are not merely passive recipients of information, but are active participants in their own learning process. It means also that the out-of-classroom experience complements and supports the central mission of the college. Whether it is in athletic competition or recreational sports or artistic pursuits, or in conversations at the residence halls or dining tables, we recognize that learning here has never been—nor should it be—limited to the classroom.

What does this synthesis mean for you as graduate or professional school students? It means that your professors are as committed to teaching and to the quality of your academic experience as those who teach only undergraduates. It means that you, too, benefit from studying within a community large enough to be intellectually vital while it remains one of a human scale—where you have an opportunity to know not only your classmates and colleagues, but also the faculty with whom you work.

What does this synthesis mean for you as a Dartmouth graduate? You too can take pride that the undergraduate program that will remain at the heart of this college is envied by many and is second to none. It means that you can take pride in the fact that your alma mater is enriched and enhanced by the presence of three of the oldest professional schools in their respective disciplines. It means that the whole institution benefits from the presence of select doctoral programs within the sciences—small programs, excellent in their own right, that enrich and enhance the entire institution. It means that you have a justifiable pride in the scholarly accomplishments of this faculty. As alumni and alumnae, your loyalty to Dartmouth—your support, your enthusiasm—has always been, and will continue to be, integral to the college's success.

And what does this synthesis mean for those of us who form the staff and administration. It means that we facilitate the mission and success of this complex institution, we steward a rare community of learning, and we use our skills to maintain and promote its many purposes. As staff and administrators you are the part of the Dartmouth family that enables it to function. Your selfless energy and your commitment to maintaining this place encourage in me a sense of confidence in our future. I am pleased to be part of the administration of such a place and to have you as colleagues.

My commitment, then, as your sixteenth president, is to affirm our purpose and to build upon our enviable strengths. I expect to pursue my vision of Dartmouth energetically and to use the persuasive powers of this office to strengthen further this great institution. And I expect to be held accountable for our success in leading Dartmouth into the new millennium. I welcome the challenge. In the seventeenth century, the Japanese poet Basho wrote, "In my new robe this morning—someone else." I do not expect to be someone else in my new robe. But I do like its fit. And I am prepared, in this new office, to take on new challenges and new roles. I look forward with anticipation and excitement to the work ahead. Together we can accomplish much.

Now I would like to take a moment to address the Class of 2002 in particular. I have had the pleasure of welcoming you individually to Dartmouth, and I am pleased to join with you on a new and exciting journey. You will share much together as a class, and through your studies, activities, and interests you will share much with others in this community. But don't forget that it was your own accomplishments and promise that brought you here. And ultimately it will be against your own accomplishments that you will be judged and that you will judge yourself—whether you have pushed yourself, stretched, and grown; whether you have availed yourself as fully as you might have of the rare and precious opportunities that this place will afford you. The burden of regret is a heavy one. Take on the burden of responsibility instead; it is no lighter, but it surely is more rewarding in the end. Emily Dickinson wrote:

We never know how high we are
Till we are asked to rise
And then if we are true to plan
Our statures touch the skies . . .

By the act of matriculation you have been asked to rise. You have become part of Dartmouth, and Dartmouth forever more will be a part of you. You will never be the same. Four years from now you will graduate

President Wright at the podium in front of Baker Library at his inauguration, September 1998.
Photo by Joe Mehling.

from Dartmouth, as tens of thousands did before you. You will go on to make a difference—in business, public service, the professions, education, the arts, and myriad other endeavors. But you should know that by your very presence here, Dartmouth itself will be changed, as well. This is as it should be. For along with me, and with the faculty and administrators, staff and graduates, you each assume responsibility for making certain that the richness of this special place endures and grows. Take on this responsibility with confidence and joy—but also share with me a profound sense of gratitude for the privilege we have been given.

We have work to do, you and I—and it is time to begin!

2

CONVOCATION ADDRESSES, 1999–2008

James Wright, following in the tradition of President John Sloan Dickey, began and ended his convocations in the same way each year, as follows:

Greetings! It has been my practice on this happy occasion to remind the community that even at an institution that operates around the year and around the world, there needs be a time and a place for us to gather, symbolically, to mark a new beginning. Today we assemble here in the annual ceremony of renewal and reunion that celebrates the beginning of another academic year and that formally welcomes into this community our newest members.

[Body of individual convocation address]

So, members of the Class of [2012], today you have become a part of Dartmouth, and Dartmouth forevermore will be a part of you. You will never be the same. But you should know that by your very presence here, Dartmouth itself will be changed, too. Take on this responsibility with confidence and with joy. But also embrace with me a profound sense of gratitude for the privilege we share as members of this special community of learning. We have work to do, you and I, and we must begin it. Welcome to Dartmouth!

. . . We convene today for an important ritual, one rooted deep in the traditions of the academy and of Dartmouth. Convocation marks the annual renewal of the academic year. It is a time for us to welcome incoming students—the Class of 2003, as well as new graduate and professional school students—and to greet upper class students, faculty, and administrators who are returning to campus. It is good to see all of you, as well as to have community members and other friends join us today. Convocations signal special moments in the life of an institution. They are times for us to challenge ourselves and to remember our great promise. This year is perhaps weighted with more symbolism than most such occasions, for we gather today on the eve of a new century—indeed, of a new millennium.

All of us are weary—or assuredly soon will be—of millennial commentary that reflects on where we have been and wonders about what is ahead. The recitation of past accomplishments and the listing of great achievements seem never-ending. The historian recognizes this as part of the continuing human search for ancestors worthy of their descendants. The prospect of a new millennium has been attended for many years by a sense of eager anticipation and even, among some, by apprehension. There is no denying that the turn of the millennium has profound symbolic importance for a wide range of groups, secular as well as religious, and that it has real implications for our technology-dependent world, which, some warn, in its Y2K confusion, may attempt to throw us not forward, but back a hundred years.

The fanfare surrounding the approach of the year 2000 has other implications for us, too. It provides an important lesson in how we interpret and understand the world in which we live. But in this place of learning, we need to recognize the artificiality of the construct we call the millennium. The movement of the earth around the sun follows a set and predictable—and countable—pattern, to be sure. Clocks and calendars measure intellectual constructs that describe this. This autumn solstice is millennial because the western calendar has chosen to describe it that way. Indeed, the arithmetic strict constructionists among us will point out that the year 2000 is millennial only because we are too impatient to wait for the year 2001!

Despite the reservations I have about all of this, the historian in me cannot pass up such an opportunity to reflect, not on the past thousand years—for that would test your patience more than would be kind—but at least on the last hundred years, and to relate to our current task some observations about this remarkable century in which we all were born. When students traveled to Hanover a hundred years ago they did so by horse and buggy or by train to Norwich. The hills around us were then largely treeless, and the pasture fence had only just been removed from the college green. Telephones had arrived in 1884 and electric lighting in 1892. The germ theory of disease was only beginning to be widely accepted, and the town of Hanover, together with Dartmouth, had undertaken the building of a public water works and a sewer system. Modern social science and the teaching of evolution had appeared for the first time in a college curriculum that was still dominated by the classics. Dartmouth was largely a school for young men from New Hampshire and the other New England states.

The turn of the last century was a time marked by high expectations. It was a time of great secular optimism; of belief in science, in rationality, in education and civic responsibility; and of belief in the inevitability of progress and in the innate human capacity for good. During the years since 1900, our society has made incredible progress in a wide range of areas. Medical advances have included the development of penicillin, open-heart surgery, organ transplants, treatments for cancer, preventive vaccinations, and the eradication of many infectious diseases. The average life span in industrial countries has grown from forty-five years to seventy-five years. We have split the atom, broken the genetic codes that shape human life, and smashed the sound barrier; we have walked on the moon. We have begun to understand the patterns that mark the history of the universe. Computer technology has given us a capacity to store, analyze, and manipulate data in volumes and at speeds that are hard for most of us to comprehend. We communicate over great distances instantaneously, and through mass media we have forged a new sense of national and international identity.

But a progressive view of the history of the past century belies the complexity of our world. While we have solved many problems, we have created still others: the vexing moral quandaries posed by our genetic understandings and capacities, growing concerns about environmental pollution, the greenhouse effect, global warming, and the anonymity of cyberspace. This century has seen the application of science and technology in horrifying ways. This, we remember, is the century of mustard gas in Flanders Field, the century of the genocidal efficiencies of Auschwitz, the century of the incineration of the very air over Hiroshima. The young British poet Isaac Rosenberg wrote, before his death in the trenches in 1918: ". . . what do you see in our eyes / At the shrieking iron and flame / Hurled through still heavens?" Rosenberg, perhaps, answered his own question when he wrote, "It is the same old druid Time as ever."

One hundred years ago, the dawn of the age of rationality and applied science was also the era when Jim Crow laws became the laws of the South. If we properly celebrate at century's end heroes such as Susan B. Anthony, César Chávez, Jackie Robinson, Rosa Parks, Alice Paul, and Martin Luther King Jr., we do so acknowledging that increased legal equality for women and for people of color constitutes a step taken, rather than a conclusion. Barbara Jordan said just a quarter century ago, "I have finally been included in 'we the people.'" If we still do not fully understand the origins of the universe or all of the mysteries of genetic structure, it is also the case that we do not yet comprehend some basic principles of human relations. We have not, in this age of reason, yet overcome hostile and negative stereotypes and caricatures, biases and presumptions that inhibit the pursuit of the dreams of this republic: an inclusive "we the people."

The long view of scholarship can be of little comfort in the face of day-to-day frustrations and obstacles. Each of us finally measures progress not by the historian's constructs, but against our own hopes and aspirations, against our own sense of accomplishment. Last June when I addressed the graduates of the Class of 1999, I quoted a line from a poem that Walt Whitman wrote toward the end of the last century. He said, "The strongest and sweetest songs yet remain to be sung." Members of the Class of 2003, much remains for you to do. This occasion reminds us of the tasks—and the opportunities—that you have and that we share. You see, we have no mold in which to cast you; you need to define your own expectations and dreams. We have a hope, though—a hope that you will never be quite satisfied with your own knowledge or your own understandings and that you will never be quite satisfied with the way things are.

Your task over the next four years, women and men of the Class of 2003, is to assess where you fit into the time and place that is yours. Dartmouth is first and foremost an academic community—a community where faculty and students work together, learn together, grapple with the uncertainties that this world poses for us, together. You now need to decide how you understand and relate to the world around you and to the others who inhabit it with you; how you will advance the beauty of human creativity; and how you will share the good fortune that becomes yours today. Dartmouth has an enviable reputation as a place where students are happy. I have two caveats about that that I would like to share with you: being happy does not have to mean being content. Second, it is fine for you to feel frustrated and unhappy at times. It really is okay! That does not make you an outlier. Rather, it makes you an adult grappling with questions about who you are and what you will be.

President John Sloan Dickey used to tell Dartmouth students each year at convocation, "Your business here is learning." This purpose has not changed, and I enjoin you to be more than merely passive observers in the process; I urge you actively to seek out and to engage the questions of our time. None of us would pretend that this is an easy assignment. You need to find a way to fit into an institution and its intellectual assumptions, even as you challenge those assumptions and as you challenge this institution itself.

The Spanish author Miguel de Unamuno once wrote, "May God deny you peace but give you glory." I would not deny you peace, but the glory is yours to find—and yours to define. To illustrate this, I think in particular of three young men who came to Dartmouth just about a century ago and of the experiences they had. Each came with a sense of trepidation, and each had to work to find his own particular niche at the college. Indeed one of them never did, and he left after only a term. However, despite the difficulties they faced when they first came here, each became an important part of the history of the twentieth century; each found his own way in the world.

Kan'ichi Asakawa was born in 1873 in Nihonmatsu, Japan, the son of a samurai. He went to university in Tokyo, and he was then encouraged to come to the United States—and, in particular, to come to Dartmouth College. Think of the difficulty of his trip and the apprehensions Asakawa must have had. Nonetheless, he graduated with full honors in the Class of 1899 and went on to get his Ph.D. in history from Yale. He subsequently came back to Dartmouth to introduce a new program in Asian studies—the first such program at the college and, probably, the first in the United States. Asakawa very likely was the first university faculty member in this country to teach Japanese language to undergraduate students.

Ten years younger than Asakawa, Ernest Everett Just was born in 1883, at Charleston, South Carolina. Descended from slaves, he was only four years old when his father died, leaving a widow and three young children. Mary Just, Ernest's mother, was a remarkable woman. She moved her family out of Charleston to James Island, where she worked in the phosphate mines, and then went on to found a black township and a school for African American children. She insisted that her son Ernest needed to pursue an education, and at age sixteen he traveled by boat, by train, and finally by stage to Meriden, New Hampshire—just fifteen miles down the road from here—where he attended Kimball Union Academy and excelled academically.

Ernest Just matriculated at Dartmouth in 1903, attracted by President William Jewett Tucker's "new Dartmouth." He did not have money to live on campus, and he found it hard to fit into a Dartmouth student body that was quite different in composition from the schoolmates he had known back in South Carolina. For the first six weeks, he rarely spoke to anyone. Like many first-year students, he was insecure and afraid that he would not be competitive academically. But although his academic accomplishments and records were at first uneven, by the conclusion of the year he had earned the highest grades in Greek ever received by a freshman at Dartmouth.

In his sophomore year, Just met Professor William Patten, chair of the Biology Department, who talked to him about his research. Captivated by this new field, Just went on to take every course the department had to offer. Ultimately, he became more involved in campus life, and in his senior year, he wrote a thesis, published two short stories and a poem, and excelled generally in the classroom. He graduated in 1907 as the top student in a class of 182. No members of his family were ever able to visit him at the college, and none saw him graduate. E. E. Just went on from

Dartmouth to secure a Ph.D. in biology and to teach at Howard University. As a scientist, he attained an international reputation. He helped to develop and define the field of cell biology. He was one of the organizers of the great Woods Hole Marine Biological Laboratory at Cape Cod.

Obviously, there are many stories, down to the present, describing students who came to the Hanover Plain feeling uncertain of what they would do and how they would fit. Yet, I expect that few have had to travel greater distances, socially or culturally, than did Ernest Everett Just or Kan'ichi Asakawa. Both worked not only within the conventions of the curriculum here, but also served to extend and to enrich that curriculum. Moreover, they spent their lives expanding knowledge, by helping to pioneer and develop new fields, and in that process they helped to shape the twentieth century.

In the autumn of 1892, another young man matriculated at Dartmouth. Coming as he did from Lawrence, Massachusetts, he had a short distance, geographically and culturally, to travel. But it still was not easy. He never quite became engaged. As he recalled later, "I didn't seem to have any sense of what I was doing. I didn't seem to think it was serious at all. . . . I sort of lost my interest." That man left at Christmas and never returned to Dartmouth as a student, although he would in after years return here many times and become a source of great intellectual inspiration to generations of Dartmouth students.

I share with you an account of that student's experience not to encourage you to leave at Christmas, but to assure you that it is in fact all right to work through your own fit. The name of that nongraduate, member of the Class of 1896, was Robert Frost. While his stay at Dartmouth was short-lived, Frost, in his long and productive lifetime, expanded our understanding — our sense of who we are and how we relate to others, our sense of the beauty of language and the world around us. Frost said in one of his poems: "The utmost reward / Of daring should be still to dare." I hope that you will, if you do not already, come to enjoy his poetry as I have, and will indeed dare to dare in your time at Dartmouth.

Certainly, this century now concluding has been richer because of Robert Frost and of Ernest Everett Just and of Kan'ichi Asakawa. As we look back on this century, let us conclude that knowledge can lead to power, but not necessarily to wisdom, that individuals can make a difference, and that much remains to be done. A Korean proverb suggests,

"Plant a tree today, even though you know the world will end tomorrow." As we face a new century and a new millennium, we symbolically plant here, at this place of learning, these trees—assuming, to be sure, a tomorrow, but as an act of faith as much as reason. This convocation represents an act of faith on your part and on Dartmouth's.

SEPTEMBER 19, 2000

. . . . Convocation serves as a symbolic occasion, one that officially marks a new academic year in Dartmouth's long and venerable history. But it also serves a specific purpose: we gather this morning to greet our newest class and to welcome them to this place of learning. Members of the Class of 2004, you will be able to date the commencement of your Dartmouth career with the beginning of a new millennium. It will always provide a ready benchmark for the beginning of this phase of your lives. But apart from the artificial construct of the millennium, you will have a more important reference point, because your undergraduate career begins in the year in which the human genome was mapped—at least, in its first draft.

There is no doubt that the conclusion of this phase of the human genome project represents a triumph of modern science and of modern scientific collaboration. For most of human history—certainly, down to the Second World War—advances in our understanding of the natural and physical world were most often marked by the lonely experimenter, by an individual making and recording observations, developing and testing hypotheses, doing analyses and calculations—the work of a Galileo, a Darwin, a Curie, or an Einstein. Science today typically involves teams of researchers, and the major scientific achievements of the twentieth century have been increasingly collaborative efforts: the Manhattan Project, the Apollo Project, the Human Genome Project. This development says much about the growing complexity and cost of science, about the need for multi-disciplinary approaches, about our ability to process massive amounts of digital information. It also says much, however, about our capacity to collaborate. In the instance of the human genome there was even an important public/private collaboration—or, at least, coordination—in the final months.

I am not a scientist. Others will need to make comments about the science and the scientific consequences of this breakthrough. Many people will spend many years sorting out both the biological meaning and the implications of this accomplishment. Yet, although much remains to be explained, the completion of this first phase has a bearing on the business before us today—the business of learning. You will quickly realize that it is in the nature of scholarship that answers inevitably lead to more questions—and often to more complicated questions. Albert Einstein insisted, "The important thing is never to stop questioning." The mapping of the human genome marks more of a starting point than a conclusion. It raises complicated questions having to do with matters such as genetic manipulation, with the development of policy, and with the allocation of resources. It forces us to confront issues having to do with acknowledging the assumptions that lead to definitions of "normal," issues having to do with variation and difference, with privacy and confidentially—with questions, indeed, that ultimately have to do with who we are and with what we can expect to be.

This scientific breakthrough promises much. But now the difficult work is before us—to use this knowledge to eradicate or ameliorate conditions and maladies that cause misery and suffering. As a society we must wrestle with vexing issues concerning the role—and the public responsibility—of modern science. How does society assign priority to working on specific projects? What role should the public play in deciding how to allocate our scarce resources? And there are many other questions to be faced including who owns the human genomic code? Already there are half a million patents pending that would claim proprietorship of various findings.

Beyond the science involved, the Human Genome Project raises critical ethical issues having to do with privacy—with our ability to protect information about our own genetic structures, about those genomic sequences that may influence our individual health or our physical and emotional development. This information relates, in turn, to questions about the delivery of medical care and the provision of insurance. Will we all have an equal claim to the medical benefits that will derive from these discoveries? Will there be "haves" and "have nots?" Knowledge about individual genetic codes or mutations may lead to employment, as well as other forms of, discrimination. There is the potential for a new variant, perhaps, on the nineteenth-century "survival of the fittest" theories, which unfortunately sought to apply Darwin's findings to society.

It is not clear how best to sort through these matters, but we all have a stake in this for surely the answers will impact us all. The questions we face concerning the human genome are not the singular responsibility of scientists. Rather, confronting them will require the creative energy of scholars from across the academy, and may best be answered by those working at the intersections of disciplines. Thus, they relate to the core mission of a liberal education—to the core mission of a place like Dartmouth. Daniel Coit Gilman, the first president of The Johns Hopkins University, hoped that "American universities [would] cherish all branches of learning. . . . Let not," he said, "our love of science diminish our love of letters." Surely, scholars from all across the academy have much to offer as we move into this exciting new period in our history.

Finally, this discovery reminds us to recognize and to celebrate the important genetic similarities of all life forms. The human genome map should cause each of us to be a little less arrogant. (Fruit flies, flat worms, and yeast cells have much the same chemical make-up as we do!) And even more than the basic similarities that cut across life forms, we need to acknowledge the common molecular structures of all peoples. Four relatively simple nucleic acid bases form the core of each of us. We each share 99.9 percent of the human genome code—meaning that the genetic makeup of any two persons differs by only one-tenth of one percent.

The human genome map has been called our "instruction book" and the "book of life." President Clinton even described it as "the language in which God created life." As we think of the marvel of this accomplishment and of the mystery that it has unraveled, however, we must avoid the tendency to genetic determinism. Above all, we need to remember that we are each very much more than the sum of our genes. We are each shaped by the many environments through which we pass and by the choices we make.

Members of the Class of 2004, every one of you is here this morning because of who you are. We selected and invited you individually—with attention to your accomplishments, your personal potential, your capacity to make this a stronger and more interesting place, your own promise to live lives that will make those of others fuller, richer, more informed. We expect much of you, as you have already demanded much of yourselves. Your choices and your commitments will continue to shape the turns your lives will take. For it is the case that our ambitions for ourselves, our values, our generosity of spirit, our capacity to love and to share, that these remain our own value-added qualities. This is true even if we learn that some sequencing of the four nucleic acids ACGT influences these.

33

Some of us have been dealt particular advantages in life; others of us have overcome disadvantages. Each of us must actively, individually, live our lives and make choices. We are not mechanically following a predestined program. Each of us must insist upon being sustained by our hopes rather than being directed by our fates. Georgia Johnson, a poet of the Harlem Renaissance, wrote:

> The right to make my dreams come true
> I ask, nay, I demand of life,
> Nor shall fate's deadly contraband
> Impede my steps, nor countermand.

Sometime in the future, science may well reveal which of us has a greater genetic propensity to excel as a poet, as a caregiver, as a good and loyal friend. I hope not. Human will and human spirit, generosity and creativity, these surely are more than manifestations of biological codes. Remember this well: You are individuals and are not categories defined by color, by gender, by other characteristics, or even by the coincidence of all being members of the Class of 2004. You each will assert your independence and enrich us by your unique qualities. We count on that. Our institutional vitality is sustained by it.

But even at this place marked by personal strengths and individual aspirations, never forget how much we depend on each other. Being independent does not have to mean being selfish or being lonely. Today, you join a community, one that derives its energy from our individual accomplishments *and* its identity from our shared values and our capacity to collaborate and to support each other. Dartmouth depends upon an implicit compact that assures mutual respect and an implicit recognition of how much each of us has yet to learn—and of how much each of us can yet learn.

SEPTEMBER 24, 2001

. . . . On behalf of the college, I am especially delighted to greet here the members of the Class of 2005. Having already shaken your hands at matriculation, I recognize you as old friends. And I'm honored to salute you as the largest class in the history of Dartmouth College—a distinction that we had not expected you to achieve and one that we intend to allow you to retain for quite some time. As one who himself can think of no place he would rather be, it is a privilege for me to welcome so many others who simply wanted to be here. What a great foundation for all of us to build upon.

As members of the Class of 2005, you have by now stored in your own mental scrapbooks your first Dartmouth memories as students—outing club trips, athletic events, class orientation activities, social gatherings, meeting roommates, making friends. I hope that each of you is already enriched by a treasure trove of happy experiences. But throughout your long lifetimes of remembering these, you will also never be able to dismiss some uninvited companions of your thoughts: searing images of horrendous tragedy and stories of courage, of suffering, and of unspeakable loss. September 2001, the month that you matriculated at Dartmouth, is destined to be more than merely a calendar notation in your personal diary.

The inhuman acts of terrorism in New York City, Washington, D.C., and the Pennsylvania countryside will forever cry out from the recollections of this time. History is now encumbered by this memory; understanding its significance will be far more complicated. While you have come to a place where we try to make sense of things, there is no act of intellectual legerdemain by which we can transform the irrational, suddenly, into the rational.

On September 11 our most common reactions were ones marked by shock, alarm, grief, and anger. For some, these feelings may have evolved into emotions of fear and of hatred. But it is critical that we not surrender to either fear or hatred. This nation may necessarily feel a lessened sense of security, indeed of innocence, as a result of this terror, but our ideals— national and human—must not be eclipsed by a pervasive sense of insecurity. We are right to be cautious—but not afraid. One cannot live a good life if it is imprisoned by fear and guarded by suspicion.

Robert Frost cautioned us, "Before I built a wall I'd ask to know What I was walling in or walling out. . . .

We all recognize that evil individuals exist in the world—individuals who have no respect for the dignity, the lives, the basic humanity, of others—or, finally, of themselves. It is, however, a complicated matter to move from knowing this to understanding and addressing it. As we cry out for justice, we must recognize that true justice requires both process and result and that the two sustain one another. Hatred does not promote these things. Never forget that those who sought to help far, far outnumbered those who sought to hurt.

The last two weeks have revealed stories of breathtaking selflessness and heroism, stories of those in airplanes and smoky stairwells, those amidst mountains of ash and rubble, stories of police and fire fighters and emergency crews, and of others who put their lives at risk—who, all too often, sacrificed their lives—to save others. Members of our broader Dartmouth community, from among our graduates and friends, were lost in this tragedy. Others from our community stepped up to help in the horrific aftermath.

It is perhaps human nature for us to wonder how we would respond if personally confronted by these things. Would we, too, display such resolute and unselfish courage? My wish and prayer for you is that you never have to discover the answer to this inquiry. Remember though there are many different types of heroism. Our society at this important juncture also needs individuals who will step forward to insist that we not extrapolate from the psychoses of a handful and harbor stereotypes based on race, nationality, or religion. Such actions will only compound the tragedy we have experienced and advance the very goals of its perpetrators.

The spirit of patriotism that is currently abroad in this land helps to unify us when we feel isolated and alone. It is a good and proper sentiment. We have reason for a sense of common pride, and we have clear need for a sense of common purpose. But as we celebrate and salute America, let us remember that our strength and our durability rest upon cornerstone values. Among these are democracy and freedom, openness and inclusion, due process and civil liberties, individual rights and individual accountability. That these values have been unevenly available and inequitably shared over the course of our history does not diminish them.

The Three-fifths Clause of the Constitution, the Alien and Sedition Acts, the Trail of Tears, Dred Scott, Heart Mountain, My Lai, these stand as reminders of when we have forgotten these basic values, of those times when we have allowed expedience, selfishness, fear, or hatred to define us. The Declaration of Independence and the Bill of Rights, Antietam and the Emancipation Proclamation, Normandy and the liberation of Auschwitz, *Brown v. Board of Education,* and a history defined by waves of immigration and by the development of a pluralist and rich society and culture— these things bear fuller witness to who we are and surely they should set our aspirations. If we have not today fully met the promise of our founding as a nation, we are insistently moving toward it. Continuing progress requires us to remember well that principles and values are not shouted slogans but must be matters that whisper in our hearts and inform our conduct.

There are those who suggest that the world of higher education is an ivory tower set apart from some real world. Let me say that this world— this so-called ivory tower, this world of ideas, of possibility, of wonder and of discovery, of embracing difference and of celebrating accomplishment—this world is indeed more real than are worlds marked by hatred, violence, and cruelty. Do not permit the cynics and the fearful to insist otherwise. Your task is to make the realities that are the everyday stuff of Dartmouth more common in the world at large. And, so, here we come to your assignment—not simply your first assignment at Dartmouth, but your assignment for a lifetime. . . . Thinking about the sort of person you will be is a far more complicated task than just thinking about your choices for employment or for subsequent graduate or professional education, as important as these matters are.

At Dartmouth, you have joined a vibrant, intellectually engaged, exciting community of thinkers. This college is not a place that you simply pass through, as part of a group of young women and men who are to be filled with canonical and fixed knowledge, and then, following a four-year aging process, officially certified as learned. Today you embark on a journey more demanding and energizing than that. Dartmouth is a place of learning that requires your full and active participation. Here, where the liberal arts occupy a central position, you yourself will share a responsibility for shaping your learning. Moreover, you will quickly discover that you have set forth upon a lifetime of learning, growing, and changing. Finite courses of study can never keep up with the infinitely expanding knowledge that will mark your lives. Nor can static learning prepare you for the unimagined challenges that your generation may face.

Your lifetimes will be shaped—as they already have been—by unfolding discoveries and by technological marvels, as we understand better the universe around us and the genetic code within us. You will need to be prepared for continually expanding your knowledge—and for unlearning things as well. Here at Dartmouth we urge you to follow a course of study that takes you along intellectual trails you never thought to follow. Here you will come to appreciate better your place in a physical and natural world, in a social and political world, in a world of natural and human history, in a world of arts and letters, of belief systems, and of human creativity. As scientific discoveries and technological advances enlarge our sense of the possible, as stunning acts of cruelty and malice constrict our hopes, we gain equilibrium more readily when we are grounded in reflections on what it is to be a human being. Our guides for this may be works of observation, reflection, and artistic representation that are as old as human records or as contemporary as the creative and insightful thinkers who provoke and enliven our lives today. John Adams assured his son, "You will never be alone with a poet in your pocket."

Just as learning to learn is a lifetime goal of the liberal arts, so is learning how to learn with and from those who are different from you. Our "Alma Mater" has lines urging the sons and daughters of Dartmouth not to let its "old traditions" fail. I urge you to assume this obligation, and to remember that the oldest and truest tradition of this college is to provide a community that is welcoming, sustaining, and empowering—one that celebrates, rather than shies away from, difference. If this was but an implicit part of our founding charter 232 years ago, it has been our explicit goal for the last century. Learning is more than a formal academic process. It is also a social and cultural journey of discovery, as you learn to cross boundaries defined by race, gender, religion, place of origin, sexual orientation or identification, and political philosophy. Dartmouth is a community, and as a community we are strengthened immeasurably by our historical commitment to being more than a transient residential neighborhood.

Here community means welcoming and belonging; it means including and supporting; it means friendship, rather than mere acquaintance. You will likely never again live and work in such a close residential community with so many people who are different from you and who have so much to offer you—just as you have so much to offer them. I call on you to cross boundaries, to learn about classmates and friends who are not like you, and to learn about yourself in the process. This surely is what education is about. And this is more than a singular experience limited to under-graduates. Those of you who best learn to handle these transactions will be enriched for the rest of your lives. You will be the stronger as a result, as will be the society in which you live. The recent census confirms what we can all observe: that this country is a bright tapestry of differences. Recent events attest to the urgency of crossing boundaries, of embracing differences, as we find and celebrate our common humanity. In a world that increasingly is global economically, culturally, and politically, this truth, this urgency, becomes ever more compelling.

September 2001 needs to be marked by more than a memory of violence and suffering. We need to grieve and remember those who have been lost, commend those who were our heroes, and comfort those who mourn and suffer. How better to do this than by dedicating ourselves to confronting hatred and rejecting stereotypes, by seeking justice and by its corollary of confronting injustice. This task is one that we must individually assume as a living memorial to the victims of these tragic events.

. . . . It is a special pleasure to welcome the Class of 2006. We are delighted that you are at Dartmouth. Each of you is here because of who you are, what you have accomplished, what you promise to accomplish, and the sort of person you are. We invited you as an individual, and it is as an individual that your achievements and contributions will be assessed, here and for the rest of your life.

We treasure your unique qualities, but independence of mind, a quality that we both value and admire, can never be an excuse for selfishness of spirit. You will all recognize in time, if you do not already, that those things which will count the most in your lives will finally derive from relationships with others. Few people ever assess a life well lived as one marked by self-absorption. Herein lies the essential tension of the academy and of life: how to pursue your own personal goals and singular efforts within a value system that is fundamentally collaborative and dependent upon sharing.

This is where the role of society and of community comes in. At their best, aggregations of individuals encourage the application of personal talents and strengths within an ethos that promotes the common good. Dartmouth is an academic community that thrives on individual achievement and merit. Our personal accomplishments are enabled by our shared and common values—values that cherish discovery and learning, innovation and change, independence and distinction, and do this within an environment that is collaborative and collegial, supportive and empowering, open and tolerant.

All communities, save perhaps the smallest and most homogeneous, have intermediating groups; some that we form or join, some that we enter at birth. I would like to spend a few minutes today talking about the latter, the involuntary groups, those to which we are assigned for categorical reasons; those determined by our gender, our sexual orientation, the color of our skin, or other racial or ethnic characteristics. As individuals we may willingly, even eagerly and proudly, identify with such a group. When a broader culture defines us based upon these traits, however, it is not a voluntary act. We lose part of our individuality. My focus this morning is on a topic that we need to become more comfortable about discussing: the cultural construct or conception of race. Racial identity can be a wonderfully positive and beneficial factor in a person's life, but race can also have negative consequences for an individual and society when it is considered to be otherness, as stereotypical, as a confining, defining, and constraining barrier.

The diversity of American society has made us richer as a nation. We have benefited immensely from the fact that, despite the best efforts of some to make the metaphor real, the so-called melting pot did not, in fact, melt and blend us into a homogeneous whole. Rather, even in moments of struggle, our differences have enriched us and our shared values have strengthened us. In the United States today, about 30 percent of the population are racial or ethnic minorities; and, indeed, in some states, like California and Hawaii, those we consider minority groups make up more than half of the population. It is long past time for us to move along the unfinished work of challenging conventional demographic and racial stereotypes and assumptions.

Our growing recognition of global interdependence underlines the importance of this task. We have in the past twelve months had the lesson dramatically affirmed that we all need to put aside stereotypes in order to advance beyond hate and fear. Last year, we had some good and heated discussions on this campus about terrorism and the ways to defend against it, about civil liberties and the challenges they face in times of insecurity, and about Israel and the Palestinians. These are clear matters for debate. And we have more such debates to come. Part of the Amidah meditation includes the prayer, "Help me to avoid shameful speech, as well as shameful silence." Debate means listening as well as speaking, and here it leaves no place for intimidation, for anti-Semitism, for anti-Muslim and anti-Arab attitudes, for racism, or for impugning the patriotism of those who challenge prevailing wisdom. The most enduring wisdom is that which welcomes challenge. The best debate is the one that tests ideas rather than asserts them.

Dealing with racial, ethnic, and religious stereotypes may be one of the most pressing challenges of your generation, and there is no better place or time than here and now for you to begin creating the future that you would like to see. I am pleased that the Class of 2006 is the most racially diverse class in Dartmouth's history. Now you need to determine what you will do with the circumstance in which you find yourself. If you take advantage of the opportunity to advance your own education, your own understanding and learning, you will also add greatly to the strength of this community—and, in the years ahead, to that of the many communities you will enrich for the rest of your lives. Just as learning to learn is a lifetime goal of the liberal arts, learning how to learn with and from those who are different from you is an essential quality that will be much in demand in this century. Here at Dartmouth learning is understood, at its core, as being a habit of the heart and mind that seeks continually to understand better and to know more, one that is never quite satisfied by answers, and that is always imagining the next questions that ought to be asked. This is the sort of liberal learning that can sustain a life well lived.

In addition to the rewarding academic life that you now commence, today you also enter a classroom without boundaries, a course of study not circumscribed by time limits, a learning environment that is as much about people as about place. With few exceptions, never before, and likely never again, will you live and work in such a small, intimate twenty-four-hour-a-day community, with so many people so different from you. If you seek out only the obviously like and like-minded, your comfort might initially seem somewhat greater, but your challenges, I can assure you, will be smaller and your learning will be the less. Johnnetta Cole wrote, "Leadership comes not only from growing up in a place called home, but from growing out into unfamiliar places."

Survey data from previous Dartmouth classes suggest that students come here wanting to transcend boundaries and to make new and different friends. The data also indicate that upon graduation many wish that they had been more successful in this task. I urge you to determine now not to share in that regret. Your four years will pass all too quickly. The faculty and administration are eager to help you in this challenge, but ultimately it will be up to each of you, as individuals and as members of the Dartmouth community, to approach one another in the spirit of openness that will make new relationships possible.

In order for you to do this, let us confront an obstacle that must be overcome, one that we shall work on together during your time here. We need to consider the way that the concept of race is used in our society and the assumptions that we attach to the very idea of race. Those in the

racial majority must scrutinize and then set aside one especially deleteri-
ous assumption: the notion that students of color are the "other." Any who
make such an assumption impose a normative system, a value judgment,
upon difference, transforming an enriching quality into a divisive and
hierarchical category. Many of you have moved well beyond this concept.
We all need to do so.

Here we have an opportunity to come together as a community and to
begin to engage in a critical, respectful examination of our assumptions
about race. The manifestation of one assumption is all too familiar: the
inquiry on the part of some whites of why black students or Asian students or Latino students or Native students—students whose identity is
racialized—hang out together. We rarely ask why less superficially identi-
fiable groups—Catholic students, Jewish students, lacrosse teammates, a
group of women or men, white students—hang out together.

I was disappointed last year to learn the results of a study, conducted
here as a senior thesis that revealed that most white students surveyed
did not acknowledge that they belonged to a race. They did not recognize
whiteness as culturally meaningful. These students seemed to have little
understanding of the privilege that they enjoyed, as whites, in a racialized, hierarchical environment, one in which they implicitly assumed
their own conduct and experience was normative.

Potentially, the most destructive consequence of this attitude in our
society, largely as part of the debate over affirmative action, is the belief
held in recent years by some whites that their accomplishments and recognition have been due solely to merit, while the accomplishments of students of color reflect an advantage conferred by race. Some of these same
individuals further see whites as now comprising a disadvantaged group.
We need to confront this view directly and consistently: Students of color
cannot be asked to bear the dual burden of presumed "otherness" on the
one hand (implicitly the inferiority of difference), and at the same time
an assumed advantage deriving from this. It is worse than illogical; it is
worse than untrue. It is corrosive of our best impulses, and it impedes our
highest aspirations. We cannot put disadvantage behind us until we fully
understand and confront advantage.

I can pretty confidently say that each of you is proud of who you are.
You surely should be. I am proud of you, too. Goodness, you have worked
hard to be in this assembly today. As I noted at the outset, each of you is

Wright with Dartmouth Hall in the background, March 2006. Photo by Joe Mehling.

here as an individual, because of what you have accomplished and for what you promise. Recognizing advantage is not to ignore personal accomplishment. One of my grandfathers was a miner. The other was a farm worker. Neither they nor my grandmothers completed high school. I am the first member of my family to receive a college degree. I know full well how hard I worked to move from where I was to this microphone. I also know how lucky I have been. I know I enjoyed an advantage. Others were surely more able, but not so lucky. And for my generation if they were people of color or women, their accomplishments were constrained by category. Let us work together to confront and move beyond the vestiges of this circumstance, and surely substantial vestiges remain.

I wish I could say that addressing these matters will be easy things for you. They will not be, and few societies or times have shown them to be so. But I have confidence in you as individuals and I have great hopes for what you can contribute to this community. Dartmouth historically has sought to move beyond category to recognize the worth and dignity of each person. Your accomplishments to date and your admission here confirm my view that you will assist in this good work. Barbara Jordan once said, "I have faith in young people because I know the strongest emotions which prevail are those of love and caring and belief and tolerance." I agree with her. We have made some progress. The senior society Palaeopitus organized a panel discussion last year on race and white privilege, and it served as a catalyst for good conversations. We must build upon this work—surely Dartmouth would be the richer as a result. And so will your experiences here be—and your lives.

. . . . It is my particular privilege formally to extend Dartmouth's welcome to the members of the Class of 2007. While I have had the opportunity to greet each of you individually, this ceremonial occasion closes the time of transition for you and invites your lifetime commitment to the good work of learning.

This is an exciting time at Dartmouth. You have arrived as we begin to advance a number of capital projects to enhance the academic and out-of-classroom experience. We are moving forward with

the construction of residence halls for five hundred students;
a dining and social center to serve undergraduate and graduate students, faculty, and staff;
Kemeny Hall for the Department of Mathematics;
the companion Academic Centers Building, which will house the Dickey Center for International Understanding, the Ethics Institute, and the Leslie Humanities Center;
an addition to the Sudikoff Laboratory for Computer Science; and
a new facility for the Engineering Sciences Center at the Thayer School.

Generous Dartmouth alumni and friends have pledged over $90 million toward the realization of these projects. And, by the time you graduate, in 2007, we hope to have completed each of them. Together, they will further enhance the academic and residential life of this college. You have joined an intellectually vibrant community.

You have also joined a community sure of its purposes and anchored by its values. In your short time here, you have already learned the songs and have heard the stories that echo throughout these hills. They proclaim a sense of community and of belonging, a sense of responsibility for other students and for your college, and a profound and enduring sense of place. The ethos of Dartmouth declares that these immeasurable, personal, even subjective things are not part of a transient four years of your life, but are now or will soon be for a lifetime "builded" in your hearts. Like those who have preceded you, you will carry from here the enduring granite of your experience.

You bring with you a wide range of ambitions and expectations. We do not expect, nor do we wish, you to be all alike; we cherish you as individuals. Despite your unique hopes and fears and experiences, we have determined that you do share with each other and with this college one thing of paramount importance: a commitment to learning. This is indeed our shared purpose, and, without it, it would be hard to justify either your or this college being here. Let us, then, today talk about learning.

A great deal of the learning that you will do here will take place outside of the formal academic spaces of classroom, laboratory, and studio—as of course it should at a residential college. I urge you to take fullest advantage of the opportunities that Dartmouth offers in the performing and creative arts and our wonderfully full schedule of public lectures. Participate in outdoor and athletic programs. Take in the beauty of the North Country; take on the pleasure of serving this wider community through the Tucker Foundation or other programs. Enroll in an off-campus program. Your class and this community include many persons whose backgrounds differ from your own. Realizing the potential of this diverse community needs your active engagement to advance your learning—and the learning of all who can learn from you.

But my focus today is on the formal liberal learning that Dartmouth advances so exceptionally. A liberal arts education is about process more than product, in that it seeks to encourage a lifetime of learning and unlearning—an intellectual impatience and curiosity that never allows you to be quite satisfied with what you know. A Dartmouth education may finally enable you to do many things with your lives, and that is good. But you will seriously devalue your opportunity here if you think of the next four years simply as a path to a job, or consider our courses of study as being discrete units that teach skills with a market value or that substantiate a resume.

Dartmouth President Ernest Martin Hopkins told his all-male student body that the primary concern of a Dartmouth education "is not with what men shall do but with what men shall be." Seventy-five years later, I echo Mr. Hopkins' advice, in telling today a class having more women

47

than men that while, of course, we urge you to pursue a career and calling that you will find fulfilling, we care fundamentally about the sort of person you will be and how you will live your lives.

Dartmouth is part of an educational tradition that has existed for at least a millennium. Our own college history dates back two and a third centuries. In the late eighteenth century, Dartmouth faculty, like those at other colleges of the time, had few doubts about the truths or texts they taught, although their certainty existed within a physical and a natural world that remained ill-defined and, even, mysterious—perhaps acceptably so. Today, while we might better understand our natural and physical world and are eager to improve our knowledge in these areas, we are less confident than were our ancestors about the received truths that anchor our lives.

The one thing I can assure you now is that your own certainties and understandings will continue to change. Most of you were born in 1985. In that year, the Soviet Union still held sway over much of Eastern Europe and apartheid still controlled South Africa; there was no World Wide Web; personal computers were new, clumsy, and slow; the genetic code was largely an abstraction; and women served only in limited roles within the U.S. military.

Your lives will continue to be marked by stunning developments in science and technology, bearing upon our understanding of the physical and natural world in which we live and about the cosmos of which we are a part—indeed, are just a particle. You need while here to continue the process of understanding these things as best we can now understand them—and some of you will begin a lifetime of expanding our understandings. None of you should leave Dartmouth without engaging with the work that defines modern science and technology. This is a critical purpose of liberal learning. But there is more.

The binary world of hypothesis tests, of experiments and empiricism, of correct and incorrect, of either/or, of if/then has limits. We have developed remarkable capacity to observe, to model, to analyze, to sort, to calculate, and to describe things—but after all of this, as scientists would be the first to warn us, we still finally need to be able to understand and explain. And the more we engage the timeless efforts by philosophers, poets, historians, artists, and writers to understand who we are and what we value, the less binary our world seems.

48

Wright at his desk in the President's Office, December 2007. Photo by Joe Mehling.

A few months ago, British Prime Minister Tony Blair said before the U.S. Congress that there had never been a time when "a study of history provides so little instruction for our present day." Perhaps. But, as a historian, I would encourage you not to look to history for practical guidance, for instruction, or for recipes for life. History, together with the liberal arts more generally, assists us in knowing that the human experience is a complicated and rich continuum and that ours is not a world that we can model and predict.

There are indeed canons, or at least timeless texts, that can guide and that I encourage you to study. But the reading of them is not fixed for all time. Who could read Othello today with the same assumptions about race that marked those of Elizabethan England? Who could disagree that the inspiring goal of "life, liberty, and the pursuit of happiness" has a fuller and richer, indeed, a more complicated, meaning today than it did in our colonial past? Who could deny that while Morrison and Marquez do not replace Shakespeare and Whitman, they enrich our reading of them, and surely expand our context for knowing? In the complicated world of the academy, which you now join, knowledge and understanding evolve and the world is seldom so simple as evil versus good, foolish versus enlightened, traditional versus modern.

The liberal arts require an engagement with the historic and contemporary work of the arts and humanities, the social sciences and the sciences, work that wrestles with understanding the human condition. If learning is an individual process, it does not at Dartmouth need be a lonely one, for you are accompanied by your classmates, your faculty, all of those who have preceded you here, and, finally, by all of humanity. The books that sit on shelves in the library, or on the virtual shelves of the digital library, the works of art on our walls, and the compositions that flow from musical instruments are also good companions—they do not shout at you, but they can quietly inform. Life that is not engaged with them is not so full.

Read and think critically. You have a role, independently, of determining what is good and what is beautiful, what is moral and ethical, and your judgments will be informed by the education you now embrace. The academy insists upon including and enabling; we value individuality and accomplishment; we depend upon integrity and honesty and upon academic freedom; we are sustained by discourse and by respect and tol-

The Wrights in June 2009 with members of the 1988 History Department Foreign Study Program they led in London. Personal photo.

erance. Eleanor Roosevelt once said, "A mature person is one who does not think only in absolutes, who is able to be objective even when deeply stirred emotionally, who has learned that there is both good and bad in all people and all things, and who walks humbly and deals charitably with the circumstances of life, knowing that in this world no one is all-knowing and therefore all of us need both love and charity." The liberal arts allow you freedom to find your own ways of knowing, but they will not allow you to believe that you do this in a vacuum or that each idea or insight is equally valid. Protecting the right of individuals to hold their own views is a cornerstone of the academy, but our energy does not derive from acknowledging the equal validity of all views.

And surely we do not suggest a moral relativism. There are finally some things that are morally and ethically good or correct—or at least things that we now believe to be, others that we hope to become understood as, good or correct—meaning as right, as appropriate, as normative. Our shared moral principles strengthen us as a community.

Your lives have already been marked by change and complexity. You have known acts of cruelty and of kindness and of sacrifice. So will you always live through and know these things. We would like to be able to assure you that the liberal arts will provide you with answers, with a road map for life, with the same confidence with which our eighteenth- and early nineteenth-century predecessors approached education. But here you will likely encounter more questions than answers—good questions, about choices and nuance, about taste and judgment, about standing for and defending those things you believe to be right. We warn you, however, that being educated is no guarantee of being wise—or being good or being responsible.

Alfred North Whitehead, perhaps in a more optimistic age, defined our task in higher education as "the creation of the future." Recognizing today our limits in controlling and shaping that which will come, liberally educated women and men nonetheless experience life with a sense of history, of ballast, of context, which enables them to cope, at worst, and to shape, at best, the way their lives play out. When we encourage you to learn how to learn, this is not to suggest that the process is independent of, or more important than, the subject. Learning is not a method, but it is a habit of mind, one that is open and inquisitive and critical, one that is informed and shaped by knowing how those who preceded us wrestled with those questions that vex us.

Moreover, learning is not a passive process—it is an engaged and inter-active one that is essentially fueled by your curiosity and your creativity. Engage here with your fellow students and your faculty and make your own tentative contributions to what we can know. William Merwin, who received an honorary doctorate from Dartmouth last June, wrote,

Inside this pencil
crouch words that have never been written
never been spoken
never been taught . . .

Each of you has such a pencil—or PC—with which you can take us where we have not yet been. You occupy a prized seat this morning—and we are so glad that you are here. My charge to you is simple: meet your own highest aspirations and your own best promise; then, as a consequence, your college and your world will each be the stronger, the richer, the more interesting.

. . . . It is my particular privilege formally to extend Dartmouth's welcome to the members of the Class of 2008. While I have had the opportunity to greet each of you individually, this ceremonial occasion closes the time of transition for you and invites you to enter upon a lifetime commitment to the good work of learning.

As is appropriate, we are all excited to be starting another academic year, the 235th time that Dartmouth has gathered for this purpose. Yet sharing thus a sense of our history, reminds us of our need today to mourn the death, even as we celebrate the life and contributions, of David T. McLaughlin, the fourteenth president of this college. Please join me in a moment of silence honoring this accomplished and dedicated son of Dartmouth. . . . I am pleased this morning to announce that the Board of Trustees has agreed to name the new Maynard Street residential complex the David T. McLaughlin Cluster in his honor. We hope to break ground this fall on this important facility, on space that the college acquired for this purpose as a result of his stewardship.

Members of the Class of 2008, you assembled here as individuals just a few short weeks ago. You now assume the additional privileges and responsibilities associated with being members of this community. Dartmouth is a historic and special community, one physically rooted on this plain along the Connecticut River, even as it reaches "round the girdled earth."

Already you have walked along paths laid out by Eleazar Wheelock and marked by Daniel Webster, smoothed by the tens of thousands of students who preceded you. You will gather together many more times—indeed in the year 2058 for your fiftieth reunion! This is what institutions are about. You are now part of a long and enduring and evolving history, one that has no end. And as you fix your place in this procession you should know too that tens of thousands of future students will follow in the footprints you leave.

These occasions afford me an opportunity to share my sense of this college, in observations shaped by thirty-five years here, teaching and learning, and also an opportunity to reflect upon the history of Dartmouth. I have in recent years talked about Dartmouth as a learning community, a place where the liberal arts provide the basis for a life well lived. I have reflected upon the importance of diversity as a critical ingredient in the educational experience. Today, I want to talk about two values that are central to our academic purpose, even as they are sometimes in tension with each other: our commitment to freedom of expression and our obligation to foster here a truly inclusive community.

This is an academic institution marked by a need to know, a passion to share what we know, and a curiosity about what we do not know. It depends upon shared values, a shared sense of purpose, and the assumption of shared responsibility. Our common purpose has little to do with what you have accomplished before you came here and everything to do with what you can accomplish—and what you can contribute to the accomplishments of others. You will learn from one another, and you have much to teach one another as well as the rest of us. You sit here in an arena full of classmates who can share with you this process of exploration. You will develop friendships that will sustain you for a lifetime. You need not be defensive about engaging with and forming essential friendships with those most like you. Life is full of stresses and tensions, and kindred souls—those who share with you a set of experiences, a common background, similar ambitions for life, tastes in music, literature, movies, recreational activities, common political values, or religious beliefs—these are comforting and supportive friends. But education finally needs to be more than simply comforting and merely reinforcing. Reach beyond your circle of comfort.

Learning is about expanding that which we know and also challenging that with which we are comfortable. College years—and, ultimately, full lives—are about testing our convictions, exploring our doubts, and engaging in debate and dialogue; these years are about challenges to certainty. Often the most fundamental dialogue is, or at least should be, with oneself. But such introspection can only follow exposure to ideas different from the ones you have brought with you. Now the opportunities for such exposure surround you.

An academic community—indeed a free society—rests on the freedom to think and to speak out. The free expression of ideas is a bedrock principle, even though not all that is thought or said is equally valid or true.

The corollary of the freedom of speech is the freedom to criticize that which is said. And sometimes this freedom to disagree becomes an obligation. If politeness and civility and mutual respect form the basis of our community, so too do engagement and debate and, assuredly, disagreement. Academic communities at their best are places that challenge more than they reinforce.

Dartmouth needs to be a place where arguments and assumptions and conclusions are tested—and, then, tested some more. This is as it should be. Dartmouth students are incredibly generous and willing to serve, concerned about moral and ethical dilemmas, and supportive of one another. Yours is a good generation—the future is in good hands. You are also for the most part incredibly polite. This is a good thing, but politeness and tolerance need not lead to a sort of intellectual or moral relativism that discourages you from challenging ideas with which you disagree. Discuss and debate. Do not accept the uninformed or the glib or the foolish as having equal validity with sound argument and the view well crafted—with the position shaped by explicit values and principles and informed by evidence, thought, and understanding.

As a historian, I regret the decline in American life of true dialogue and debate on fundamental matters. Our society segments itself too readily into enclaves marked by like-mindedness. Those times when we engage in debate about real differences or expose ourselves to those differences are all too rare in our society. We watch television stations, listen to talk shows, read publications, and journey to websites where what is presented serves only to reinforce what we already think, rather than to challenge our views. Attitude and ideology become more important than analysis and fact. Ideas are not things that prevail without context and contest. They need to be challenged and tested. Otherwise, they stand at best as attitude or opinion—or as prejudice.

The current election campaign underlines and sadly exemplifies my concern. There is a tremendous free range of ideas in this country, unfettered by law or convention. In this respect we have met the highest hopes of the political leaders and philosophers who founded the republic. But we surely have not met their ambitions for informed debate—Thomas Jefferson talked about the "boisterous sea of liberty." The American people deserve, and indeed need, a more substantive engagement of the real issues that confront our nation and our world. Discussions and calculations about red states and blue states, about tactics and polls, about funds raised and spent, about personal biography—as well as vicious smears that are cloaked in the wink of innuendo—these reduce the great issues of a great republic to a board game. The loser will not be one or another candidate. We shall all lose, because we will have allowed ourselves to be distracted from matters of substance. We deserve better, but we will have it only by taking on the civic responsibility of insisting upon better.

The long-term health of our political system depends upon the engagement of the young, upon your engagement. Your freedom to do as you wish with your life entails a cost: a responsibility to advance and enhance the life of the republic. Our history is full of the evidence of those who have paid the greatest price for you to have this gift. Talk to one another about the issues of the present political campaign. I suspect you will do a better job of wrestling with the profound issues of our time than the campaigns of any of the candidates now standing before us promise to do. Debate the ideas, not the personalities. The candidates will want to persuade you to accept their vision of the future—but remember this is your future they are discussing.

How do we engage in rigorous discussion of real issues in an atmosphere of respect and civility? How do we debate and disagree and challenge and still make this a community that is welcoming to all? This is the fundamental tension of American life—dating back to our defining documents, a Declaration of Independence, which affirmed life, liberty, and the pursuit of happiness, and a Constitution that shaped a government with power to direct and restrain. The first amendments of that Constitution provided protections for the individual from the government, and throughout our history citizens and the courts have sought to relate these powers and protections to the complicated interactions of a heterogeneous, vibrant, and sometimes contentious society. We have not always lived up to the promises of our founding. Liberty and equality, freedom and order, these abstractions that we applaud are marked by inherent tensions, mutual contradictions even, that we juggle constantly.

This brings us full circle. It writes large our own task. At Dartmouth no code or regulation restrains the right to the free expression of ideas. If it did we would lose something critical to our intellectual purpose and to our core values. But as a place of learning, the college too has a right, in-deed, a responsibility, to champion those ideals that shape us. We stand for certain fundamental things: the rigorous pursuit of knowledge and an openness to new ideas, academic freedom and a spirit of inquiry, in-tegrity and honesty, individuality and inclusiveness. We are sustained by vigorous discourse, as well as by respect and civility. Now, your right to challenge these values, or any others, is clear. But as president I assume the obligation to define and defend them and to protect here a learning community that welcomes us all—a community where, regardless of our race or gender or sexual orientation, we are all respected and valued, and one in which different political and religious views are encouraged.

Some critics suggest that the academy is marked by a particular ortho-doxy, a political correctness, although these same critics are frequently the most certain, even absolute, about truths—about what we should learn and about how we should know. If sometimes we seem more certain than we have a right to be, we also understand that the world is marked by change, and the tensions that often and necessarily follow change are seldom so simple as to be resolved by slogans. We recognize well the elu-siveness of the truth that we consistently seek. Standing for something while resisting the comfort of orthodoxy is complicated, but it is a neces-sary part of our work. As we welcome you into this academic community, I enjoin you to embrace both the free expression of ideas and the principle of community. It won't always be easy to balance them, but the struggle to do so is a fundamental part of a Dartmouth education.

At convocation in the fall of 1950, President John Sloan Dickey chal-lenged David T. McLaughlin and his fellow members of the Class of 1954 to remember that they were the "stuff" of this college—and what they were, Dartmouth would be. David McLaughlin surely spent the next fifty-four years making his college the better. While an undergraduate student, he was a star football player, president of the Junior class, a member of Phi Beta Kappa, and the head of the undergraduate student government. His was a long career of accomplishments; he assumed responsibility. As a student he joined President Dickey, the faculty, and other students in in-sisting that Dartmouth become a more open place. As a trustee he had the privilege of voting on behalf of the motion to make Dartmouth coeduca-tional. He always insisted that our purpose was to enhance Dartmouth for students not yet admitted-or not yet born. Now, the baton is in your hands. You are not consumers of an education here; you are colleagues in an institution committed to learning, and you are the beneficiaries of a legacy passed along by generations of Dartmouth graduates. Your obligation to them is to leave the college stronger still for those who will follow.

. . . . This morning, we share in a ritual that is as ancient as the academy at a place that is older than the Republic, and here we extend to the first-year members of this community an embrace that will be as enduring as the granite of the North Country. Members of the Class of 2009: Welcome! The air is electric with a new class in town. Quite aside from the pomp and ceremony, for most of us the true excitement of this assemblage is less about reflecting on the tradition and history that mark this day than it is about the anticipation and excitement that enrich it. '09ers, you bring much to this occasion, and we are caught up in your own enthusiasm for the journey that starts here.

As we begin another year in the history of this college and as our newest members begin an important stage in their lives, our mood of celebration is muted by nature's most recent cruel reminder of the fragility of human plans. Our attention necessarily is distracted by the tragedy on the Gulf Coast. Katrina, a random name associated with a random meteorological event, will evermore recall catastrophe. You would need to go back to the San Francisco earthquake of a century ago to find in the annals of this country a natural disaster as broadly and fundamentally devastating. We join in grieving for those who have been lost. Our hearts and our support go out to all who have suffered and who will endure suffering and dislocation and mourning for some time. Let us join together to resolve to reach out to them in whatever way we can. And let us share now a moment of silence, a moment to reflect or to pray. . . .

I would also like to extend today a special greeting to those students and faculty from institutions in New Orleans and the Gulf Coast who have come to us this fall. You are most welcome here, and we are indeed enriched by your presence. You have become a part of this community, and we shall consider you such even when you return to your home institutions. Your Dartmouth association is for a lifetime.

For 236 years now Dartmouth College has convened to go about the good work of learning. Since before the American Revolution, in an unbroken path to this moment, students, faculty, alumni/alumnae, staff, and officers of this college have collaborated and committed themselves to provide the best education possible. Here, students are not consumers of an education, but rather are beneficiaries of a rich and generous legacy, one that for each and every one of you has been shaped and subsidized by those who have preceded you. Few gifts that you will receive in your lifetime will ever exceed this one—this Dartmouth education.

Now, in turn, you assume three responsibilities. The first one, and it is one not ever to be taken lightly, is to take fullest advantage of the opportunity that it is your good fortune to have. Here you may study all that is now known, and here you find an environment and a faculty who will share with you a curiosity and a passion to extend that which we now know and to discover that which we do not. Pursue this opportunity fully; reach out to new areas of learning; expand your comfort zone; seek out and engage people whose views and interests differ from yours; understand the selfless generosity, the helping hand, that makes a true community—and as a corollary, recognize the even more complicated step of learning to accept help when it is extended to you. That reciprocity is an essential mark of a true community of true equals and true friends. You of the Class of 2009 commence on this date a voyage of liberal arts learning that will occupy you for a lifetime; and it is one that will enable you to make choices that fulfill best your own interests, your own aspirations, your own needs. Take it and run with it; it is yours. And don't ever underestimate the special opportunity you have.

But there were two other responsibilities you incur today. (With such a generous gift, of course there must always be a "But . . . !") While I hope and expect that your education here will enable you to fulfill your dreams and to pursue the career that you wish, Dartmouth is also about more than you and what you will do in your life. Dartmouth is here because for over two hundred years people have had a special hope for it. And you, members of the Class of 2009, are here because we have a special hope for you: that as a member of this fellowship you will assume a lifetime responsibility to make this school the stronger, as well as a companion responsibility to make the world the better. The former, the work of always advancing this college, cannot be an act of institutional self-indulgence either. Last year Dartmouth was identified as one of the world's great enduring institutions. This is a very special recognition, in which we justly take pride. But finally our purpose is about more than merely enduring, simply hanging around.

Dartmouth can be justified only if it continues to do what it has done so well for so long: educate students who embrace teamwork, assume leadership, and understand the obligation that accompanies their good fortune; Dartmouth graduates readily understand and accept responsibility for the world in which they live. A natural disaster has provided you a pre-matriculation opportunity to understand the nature of your life assignment to contribute to the world in which you live.

Following Katrina's savage assault, it was not just levees and buildings and infrastructure that were destroyed, but lives were lost and hopes and dreams were shattered. Rebuilding the latter for those who survive and sustaining those who mourn will be by far the hardest task. This college, this community, has stepped up to help in this work. But our response to Hurricane Katrina must involve more than helping to rebuild that area—it is about more than plywood and new clothes, as critical as these are. We all, your generation and mine, face a far harder assignment. This natural disaster exposed levels of poverty and racial disparity that a good society simply must confront. We need firmly to resolve to address these issues.

I am accustomed to the generosity of the Dartmouth family and to the generosity of the broader community of which we are a part, but I am in this instance profoundly struck by the reminder that the toughest of times brings out the best from the best. You have already learned in your lifetimes that the test of human society is not the impossible task of preventing all bad things. Rather, the test is how good people respond to bad things. And I am always inspired by the response, by the generosity of the young.

When I was your age I was in the Marine Corps, having joined when I was still seventeen years old. Since I believe I am the only Marine ever to serve as an Ivy League president, I have long recognized my good fortune, and recently I have recognized perhaps a singular responsibility. This past summer I visited with the Marines being treated at the Bethesda Naval Hospital, each of whom had been very seriously injured in Iraq. I thanked them for their sacrifice, and I encouraged them to pursue their education, encouragement they did not, in fact, require. Several of them had enlisted following 9/11, withdrawing from school to do so, and are now ready to resume their education. On the occasion of that visit, I also learned from these hospitalized Marines, as I always do from young people. I was moved by their stories, impressed by their courage, and inspired by their enthusiasm to live lives that make a difference. It was I who was the beneficiary of my visit to them.

But, you know, those Marines at Bethesda are part of an inspiring generation—yours. As long as there have been people my age, they have assumed as a matter of privilege the right to wring their hands and to fret about people your age. Their metric is typically set at how they remember their generation when they were you. And you know already from your own experience how that comparison will typically end. The odds are not with you. All I can say by way of reassurance is that it has always been so. Even the noble Socrates once wrote, "Children nowadays are tyrants. They contradict their parents, gobble their food, and tyrannize their teachers." I do not join in worrying about you. I have had the advantage of observing your generation closely, and I do not fret for the future of this Republic or for the extension of human decency and generosity under your care. There will be no hand wringing from this platform—instead, I raise my hand in salute for what you have already done, and I am heartened by the promise you bring here with you.

The work of Dartmouth students just in the past year or so affirms this promise. Students have been involved in projects ranging from a local Habitat for Humanity house to clinics in Central America and Kenya, to tutoring in local schools, to the Tsunami relief effort last winter. Campus Compact and the Princeton Review recently named Dartmouth a "College with a Conscience," because of its exemplary record of service and the extent of student engagement in outreach activities. Through the programs and activities of the Tucker Foundation, approximately 60 percent of undergraduates are involved in helping others. Last year, senior Rebecca Heller received the Campus Compact Howard R. Swearer Student Humanitarian Award for her service work. She volunteered with AmeriCorps and developed a program called Harvest for the Hungry that addressed hunger in the Upper Valley.

Our graduates also affirm this commitment and have inspired the culture here by the lives they lead. Last year a record 11 percent of the graduating class applied to participate in Teach for America. Since its inception under President John F. Kennedy, nearly forty-five years ago, 500 Dartmouth graduates have worked within the Peace Corps, and this past year a record number of Dartmouth graduates joined that organization—the second highest participation rate in the country. A number of other graduates have joined the military, some through ROTC and others through officer training programs. Nathaniel Fick of the Class of 1999 served in Afghanistan and Iraq as a Marine platoon leader and is now heading for a career in government service.

We take seriously here President John Sloan Dickey's invocation "The world's troubles are your troubles. . . . and there is nothing wrong with the world that better human beings cannot fix." In order to perform public service it is not necessary, of course, to devote yourself to a career in public service. This society is surely the better because of all of our graduates who have excelled in business and the professions and who have also assumed responsibility for helping to make their communities and their world the better.

You have joined a proud Dartmouth tradition, as you have enriched it already by your commitment to helping in the aftermath of Katrina. Your willingness to assume this task is consistent with the contributions that you have already made in your home communities and in your secondary schools. Everyone has a contribution to make, and it is up to you to decide how you will make yours. Your reputations and your work have preceded you. The world is in good hands—and if terrorists and the venal, the cynical and the selfish, get the headlines, they do not represent us, so long as we insist that we will not allow them to do so. They surely are not the majority of humankind. They are not our future. The young Marines at Bethesda are, the most committed teachers in the poorest schools are, the people who work with Paul Farmer are, the people who have stopped their own lives to contribute to the rebuilding of the lives of those on the Gulf Coast are, Sarah Billmeier, Nathaniel Fick, and Rebecca Heller are. You are.

A few minutes ago we joined our quite independent modes of reflection in a common gesture: a moment of silence to consider and to hope and to pray for those who suffer. That moment was more than symbolic. Its power came from the unity of purpose and the shared hope for the good. This shared hope, this collective commitment, followed by generosity of action, is what encourages my sense of pride and underscores my sense of optimism.

. . . . Our shared welcome today focuses particularly on the Class of 2010. We have been waiting eagerly for your arrival since last spring, and your presence here affirms the high expectations we have for you. You will make a good place the better, and that is perhaps the most that we can ask of any class. Whatever we ask of you, however, must necessarily be far less than you ask of yourselves. If you have not yet sharpened your own hopes for what Dartmouth can enable you to accomplish, please do so.

You come here from many places, and each of you has had your own distinctive experiences that have shaped your memories, as well as your hopes. Collectively, you come here with 1,081 sets of dreams. Pursue them resolutely, but also reflect on them carefully. At Dartmouth the liberal arts curriculum, the faculty and administrators, your classmates and other students, and the very culture of this place will allow you to think about what you wish to do and what you seek to be, and they will encourage you to pursue these goals. How you will lead your lives is not ours to chart, but since we care about you and we care about the world in which you will pursue your dreams, we are more than disinterested observers.

Your dreams will surely include your own personal ambitions for success. Go after them with enthusiasm and enjoy reaching them with tremendous satisfaction. But as you already know, of course, a good and full life entails more than self-accomplishment. It also means a life shaped by conviction and by purpose. What it is you will do with your life is an important question. And what it is you will stand for in your life, the values that you will embrace, is an even more fundamental one.

Values are more than abstract concepts of good; they are principles that shape the way we conduct our lives. They must come from within each of us, because imposed values are not values; they are prescriptions. Now, you were not a blank slate upon which values and beliefs have somehow grown spontaneously. Influenced by society and culture, by history and religion, by teachers, family, and friends, your values are nonetheless deeply personal and intensely held. They are yours—and they define you.

The question here is less about what you believe, although we do care about that, than it is about how you negotiate the complicated relationship between your personal values and the community—indeed, the world—of which you are a part. Unless you choose a life of full isolation, you will need to relate to and live within a world of differences. This is eased to a degree because while values and belief systems are deeply personal, they are rarely unique. Often, in fact, many are widely shared and reinforced as parts of a broader community of philosophy, belief, purpose, or culture. These, in turn, provide an important voluntary element of cohesion within a society or group. Sharing values without accepting a stifling shared conformity and arrogant exclusivity is a tenuous, and sometimes tense, balancing act. In this country we are the beneficiaries of historical success, most of the time, in negotiating this balance between personal beliefs and common values. The historic success of American society has been its openness to the new and the different, sometimes reluctantly open, to be sure, sometimes inconsistently so in relating practice to principles.

The first lesson of history is really quite simple: Learn from the worst and aspire to the best. It is the history of this country's best instincts and best values that should provide the legacy that is our inspiration. In this republic, democracy and equality, freedom of speech and religion, as well as of the press and of assembly, economic freedom, valuing the individual and his or her independence, embracing a culturally rich heritage of immigration, and a generous approach to the world, these are the best hopes of our heritage, the building blocks for a strong and enduring nation. Embedded in our constitution and our culture, they are fundamental and essential parts of who we are.

Freedom of speech is at the core of our value system, and yet, unless accompanied by independence of mind, it is but a shadow of what the founders of this nation dreamed. Freedom of speech is less meaningful if the speakers are unwilling or unable to think and speak freely. Your generation needs to confront a real problem, which is—as Paul Simon and Art Garfunkel, two of the poets of my generation put it, "People talking without speaking / People hearing without listening." Through fear or politeness or apathy, too often we yield the floor to positions shaped by self-righteousness, intellectual inflexibility, and intolerance, a mindset held by those whom philosopher Eric Hoffer described as the "true believers." Hoffer and his generation were concerned about the specter of

66

Hitler and of Stalin, about what he called fanaticism, secular as well as religious. Today, unfortunately, we have other examples wherein absolutism and intolerance lead to repression, murder, terror, and genocide—where preachers and demagogues attempt to justify the unjustifiable. Hoffer wrote, "To be in possession of an absolute truth is to have a net of familiarity spread over the whole of eternity. There are no surprises and no unknowns. All questions have already been answered, all decisions made, all eventualities foreseen. The true believer is without wonder and hesitation." Wonder and hesitation, curiosity and uncertainty, these are exactly the qualities that a liberal arts institution exists to foster: The confidence to admit to not quite knowing, coupled with the capacity to search in order to know—and the perspective to realize that any answer may at best be an approximation of the final answer—these are the values of the university.

College campuses should resonate with mutual respect and difference, with free speech and free thought, with the sense of "wonder and hesitation" that Hoffer worried about. As Mahatma Gandhi once cautioned, "It is unwise to be too sure of one's own wisdom. It is healthy to be reminded that the strongest might weaken and the wisest might err." One of the criticisms of the academic world is that we too readily accede to a satisfying like-mindedness. Political correctness is a label these critics use to describe our world. The academy is far more intellectually and philosophically diverse than this suggests. To be sure, we need to resist those qualities of certainty and intolerance that our critics point to and, sometimes accurately, caricature. If we are not monolithic, neither should we be monophonic. We need to be open to all ideas, and we need to resist all stereotypes. The sharpest critics of academic culture are often far more confident in their world views and answers than are members of the academy. One might even say they are in that sense more "politically correct." Nevertheless, let us deal with ourselves first. We need steer clear of any easy path through life that would enable us to avoid being challenged intellectually. And by challenged intellectually, I do not mean the incremental process of learning that which we had never known; rather, I refer to the dialectic of rethinking that which we think we know, and of challenging our deepest beliefs. Dartmouth needs to facilitate that challenge, but you yourselves, as students, must undertake it.

Our world today is marked by ease of communication and instant information. It is easy to select circles of friends, sources of news, blogs and talk shows, all of which will salute one's unwavering good judgment. These mutually reaffirming and sometimes remarkably self-satisfied collectives frequently do not seek to engage in debate, but merely to reaffirm positions. Too often, they use sarcasm and volume to dismiss those who are not likeminded, rather than engage in true intellectual discourse. Nodding agreeably to such exercises of freedom as these may, ironically, make us less free. They surely render us less tolerant of difference. Skepticism, reason, and logic are values that can inform and enable us to grow. They have no relationship to cynicism, emotion, and dogmatism. Even in our free society, we need to acknowledge the decline of a tolerance for difference. Our political system is increasingly marked by polarities, rather than by a sense of accommodation, respect, and compromise. Those whom a former generation might have considered statesmen are dismissed by the absolutists of our time as sellouts. We engage infrequently in true debate, and compromise is a pejorative concept to those whose lives are marked by ideology and rigid intellectual conformity. Slogans are often more important than ideas. And hard evidence sometimes has no role in shaping harsh generalizations.

Beware the easy and soothing hatred of the demagogue who can make your problems someone else's fault and their solutions appear simple and painless to you. Beware those who can always articulate fundamental principles and values in ways that obscure and advance their own self-interest. And beware those who mobilize the legions at Armageddon for every debate of policy or priority, those for whom every difference becomes a moral imperative, for they cheapen the very concept of morality. Here in the United States, we have a long and rich tradition of supporting freedom of religion. For many, religious values are more than matters that shape and enrich private lives, they are also central to informing public life. Some belief systems include a spiritual mandate to convert, and in a free society of free choices, the right to do this is protected. But proselytizers must recognize the reciprocal rights of those who decline to be converted.

Religious spokespersons who do not acknowledge the marvel and complexity of science and the essential nature of individual freedom may think as they will. Ours is indeed a free country. But when they insist that private beliefs should substitute for empirical knowledge in the schools, both scientific progress and the freedom to learn is imperiled. As we protect for religious assemblies and religious schools the right to teach and to believe, so need we protect for public schools and public forums the right not to believe. Intellectual, political, cultural, and religious freedoms are the sources of the energy and independence of our society today. They must not become the selective rights of some, which when fully exercised, restrict the rights of others

So we return to your task, members of the Class of 2010, and to our purpose. It is no accident that the liberal arts are central to a free society, just as only a free society enables the liberty essential to the liberal arts. At our best, Dartmouth will challenge you over the next four years to understand yourselves as actors in rather than observers of a rich historical and cultural tradition, as members of a world of interdependence, of a physical and natural world of which we know much even as wonderful mysteries remain, as beneficiaries of a tremendous and diverse heritage in the arts that you can augment and expand, and as individuals with independence of mind and a willingness to accept responsibility. Curiosity and discovery, a questioning attitude toward answers—these should mark your education here and your lives of learning hereafter. Lord Byron reflected, "If I am a fool, it is, at least, a doubting one; and I envy no one the certainty of his self-approved wisdom." As you properly doubt others, remember to doubt yourself—especially when you feel most confident.

All we can assure you here is that your century and your lives will be filled with challenges. Those of you who will excel and who will make your own lives the richer and your world the stronger, will be those who know—tempered by a healthy sense of humility—what they stand for and learn how to affirm, while respecting and learning from those whose beliefs differ.

. . . . I would like to welcome the Class of 2011 to Dartmouth. A few days ago in my office at your matriculation I told you how pleased we are that you have joined this community of learning, this community of warm and enduring friendships. And I am especially proud to welcome here the military veterans who have chosen to join the Dartmouth fellowship; we salute your courage and are enriched by your presence.

The Class of 2011 is larger than we intended because more of you wanted to accept our admissions invitation than we had anticipated. This is not a bad circumstance! Each and every one of you is here because this is where you want to be. And each and every one of you is here because we wanted you to be here. You are also more diverse in background, race, and economic circumstance than any previous Dartmouth class has been, and there are more international students than we have ever heretofore matriculated. At Dartmouth we have a tradition of urging students to learn from each other—and in this arena today is the base for a wonderful and rich learning experience.

This exciting opportunity is partially a result of the serendipity of history; thousands of individuals making the decisions and choices that bring us to a common place now sharing a common purpose. But the range and richness of your Class is not just an accident of history—it is also the result of a sense of purpose deeply embedded in the history of Dartmouth.

The college charter issued by King George III in 1769 provided that Dartmouth College be established "for the education and instruction of youth of the Indian tribes in this land," and also for "English youth and any others." There was no school of the period that embraced so inclusive a purpose. The Mohegan Indian Samson Occom stands alongside the Reverend Eleazar Wheelock and New Hampshire Governor John Wentworth as a founder of Dartmouth. While no group owns this institution, if any group has a historic relationship with this college it is surely, as our charter reflects, the members of the Native American tribes of this land. In this, the 238th year of Dartmouth, we extend a special welcome to those who descend from our first students, and whose presence here both reminds us of our legacy and enriches our community.

To be certain, the charter also contained typical eighteenth-century British and Christian condescension toward the native peoples and too quickly the college slipped away from a commitment to Native American education. The Dartmouth of the nineteenth century became a more homogeneous place. But even then, Dartmouth stood out as a school that was accessible and welcoming to the poor farm boys of the New England North Country—and a school that admitted an African American student, Edward Mitchell, in the 1820s, far earlier than any of what would be our sister Ivy colleges. And the matriculation of Mitchell was not a singular occasion, for the college admitted several other African Americans before the Civil War—individuals like Jonathan Clarkson Gibbs of the Class of 1852, who subsequently opened a school for freedmen in North Carolina and helped to organize the Reconstruction governments in Florida, where he served as Superintendent of Education and Secretary of State.

There was also Charles Eastman (Ohiyesa), a Dakota Indian, who graduated from Dartmouth in 1887, went on to earn a medical degree from Boston University and, then, moved to the Pine Ridge reservation in South Dakota, where he tended to the victims of the Wounded Knee massacre. Over the course of his long career as a doctor, lawyer, and writer, he became one of the most respected advocates for Native peoples and Native wisdom. As someone who straddled different cultures he believed that "the [person] who preserves his selfhood ever calm and unshaken by the storms of existence . . . [has] the ideal attitude and conduct of life." I hope that as you look to learn from your classmates, you will also preserve your own identity and sense of self.

President William Jewett Tucker led Dartmouth into the twentieth century by expanding the student body and by seeking even greater diversity. The founder of Asian studies in the United States, the Japanese student Kan'ichi Asakawa, Class of 1899, and the scientist who established the field of marine biology, E. E. Just, the son of slaves and a member of the Class of 1907, embodied the Tucker vision. Still later, President Ernest Martin Hopkins in the 1920s argued for the educational value of diversity, believing that students learn from each other and that their learning is enriched by having students whose backgrounds and experiences are different from their own. Each president succeeding Mr. Hopkins has shared this belief. And this commitment to the educational value of a diverse student body represents well the Dartmouth of today, building upon outreach in recruiting that was initiated by President John Dickey in the 1960s and upon a reaffirmation of Dartmouth's commitment to Native American education championed by President John Kemeny in 1970.

This is the legacy that you of the Class of 2011 now inherit, but it is not an artifact to be passively admired or a process that was concluded deep in our history. It is a value and a purpose that each Dartmouth generation must reaffirm. And those who would claim that Dartmouth only recently discovered the educational value of diversity do not understand the richness of our past. Last year at Dartmouth, students, faculty, and staff asserted most clearly that all members of this community are welcome here. This is a powerful message that needs to be constantly and consistently reaffirmed. And then it needs to be embraced and lived: merely stating it is not sufficient.

Dartmouth's commitment is in the context of a larger national debate. The current political and legal environment is one in which programs that seek to extend diversity are under siege by those who argue that any exercise of affirmative action to address systemic or societal bias is in and of itself a form of bias. I would surely agree that the concept of race neutrality as asserted by these critics of affirmative action is an important legal principle. However, until our society is race neutral in its assumptions and practices and in its opportunities, the legal principle can stand as barrier against, rather than facilitator of, the justice and equality and access that is promised. In our society there are still too many individuals who, and institutions and cultural norms which, use race or origin to define and not merely to describe. And these definitions can be confining, if not indeed crude and demeaning as well.

The political scientist Robert Putnam has developed the concept of "social capital," to describe a society marked by trust, collaboration, and civic responsibility. In the 1990s, he worried about an erosion of social capital in modern society. In subsequent research, he focused on the relationship of diversity to social capital. And in a paper he published earlier this summer, he reported that, in fact, diverse communities have less social capital than do homogeneous communities. These findings have provided opportunities for critics of diversity and affirmative action to point out the fallacy of the principle that a diverse community is a stronger

72

community and, also, to question whether actively moving toward diversity is a valued social and legal objective.

So, it is essential that we ask ourselves on this September morning whether all of this—the legal, constitutional, political, and cultural challenges of our time, the pessimism suggested by the Putnam research—whether all of this means that Dartmouth should back away from its historic principles and assumptions? Having raised the question, I shall take the opportunity to provide an answer: No, to me it surely does not. This college's legacy and responsibility are richer than the cycles of politics. Our commitment to the nature of this learning community is older than the formation of this Republic.

The fundamental principle underlying this college and the liberal arts in general is to examine assumptions, to respond to new ideas, not stubbornly to hold to what we once thought to be true. The Putnam research makes more, rather than less, urgent our historic purpose. The appropriate response to these new findings cannot be to strive for homogeneous communities, which may, in the short term, have more social capital, but will surely not, in the long term, provide the intellectual excitement, the general stimulation, and the preparation for a lifetime of learning that Dartmouth seeks—as it has always sought to engender. The assignment for you members of the Class of 2011 is not to deal with the tensions of diversity by resisting diversity. Your world will not be one marked by insular communities or isolated societies, cultures, or nations. The leaders and contributors of your generation will not be those who seek the safe social capital and the bland intellectual capital of likeminded homogeneity and the temporary comfort of isolating themselves with those who will never challenge them.

Dartmouth's historic task and current mission is to educate young women and men who can create diverse communities with abundant social capital. No one should assume this will be an easy task. But this is the assignment of your time and of your generation. Abraham Lincoln said, "We cannot escape history." A world marked by change is not a forgiving or patient place. I believe with great confidence that we have here in this auditorium those who will realize Dartmouth's mission and who will make a profound difference in the world.

. . . Today I want to talk about leadership, not only about the qualities of leadership needed in this, your century, but also about your responsibilities to exercise leadership in a world that desperately needs it, and why leadership is rooted in a liberal arts education. Over the next six weeks the presidential election campaign will generate significant argument and commentary that will focus on leadership. Most of us hope for an improvement in the tone and content of this campaign, so that there is more in the debate that is intellectually revealing, more that argues the specifics of given positions, more that truly allows us to assess the candidates in terms of the qualities of wisdom and of character required for leadership in this era of history. We yearn for an acknowledgment that difficult situations often require difficult solutions. Our democratic process would be enriched if candidates would restrict their statements and their spots to explanations of their own positions and would declare a moratorium on describing their opponent's records and views!

Your generation can indeed play an important role in challenging those who would aspire to be our leaders. Challenge them to exercise appropriate qualities of leadership, including a commitment to civility and integrity in their own campaigns and by their surrogates. And you can challenge one another and your fellow citizens to distinguish between true leadership and manipulation and pandering. Indeed, the skills and perspective and knowledge that will enable you to do this effectively are precisely those with which we are concerned in your education here at Dartmouth.

How does a liberal arts education relate to leadership in the twenty-first century? And what specifically are the goals of leadership that we hold for the members of the Class of 2012? Let me assure you that I do not seek to channel you into careers or ambitions where you will be a political candidate or otherwise serve as the head of some activity or some enterprise. Many of you will do those things, as Dartmouth graduates have a remarkable record of doing. My hope for you and expectation is quite simple: that whatever you do, by virtue of your capacity, your character, and your vision, you will earn the respect, support, and cooperation of your peers in making a significant and positive difference in the world. If this sounds audacious, it is. But Dartmouth tries to do no less, and we expect no less of you. As Emily Dickinson urged, I hope you "dwell in possibility."

This college's mission is to recruit the best students and to provide them with a learning environment that will encourage in them the confidence, the capacity, and the character to assume responsible leadership for their generation. This community of learning is prepared to help you achieve not only that responsibility but also to assist you in reaching your own dreams. You will encounter here a remarkable faculty, who are leaders engaged in defining the boundaries of their own scholarly fields. They are eager to challenge you, to enable you, and to join with you in the process of discovery. The staff here is deeply committed to you and your experience. And alumni/ae, community members, and other students are all prepared to assist you. Our aspiration for you is that whatever your life choices may be, you will lead in a world that cries out for positive change.

I hope you will take full advantage of this community and of all that a liberal arts education can offer you. I have no hesitation in asserting that the liberal arts offer the best possible preparation for leadership today. In this era, although we surely need expertise and specialization, no one who aspires to leadership can afford to focus too narrowly, at the expense of attaining a broad perspective. Those who would lead must draw from a wide and fluid understanding of context. Your understanding of the world and of yourself will be enriched by encountering people whose tastes, experiences, and views of the world are different from those to which you are accustomed and most comfortable. The liberal arts challenge custom and comfort, even as they introduce us to the great wisdom of history and of our time. Moreover, what you will learn here is that learning never ends.

There is a conventional understanding of leadership as a synonym for authority, for command and control, for a rigid hierarchy. This is not how we understand leadership at Dartmouth; it is not consistent with the values of the academy—and I assure you it will not be a model that will work during this, your century. The Reverend Desmond Tutu refers often to the South African concept of "ubuntu." He says this word indicates the understanding and acceptance that we become a person through other

75

persons. Reverend Tutu says, "We can be free only together. We can be human only together. We can be prosperous only together. We can be safe and secure only together."

Such understanding of shared engagement in common causes lies at the root of the leadership needed today, for it brings with it humility, a fundamental respect for others, and a deep sense of responsibility that motivates action. This does not suggest a rudderless organization or movement directed vaguely by the lowest common denominator of its membership. The Boston Celtics, 2008 NBA champions, used "ubuntu" to affirm their common purpose and shared leadership. Indeed, modern United States military officer training emphasizes leadership and initiative at the tactical level, rather than hierarchies of authority constricting spontaneity and creativity. It is from this sense of shared responsibility that leaders emerge.

You each have the capacity for responsible leadership in voluntary organizations and in a democratic society. Dartmouth seeks to advance and enrich leadership skills that are based on an ability to work as part of a group and built upon personal qualities such as a lifetime capacity to learn—and its companion, even more elusive, the capacity to relearn and even to unlearn. Here we encourage leadership that is based on curiosity, the willingness to adapt, and, most critically, leadership fortified by qualities of character that are defined by clear values and principles. John Sloan Dickey, who served as Dartmouth president from 1945 to 1970, often referred to Dartmouth's purpose as the education of students whose lives would be marked by competence and character. Fundamental values and principles should not be subject to the whim of expediency, of negotiated compromise, or the lure of personal advantage.

Leaders who do not stand firmly and consistently for anything other than their own advancement will eventually find it difficult to inspire anyone to stand with them. Knowing what you stand for yourself is the essential first step toward leadership. But there is a complicating corollary to this: women and men who truly lead also understand that in a rich and diverse society many personal beliefs and values are indeed finally that. They are personal, and they have no more objective claim to priority than others. Acknowledging and accommodating the beliefs of others is not subordinating one's own. In a pluralistic world, not all differences of opinion should be elevated to a test of fundamental values. Compromise.

Compromise on important matters of policy, of priority, and strategy is at the core of democracy and of any effective group. Related to this, leadership will flow to those who can best adapt to change. Now adapting to change does not mean necessarily liking the change; it means recognizing it, even anticipating it, and accepting the consequences of it. The narratives of history are littered with failed leaders who insisted they would not adapt to the demands of their changing world.

Leadership is about understanding the distinction between ends and means. However, it is about also understanding that the means that we adopt, the processes we follow, reflect even more profoundly than do our goals the values and understandings that define any group for the long term. Adjusting tactics, adapting to a situation, this is a valued quality. But it is not a mark of leadership to subordinate the principles that define us in order to produce a short-term accomplishment.

Leaders are marked by an understanding of the richness and the potential of the human condition and a sense of responsibility. If you will lead, you need assume responsibility, first for yourself and those who love and depend upon you; secondly, a sense of responsibility for your group, your organization, or institution; and finally, a sense of responsibility for others. The latter, I would argue, is an essential quality of leadership. There surely have been ungenerous leaders—but their leadership has been almost by definition, that of command and control, rather than the respect and the voluntary deference that is extended to individuals of competence and character.

There is no doubt that leadership in your century will be extended to those who are creative, intelligent, disciplined, and focused—to those who can inspire, who articulate and live a set of values. Leaders will be distinguished by courage and strength. Courage and strength are qualities that are quietly held, and they are widely recognized. Caution may be important; timidity is not. Leaders do not categorically avoid the dreaded slippery slopes of life. They learn to navigate the slippery slopes of life. At Dartmouth you will have the opportunity to develop your capacity to lead. A liberal arts education is a wonderful intellectual grounding in the skills that will enable you. Here we encourage cooperation, teamwork, and collegiality. These are not barriers to assertive leadership, but they are the building blocks of modern leadership. Being a member of a community where student leadership is encouraged and expected will provide

77

you opportunities to enhance your own abilities. In the classroom, on the playing fields and in the arenas, within student organizations, in our service activities, and in the performing and creative arts, Dartmouth looks to student leadership that values collaboration, creativity, initiative, and responsibility.

This past summer I met with presidents of our coed houses, the fraternities, and the sororities, and we talked about leadership. I told them that they were receiving a good introduction to the complexity of leading individuals who considered themselves at least their equals and who had no interest in simply being led. That is a quality of this entire community, indeed of American democracy, not simply of these organizations. But as you learn here how to lead, you must also learn how to follow—not as a subordinate, but as a colleague. If this skill doesn't come easily, that is understandable—you are here because of your potential to excel and to lead.

But if you will only lead—if joining a group and following leadership is something that you are incapable of doing—then, I would suggest there is little likelihood that you will receive true leadership opportunities yourself. Aristotle argued that if you cannot learn to obey, you will never have the opportunity to command. You might create, organize, and run your own company or group, but even then, promoting the individual strengths and independence of members of your organization is essential. Moving beyond control to instilling a shared purpose is what distinguishes a leader; it is what can elevate a pickup game in a park to a focused, disciplined, championship team.

I count on you, and I believe in you. In fact, this summer I stepped into a national debate because of my belief that students, eighteen to twenty-year-old young men and women, should be considered adults. My test for adulthood has to do with maturity, with perspective, with responsibility. Individuals may fail to meet these expectations regardless of their chronological age. You are the fortieth class that I have welcomed to Dartmouth as teacher and administrator. Yours is a mature and responsible generation. I am more than willing to place my bet on you.

3

SELECTED SPEECHES ON
VARIOUS TOPICS, 1999–2009

ADDRESS TO FIRST-YEAR STUDENTS,
SEPTEMBER 15, 1999

Welcome to Dartmouth. . . . We were impressed early on by the Class of 2003. As the class formed last spring it was clear you would be a special group. And over the last ten days you have begun to display your creativity, your abilities, your tremendous energy. But while we celebrate you collectively—and celebrate our good fortune in having you here—we keep in mind too that your collective identity cannot, and should not, mask your individual strength.

Each of you is here because *you* want to be here. But never forget either that each of you individually is here because *we want you, individually*, to be here. We invited you, as a person, from among thousands who applied for your seat on this floor for this occasion. We wanted you to be part of this special community because we thought that you had the requisite curiosity and intellectual vitality that enriches an academic community. Dartmouth is more than a place for passing on received knowledge and traditional wisdom. While clearly we have much to learn from those who have wrestled with these very problems before, at its core Dartmouth is not a place for recitation but a place of learning—and equally, a place of unlearning.

You will hear much in the next few weeks and few years about Dartmouth as a community. And it is that. Indeed, it encompasses a number of communities of various types and interests. We have much in common. And yet we are assuredly not all the same. What binds us at Dartmouth is our commitment to a community of learning. That's the type of community that brought you here, the type for which you studied so hard and sacrificed so much, and the part that will always endure: Dartmouth as a community of learning.

Over the past several days you have come to know some of Dartmouth's traditions. Susan and I were pleased to join some of you at Moosilauke on Tuesday. Those of you who elected to go on a trip have danced the "Salty Dog" and begun to learn the lines of the "Alma Mater." You have eaten green eggs and ham. You have brought on a magical indoor rainstorm.

President Wright at Moosilauke Ravine Lodge with students, following their Dartmouth Outing Club trips during orientation, September 2008. Photo by Joe Mehling.

And you have come to know about the special place that the outdoors holds at Dartmouth. Over the coming year you will learn still more traditions—the bonfire and winter carnival, tea in Sanborn, sledding on the golf course. Part of coming to Dartmouth is learning these traditions, becoming part of the Dartmouth tradition. But don't let any of these limit you or inhibit you from making the most of your Dartmouth experience.

Traditions are only useful to the extent that they help us to shape our sense of our community. The value of concepts such as "community" and "tradition" is that they give us a sense of continuity and of context. They help set our identity. But these concepts also change and evolve. As you begin to shape the Dartmouth culture in your own image, as you begin to put your own stamp on those Dartmouth traditions, do so in ways that are open to your classmates, that are inclusive rather than exclusive, that allow you to reach your full potential rather than hinder you in that pursuit.

One of the challenges that you will face over the next few months and years is how to carve out your own particular place at Dartmouth, and how you negotiate between your own personal values and those of your classmates and other members of the Dartmouth community. There are many different ways of becoming "green," of becoming part of the Dartmouth fellowship, and all of them allow you to retain your individuality. Our institutional lifeblood requires collaboration, a sharing of common academic values. It also requires an environment that sustains independence of thought.

Certainly, the most important Dartmouth tradition is that of learning. It is this tradition against which all others must be tested, that of teacher and student, learning together. When all is said and done, it always comes down to this: teacher and student, learning from each other. Dean of Faculty Edward Berger has 350 faculty colleagues. They are eager to assist you as you make your academic plans. The libraries and laboratories, the galleries and studios, the classrooms and offices, these resonate with all that human beings can know and can do, or at least now know and now can do. Here is the seductive spell of learning and the trauma of unlearning, and finally here is the sustaining intellectual agony of not quite knowing, of being uncertain of results, and not contented with answers.

My colleagues on the faculty are very aware that we are educating you to live your lives in the twenty-first century. Naturally, we would like to be able to tell you exactly those things that you will need to know to cope with the problems, to meet the challenges, and to thrive with the opportunities that this century and your lives will present you. But as a student of history, I can assure you that a hundred years from now someone from the edge of the twenty-second century will look back at this time and smile about how little we knew and how little we even suspected.

It is impossible to know quite how your lives—and your four years here—will unfold. We all have high expectations and hopes but as that great sage Yogi Berra once said, "Forecasting is very difficult, especially when it involves the future!" You are the ones to make the choices, and you are the ones who need to live with the consequences of those choices. So choose wisely, and choose carefully. As one of our alumni, Theodor Geisel, whom you know as Dr. Seuss, has said:

> You have brains in your head.
> You have feet in your shoes.
> You can steer yourself
> Any direction you choose. . . . .
> *And YOU are the guy* who'll decide where to go.

Dartmouth is a residential college—a college where we bring people together from many, many different places, and ask them to get along with each other, to learn from each other, and to forge a sense of community. Much of your Dartmouth education will take place in the classroom, the studio, or the laboratory. But an equally important part of your education takes place outside of the classroom. You will learn much from each other and from other Dartmouth classes and from this special place.

Mark Twain once said: "Twenty years from now you will be more disappointed by the things you didn't do than by the ones you did do. So throw off the bowlines. Sail away from the safe harbor. Catch the trade winds in your sails. Explore. Dream. Discover." You too should stand ready to take risks—academically and socially—and challenge yourselves to get involved in new things. Three years from next June as you walk up the aisle in front of Baker Library to receive your diploma you do not want to regret some choices made, some roads not taken, some courses and fields not studied. Stay true to your individuality. Take different classes; make new friends; embrace new experiences; explore the full range of options that Dartmouth has to offer. "Explore. Dream. Discover." Remember too, that the Dartmouth spirit is, in the words of President John Sloan Dickey, a "joyful spirit." As you wrestle with new ideas and new concepts, as you struggle with new courses and subjects you have never taken before, as you challenge your faculty and yourselves to rethink the given canons, always remember that "those who miss the joy miss all."

I look forward to welcoming you individually this coming Sunday at matriculation and to working with you over the next four years. Dartmouth is a work in progress, and we all have a responsibility to ensure that it reaches its full potential.

Let me end with another verse from Dr. Seuss:

And will you succeed?
Yes! You will, indeed!
(98 and ¾ percent guaranteed.)
KID, YOU'LL MOVE MOUNTAINS!

The mountains surround us—physically as well as intellectually, hanging over this valley, and woven into this College on the Hill. It is time to start moving them. Welcome, once more, to Dartmouth. We are so pleased to have you with us. We are so pleased to be in your good company.

REPORT TO THE GENERAL FACULTY, OCTOBER 18, 1999

This annual occasion provides the president and the faculties a valuable opportunity to reflect upon some of the things that we have undertaken and some of the opportunities that we share. The exercise of working through these things and discussing them with you in this hall is an important one for me and it, in turn, gives me a chance to hear your ideas and your concerns.

The last year has been a full one for me—and one that has been both stimulating and positive. Over the last fifteen months I have tried to take advantage of opportunities to know better those areas and activities of the college that I have not experienced so fully before as a faculty member or administrator in the arts and sciences. Through this I have come to appreciate even more the rich range of activities that mark this place. Looking ahead, I would like to solicit invitations to join department and program faculty at lunch or other occasions so that we can share ideas.

In my inauguration in September of 1998 and in my report to you last year, I stressed three themes for my presidency: our need to enrich the out-of-classroom experience; enhancing the research strength of the faculty, while protecting the teaching environment of Dartmouth; the importance of diversity to this community.

One year into my presidency, I would like to reflect briefly on each of these. I have had many discussions about each of them and have certainly learned more about their complexity. I also have absolutely no doubt about the importance of continuing this three-fold focus. Moreover, they are not unrelated, discrete arenas. Dartmouth is a residential academic community, a place of learning. That is the core description of this place and the core value that we need to further protect. A strong learning environment is one in which students and faculty join together to try to understand vexing problems and issues—be they at the boundaries of our disciplines or at the core. Dartmouth is a place where we learn from each other, and this learning is strengthened by our different backgrounds, experiences, ideas, and aspirations. And it is a place where an important part of learning takes place outside of the classroom, and we need to make certain that our environment is as rich as it can be in this regard.

Let me start by talking about the student life initiative given that it has dominated so much campus discussion for the past few months. The Dartmouth that I came to in 1969 was a smaller, more homogeneous, all male place. Now the study body and faculty are significantly larger; we're far more diverse and half of the students are women. There is a far richer range of activities on the campus. This initiative is about recognizing these changes, it is about addressing long deferred capital needs, it is about making fully available the special strengths of Dartmouth, and it is about ensuring that the residential and social system supports and enhances the academic mission of Dartmouth. It is about affirming the importance of community, the importance of inclusiveness, the importance of alternatives and options, and the necessity of addressing issues to do with the abuse of alcohol and other drugs. Indeed, these matters are being discussed on most campuses in the country today, and it is time for us to face up to them here. The committee charged with discussing this is chaired by two trustees and includes faculty, students, alumni, and administrators. It is a strong and diverse group committed to this process, and I would like to thank them for their hard, and I know at times, stressful, work.

We know that we need more residential space so that we can house all the students who wish to live on campus, as well as to relieve some overcrowding of rooms, and to provide greater continuity for students so that they do not need to move rooms quite so frequently. We also know that we need to provide students with an enhanced and enlarged student center. But this initiative is about more than bricks and mortar. It is about changing the culture here so that the out-of-classroom experience is inclusive of all students. The trustees last February committed to providing the resources to allow us to meet the vision of an enhanced residential and social system at Dartmouth. A further important part of the committee's assignment is to look at graduate student needs, and there is a graduate student member on the committee. This is, I believe, the first time that graduate student needs have been addressed by such a committee.

The Committee on Student Life plans to present its recommendations sometime toward the end of the fall term. Speculation about what those recommendations will be, while understandable, is premature. Once the committee issues its report we will all have an opportunity to discuss it and provide additional guidance to the trustees before they take final action on the recommendations next spring. I expect to participate in this process in ways that will assure us of some real progress in this regard. I do not wish to repeat the history of previous attempts to make changes. My expectation is that this committee's recommendations will be comprehensive and bold. They will force all of us to think again about our culture and the way that we organize some activities here.

People have asked me if I see the Student Life Initiative as my legacy as Dartmouth's sixteenth president. My response has been that it is far too premature for me to be talking about legacy—and as a historian I also recognize that I will have little role finally in deciding and defining what my legacy ultimately is. But I have said that I am a faculty member, an academic; I have a lot of things that I seek to do, and I would be disappointed if my legacy did not include a significant strengthening of Dartmouth's academic programs. Obviously, part of that initiative includes the strengthening of the out-of-classroom experience, and I would take great satisfaction and pride in such an accomplishment.

While student life may have dominated many conversations over the past few months, let me emphasize that it is not the only thing on our plate. Nor is it my only priority. The protection and enhancement of the quality of this faculty is a critical objective of mine, and I intend to work with you to make the faculty that we have more competitive and even stronger. I have always believed, and continue to believe, that however Dartmouth is ranked by *U.S. News & World Report* or other ranking agencies, we rank among the top ten institutions in the quality of the undergraduate experience that we offer. And, as I think about what is important in undergraduate education, we rank nearer the top of those ten institutions than the bottom. Our professional and graduate programs are also strong and provide an intellectual vitality and excitement to our overall program. We need to continue to improve our programs and strengthen the scholarly work of the faculty—but I never doubt that we begin from a position of strength.

This past year we made a first step in this regard by giving a special increment to Dean Berger for distribution to the arts and sciences faculty, where salaries have been lagging. We will continue to watch and protect faculty salaries, including those in the professional schools, as well as those for our staff and administrators. Dartmouth's strength lies in large part in the quality of the people who sustain the good work of this place.

I will also look at ways to support and encourage still further interdisciplinary teaching and scholarship. We do not currently provide the level of support that we should for some of the academic programs. We demand a lot from them both in terms of the courses that they teach and in the level of intellectual stimulation that they bring to this campus. In addition to formal programs, we need to follow up on the exciting new initiative for the Humanities and the establishment of a Humanities Center. I am very pleased that Professor Jonathan Crewe from the English Department has agreed to direct this center. And clearly, the Rockefeller Center and the Dickey Center both also play a critical role in bringing faculty together. But as we consider interdisciplinary programs and research, we also need to protect the departments and the disciplines. They continue to provide the most important way we have of organizing ourselves, our efforts, and our intellectual energy.

Related to the active research strength of Dartmouth is our commitment to a strong teaching environment. We have a well-deserved reputation for the strength of our teaching—your teaching. Nonetheless, we could do more to strengthen this commitment. We need to explore in the near term ways of providing more support for teaching innovations and for pedagogy. A number of years ago, Professor Marilyn Reeve used to provide a class for faculty that aided them with lecturing and presentation skills. More broadly, she worked with the faculty and members of the administration to help them feel more comfortable in public forums. We need to have something like that again. We also need a better system of teaching evaluation, as well as a place that can provide support for people looking for evaluation and assessment of techniques and pedagogical experiments. Finally, we could do more to help faculty develop new teaching techniques and to introduce new technology into their teaching. I have had one discussion already with a foundation about supporting such services for faculty. I will continue to look for ways to do this.

We also have significant facilities needs within the academic program. Over the past ten years we have made major investments in this area. We opened Burke Laboratories, Sudikoff Laboratory, and we developed a master facilities plan for the arts and sciences. This past year we dedicated both the Rauner Special Collections Library and Moore Hall, the

home for psychological and brain sciences. We also started work on the
Berry Library; Whittemore Hall at the Tuck School; the Fairchild Science
Center, which includes an addition to Wilder Hall and the renovation of
space in Fairchild and Steele; and the Silsby renovation project. We are
in the planning process for Kemeny Hall, which will house mathematics
and computational science, and, finally, we are in the very early stages of
discussions for a new life sciences building and an expansion of our performing arts facilities. Through the generosity of several friends we are
upgrading some athletic facilities—the Fahey-Sculley turf field, the Boss
Tennis Center, the skiway lodge. One of the distinctions of a strong institution is the provision of first-class facilities for faculty and students.

I told one group of alumni recently that knowledge is a growth industry. New fields such as molecular genetics do not replace that of plant
physiology—an old and enduring field of scientific inquiry; new research
on Norman Mailer or Toni Morrison does not replace a focus on the writ-
ings of Emily Dickinson or Charles Dickens or William Shakespeare; new
courses on postwar Japanese history do not replace traditional offerings
in medieval history. While the expansion of knowledge and the emer-
gence of new fields are at the very core of the university, they nonetheless pose some difficult dilemmas for those of us charged with the administration of this very dynamic place. Dartmouth's academic program
has always changed and evolved. It needs to do so, if we are to remain a
vibrant and vital intellectual community. While we need to stand ready
to seize opportunities in new areas and to support with seed money new
ventures, we also need to have a sense of vision as to how we will develop
as an institution. We will face some difficult choices in the years ahead as
we embrace some choices and decide that we cannot embrace still others.
These decisions must be informed and guided by a process that includes
significant faculty consultation and involvement.

Over the last year we have undertaken a number of projects, studies,
and conversations to start this process. Among these, of course, have been
the important self-studies and assessment we prepared for the reaccredi-
dation committee that will be visiting here in another week. Chaired by
President Hugo Sonnenschein, of the University of Chicago, this group
will meet with faculty, students, and administrators and will give us feedback and calibration that will provide some terribly useful information
for us. The self-study part of the reaccreditation process has been enor-

mously helpful to our thinking in several areas. Each of the committees has provided us with a thoughtful report and important recommendations on how we should proceed, and I would like to thank the faculty and administrators who worked so hard on them. The committee on undergraduate research, chaired by Mary Lou Guerinot, has taken a hard look at the research opportunities that we provide our students and has compared that to our peer institutions. It is clear that while we have made significant strides in this area over the past ten years, there is room for still further improvement. In 1999, 327 students participated in noncredit independent research programs and about 45 percent participated in either independent research or research for credit. I have thought for some time that we need to provide more opportunities to interested students earlier in their Dartmouth career and that we need to structure those experiences more than we currently do.

The self-study on computing has forced us to confront some issues in this area and has helped to map out a plan for how we can recapture our traditional leadership role in this arena. Dartmouth has traditionally been a leader in the field of computing; many of our students come here specifically to study computer science or, more generally, to enhance their computation skills. The self-study committee looked at both the academic program and the overall computing environment at Dartmouth. Both are areas where Dartmouth can have a substantial impact. The accreditation report has provided us with a key starting point as we decide how to move forward in this area. Similarly, the committee on internationalism has made some important recommendations regarding our foreign study programs, the way our curriculum is structured, and ways in which we can encourage greater international involvement on the part of our faculty. . . .

The Tuck School has undertaken, with the assistance of outside consulting advice, a thorough examination of that school's activities and an assessment of how it compares to other institutions. Dean Danos has been working with the faculty to bring forward a set of proposals in the near term, perhaps even for action by the Board of Trustees at its fall meeting, to begin to position Tuck in an even stronger place. This will include an expansion of the faculty and student body, as well as an extensive review of the curriculum.

The dean of the Thayer School, Lewis Duncan, has initiated a process with that faculty to begin to look at some needs that the school is going to have in the future. There are some important issues of size and scale that need to be addressed, and there are some concerns having to do with space that will become an important part of our discussion. The Thayer School also faces questions regarding the role of sub-disciplines within engineering and the role of engineering within a liberal arts tradition.

Dean John Baldwin, of Dartmouth Medical School, has undertaken a terribly important initiative to strengthen the ties of the Medical School with the Clinic and the Hospital, and also to build more intellectual bridges to arts and sciences, Tuck, and Thayer. The new Department of Genetics is an important step in this regard. While housed in the Medical School and an important part of basic science research at that school, it will also have a reach into the clinical activities of the faculty as well as the arts and sciences. Dean Baldwin and Dean Berger have developed a plan to make genetics courses available for Dartmouth undergraduates, which will be an important enrichment of the curriculum.

As these various processes, reports, and discussions move forward we need to find ways to pull them all together and assess the common themes that appear in them. I have asked Provost Prager to work with the deans to do this over the next year. And, clearly, each of the separate faculties will also need to have discussions regarding specific issues and priorities that relate to them. As we look ahead, there is no doubt that we will be initiating another capital campaign within a few years.

It is my expectation that the capital campaign will be one that will focus primarily on academic life. Obviously what we set out to do is constrained by the resources that we have or can expect to have available. We cannot do all of the good things that we want to do, and yet, we have to continue to provide support for the new and innovative ideas that you and others bring in. We need to think how best to invest current money as well as incremental money. The planning processes already under way will help us as we make these important decisions. They will provide an important framework for us as we assess the academic priorities for that campaign.

Finally, let me spend a few moments talking about the importance of diversity. I would like to compliment Dean Karl Furstenberg and all of his colleagues on their significant accomplishments in recruiting the most diverse entering class of Dartmouth College in our history. The financial aid initiative that we announced last October certainly helped with under-graduate recruiting and allowed us to compete with most of our comparison schools. We have had some success too in recruiting a diverse and rich range of graduate as well as professional school students. Finally, we have done well in recruiting faculty and in filling administrative positions this past year. Certainly, there is still room for improvement. It is so important that we all attach a very high priority to our efforts in this area and that we recognize that those efforts are never quite complete. Each year we must return to and renew this effort.

I cannot think of a more exciting time to be president of an American college or university than the present. We are, in this country, now participating in some basic debates, constitutional, political, cultural, and intellectual debates, that get to the very nature of American higher education. These have to do with how we constitute membership in our community, including the importance of diversity and affirmative action. They have to do with the way we define communities in places that are increasingly rich and diverse. They have to do with the abuse of alcohol and drugs, and especially we're seeing this debate on college campuses, which by their very nature cannot police individual behavior. They have to do with basic debates about the cost of higher education and the priorities of academic institutions. They have to do with the importance of basic research and the periodic public insistence on some accounting for research activities. They have to do with the perceived tradeoffs between research and teaching. They have to do with the way that universities and colleges expand their international and global activities for a world that's increasingly marked by globalization. And they have to do with the way that we use technology. They have to do with the impact of the digital revolution on the way that we organize our activities. It is not the case that our work can take place in cyber space. But it is the case that a lot of things that enable and enrich our work are part of the cyber revolution.

And while these are all parts of a broader national debate in higher education, they are also very much a part of a discussion that we are having at Dartmouth. We are in the middle of some pretty basic issues having to do with who we are, what we aspire to be, and how we pay for that. What an exciting time to be here. I look forward to discussing these opportunities with you.

CLASS OF 1950 REUNION LUNCHEON, JUNE 10, 2000

. . . . The return of the fiftieth reunion class is always a particularly special moment in the annual life of the college. . . . When you matriculated in 1946 you were the second largest class in Dartmouth history; four years later, you were the largest graduating class. More than half of the students in your class were veterans returning from the Second World War to complete their studies. Over 300 Dartmouth men lost their lives in that war. Joe Medlicott, Class of 1950, said, "It was tough to wear beanies and wrestle in the mud if a year earlier you were flying over Tokyo in a B-29." Obviously those who came back from the war were changed by the experience. Others of you were "civilians" and came to Dartmouth straight from high school. Indeed by your senior year, only 3 percent of incoming students were veterans.

Some of the issues the college faced in the four years you were here were similar in many ways to those we face today. The *Dartmouth* took the initiative against fraternity discrimination clauses; they conducted a poll among students and found the vast majority of you opposed these clauses. There was also a need for better science facilities and an arts center, more housing including housing for married students, more scholarship aid for needy students, and changes to the curriculum. The faculty changed the language requirement and also dropped mandatory class attendance—although this last change came in the spring of your senior year and came just a little late. Or perhaps some of you had earlier exercised the option.

The years between 1946 and 1950 were the years of Perry Como and Ethel Merman, Nat King Cole and Frankie Laine; songs like "There's No Business Like Show Business" and "Rudolf the Red-Nosed Reindeer"— written by a Dartmouth graduate; Dr. Spock and Dr. Kinsey; President Truman in the White House. The first long-playing record was released in 1948—most of today's students have probably never even played one. But your college years were also years that saw a deepening Cold War with the Soviet Union, the fall of China to the Communists, and the development of the H-bomb. Within weeks of your graduation you were stunned by the start of a war in Korea. A war in which many of you served, and two from your class gave their lives (Alan Tarr and Wilfrid Wheeler). Those were difficult and tense years. A new world order was in the offing, and the United States had new and larger responsibilities.

As a class you were the first to matriculate with John Sloan Dickey as president, and you had the privilege to see that great man take over the stewardship of Dartmouth. At that first convocation, in September 1946, President Dickey told you that "calmer moments always come in life and, . . . it is out of those calmer moments that come such understanding and wisdom as a man gets." Mr. Dickey, in what would become a signature line, urged you to remember that "the world's troubles are your troubles." He went on: "The world's worst troubles come from within men, and there is nothing wrong with the world that better human beings cannot fix." This address is printed in full in your reunion book.

John Dickey insisted that Dartmouth students take an interest in the wider world and he encouraged you to care about issues. The most important issues for the foreseeable future, he said, were international. The Great Issues Course, implemented in 1947 as a requirement for all seniors, grew out of that belief. Through this course, generations of Dartmouth students grappled with the pressing issues of their day. They learned about the problems the world confronted, and they listened as visitors from a range of backgrounds shared their perspectives. In your senior year, the speakers included the president of Radcliffe, W. K. Jordan, Lewis Mumford from Columbia, Hodding Carter, then the editor of the *Delta Democrat Times*, and Lyman Bryson from CBS.

As we enter the twenty-first century, this commitment to a wider world remains an even more critical part of Dartmouth. There is no doubt that the world today is a different place than the world you graduated into in 1950. But while the world may have changed, international issues remain of central concern, and, of course, our students are graduating into an increasingly borderless world. We cannot afford to neglect this part of our students' education, and we must be aware of our responsibilities in this area. I am certain that as Dartmouth looks to the future and begins to think strategically about directions we will move in, international concerns will be at the top of any agenda. Internationalism was one of the areas I chose to focus on for our accreditation report.

We already do much in this area, and we will need to build on these strengths. Our students participate in off campus programs around the world in numbers that far exceed those at our peer institutions. Over 50 percent of our students participate in one or more of these programs—in Europe, Asia, Africa, and South America. Moreover, these programs are staffed by Dartmouth faculty and are an integral part of the Dartmouth curriculum. We must think about how to enhance and protect these programs, as well as how to integrate them still further into the on campus curriculum.

The Dickey Center for International Understanding, which many of you supported and for which Sandy McCulloch has played such a critical role, has brought international issues to the forefront of campus dialog. Formed in 1982 as an endowment to foster concern for international issues, the center encourages interdisciplinary work and collaboration across the institution. The Dickey Center is now poised to play an increasingly important leadership role as we seek to increase our international profile still further and to make Dartmouth known as a center for international studies.

The Board of Trustees has also charged us to establish a World Cultures Initiative to provide both academic and social programming for all students. The *Dartmouth* recently included a special supplement on this initiative in which they quoted from several students. Let me just draw on comments made by two students, members of the Class of 2000. Olivia Carpenter, the president of the Afro-American Society, noted that "cultural awareness needs to pervade everything we do on this campus. It needs to pervade academics; it needs to be part of social life." And Omar Rashid said, "In reality multiculturalism is part of everything in our life, everything in the real world, everything in all academic departments." Olivia and Omar have captured the essence of what I would like to see this initiative foster. We need a place or center on campus that assumes the responsibility of bringing issues of diversity and internationalism to the forefront of campus life—not for just some students, but for all students. We do not have a particular model in mind for this yet, but I will be appointing a committee of faculty, students, and administrators to develop more fully this idea.

The Amos Tuck School of Business at Dartmouth is partnering with Oxford University's Templeton College to offer a global version of Tuck's

one-month business education program to a select group of college seniors, recent college graduates, and some postgraduates with Ph.D.'s
in the fall of 1998 at Oxford. The Tuck School has also partnered with
business schools in Paris, Frankfurt, and Tokyo. Dean Paul Danos is aggressively looking for still other international opportunities including
partnerships.

These are just a few of the things that we are doing in the area of internationalism. We will continue to build and enhance these programs even
as we look for opportunities to create still others. This is a path that John
Dickey set us on as an institution fifty years ago, and I am committed to
continue to strengthen that legacy. In 1950, as you prepared to graduate,
President Dickey returned to the theme of responsibility when he left you
with one piece of advice. He asked of each of you that "as you press[ed]
forward, [to] pause and look up to see the interest of others as you see
your own." President Dickey would be proud to stand here today with you
and to know all that you have done in the interest of others over the past
fifty years. I am proud to stand with you today. You are good and inspiring
company.

LIBRARIES IN THE CYBER AGE, JULY 12, 2000

President Wright, invited by the Friends of the Library to take part in a speaker series, delivered the following remarks at Colby-Sawyer College.

I am delighted to be here at Colby-Sawyer College today. . . . By training and disposition I am a historian and not a cyber specialist of any sort. So those who seek guided tours of the evolving digital world will be disappointed. My guided tours include history lessons. I am not a library specialist either. I am a user, a confirmed compulsive, addicted, lifetime and heavy user of books. And while I certainly share enthusiasm for the cyber library, I confess to an old-fashioned pleasure derived from the look of books on shelves and the feel, the almost sensual feel, of a book in my hand.

As we know, libraries in various forms date back thousands of years and for the last millennium at least have represented the intellectual heart of our academic communities. The earliest was perhaps the collection of clay tablets in Babylonia dating from the twenty-first century BCE. For most of this long history, libraries tended to be exclusive institutions reserved for a wealthy and powerful elite. But increasingly libraries have played a civic role as literacy expanded and access to ideas and information became more democratic—became, indeed, the hallmark of a free society. The evolution of the free public library is one of the great accomplishments of the modern age. Benjamin Franklin was one of the first to recognize the need to open up libraries to the general public, and he started the Library Company of Philadelphia in 1731. His list of authors included Bacon, Dryden, Locke, Milton, Pope, Swift, and Defoe. The Public Library movement flourished in the mid-eighteenth century and resulted in the establishment of seventeen public libraries. But despite the efforts of these few visionaries, books remained expensive and scarce. Indeed, those few libraries that did exist generally charged a fee for their services. Franklin's library subscription cost £11 in 1750—a substantial sum of money.

Thomas Jefferson, a private collector, also saw the need for the development of public libraries. He once wrote, "I have often thought that nothing would do more extensive good at small expense than the establishment of a small circulating library in every county, to consist of a few well-chosen books, to be lent to the people of the country under regulations as would secure their safe return in due time" (1789). He believed that "whenever the people are well informed, they can be trusted with their own government; that whenever things get so far wrong as to attract their notice, they may be relied on to set them to rights." This year marks the 200th anniversary of the Library of Congress, the largest library in the world, established in 1800 as a research tool for the Congress. When the British burned the library to the ground in 1814, Thomas Jefferson sold Congress his library, which then formed the basis for a rebuilt Library of Congress.

Our own experience with libraries at Dartmouth may be instructive. It certainly illustrates the changing nature of libraries. At the founding of Dartmouth College, the library collection consisted of about 300 books, many of them religious tracts, housed in the personal residence of Bezaleel Woodward, Dartmouth's first librarian. By 1800 the college had about 4,000 books, similar in size to the library at Princeton, although far short of the 15,000 books at Harvard.

Access to the library collection in the early years of Dartmouth's history was severely limited—students and faculty alike could use the library between 1 and 2 pm on Monday and Tuesday afternoons only. Only five students could enter the library at any one time, and a strict hierarchy existed regarding the number of books they could look at. Freshmen were limited to just one volume, while sophomores and juniors could look at two, and seniors three. But no one could take down a book from the shelf without the permission of the librarian. And the students needed to pay a fee for any book they removed from the library.

These restrictions remained in place with little variation for most of the nineteenth century. Indeed, in 1859 Librarian Oliver Payson Hubbard decided to close the library altogether to students. He noted that little good came of letting undergraduates have free run of the library. They tended, he said, to wander around aimlessly and would then ask him what books they should look at. At the end of the first term without the library, Mr. Hubbard recommended that the college continue to keep the library closed. He reported that "no inconvenience whatever had resulted" from the closing and indeed the uninterrupted peace provided him with the time in which to catalogue the books. There was clearly little relationship in his mind between books, students, and learning! The scary thing about this is that there was no apparent protest from the students, or indeed from their faculty! Although this early history is troubling and even funny to modern ears, it represented a common attitude—that books were things to be collected, that the principal purpose of libraries was to store and catalogue these collections.

While the Dartmouth Library and most of its counterparts were doing little to increase interest in reading, fortunately the public library movement continued to grow. In 1803 Salisbury, Connecticut opened the first free library for children, and in 1833 Peterborough, New Hampshire established the first in the country tax-supported open free library. The Boston Public Library followed in 1844. It moved into its current location on Copley Square in 1895, designed by architect Charles Follen McKim as a "palace for the people." The late nineteenth century saw tremendous advances in the democratization of the library. The American Librarian Association, founded in 1876, tried to foster "the best reading for the largest number at the least expense." And in 1895 New Hampshire once again led the nation when the state legislature passed a law requiring towns with public libraries to provide them with tax support. Previous to this time, local tax support had been entirely voluntary, and thus, perhaps, a little uncertain. In the last decade of the nineteenth century Los Angeles, New York City, and New Orleans all established free municipal libraries. Private philanthropy also played an important role. Andrew Carnegie donated over $50 million to support public libraries and hundreds of communities benefited from his generosity. His gift encouraged other philanthropists and municipalities to provide similar support.

A number of factors converged to permit this fundamental shift in the use of libraries: the expansion of literacy and the growing recognition of its importance to a free society, the development of sophisticated printing equipment that greatly reduced the price of books, and a growing belief that culturally diverse immigrants had quickly to begin to share in some common values.

The new public library had open stacks, standardized lending practices, and children's rooms. They opened for millions of ordinary people a world of learning and reading pleasure. What had been kept for a select few was now available to anyone who could make it to the library. And branch and mobile libraries later made this world still more accessible.

And indeed the public did flock to these new libraries. Today, the evidence suggests that our libraries are doing very well. In 1998, the last year for which we have information, New Hampshire public libraries lent out over 8 million books, dealt with over 800,000 reference transactions, loaned 70,000 books through interlibrary loan, and saw 400,000 people attend their programs.

The expansion of the public library system in the late nineteenth century coincided with another important transformation, a change in the academy. The modern university put new emphasis on scholarship and the development of new knowledge rather than the simple transmission of received knowledge. Learning at all levels came to value exploration rather than recitation. Colleges began to encourage their faculty and students to engage in research. This in turn led to an outpouring of scholarly publication that gave new importance to the role of librarians in cataloguing and collecting this research as well as guiding both faculty and students through it. The act of negotiating libraries became far more complicated, and professionals needed to assume a role and responsibility as guides and colleagues for users. Librarians were now more than cataloguers and protectors.

Today, knowledge is a growth industry. The Dartmouth library acquired its millionth book in 1970—Anne Bradstreet's *The Tenth Muse Lately Sprung Up in America* (1650). It had taken 200 years to build the collection to that size. The library added its two millionth acquisition in 1994 with the collection of British illustrated books created by Edward Sine, a Dartmouth graduate. It took Dartmouth just twenty-four years to double the collection, or one eighth of the time it had taken for the first million. Today the library has 2.3 million volumes. The Library of Congress has 18 million books, 2 million recordings, 12 million photographs, 4 million maps, and 53 million manuscripts. The library has 530 miles of bookshelves. Literacy has never been higher in our society, and the average American buys twice as many books today as in the 1940s (*USA Today*, January 2000). At Dartmouth we got a glimpse of just how enthusiastic younger students are for the written word, when J. K. Rowling came to receive an honorary degree. Hundreds of them turned out for the public reception, many with copies of her books clutched in hand. Hundreds more lined up outside of bookstores across the state on July 8 to get their copy of volume 4 in the series.

In addition to an increase in the numbers of books published, we have seen a steep increase in the cost of many conventional publications. The Association of Research Libraries reported that 121 American academic libraries spent 124 percent more on journals in 1996 than in 1986 but got 7 percent fewer titles for their money (*Economist online*, January 24, 1998). And the situation is still worse today. But while we are getting fewer volumes for our money, we need to subscribe to more and more journals. Where a discipline used to have one or two key journals, there are now dozens of journals that serve the faculty and students of any one discipline.

The proliferation of books and materials, their increasing cost, the wonderful success we have had in expanding educational opportunities and literacy, and the increased demand for these materials have led to a real dilemma for libraries and academic institutions: How to bear the expense of purchasing, cataloguing, and storing, of making readily available materials that are growing at a rate that is almost beyond our capacity to keep and to use? New technologies provide an obvious solution to the increase in both the volume and cost of published materials today. In addition to books and journals, the library collections at Dartmouth and Colby-Sawyer now include audio and video recordings, microform records, and a broad array of numeric and textual digital resources stored electronically on CD-ROM, DVD, laser disks, and on computer servers located throughout the world. And today, every library—the Library of Congress, Dartmouth's Baker Library, and the Susan Colgate Cleveland Library at Colby-Sawyer—has computer portals to connect to the Internet and the wealth of information that is now available online. This represents the most fundamental shift in libraries since the development of printing. Now people refer to "virtual" libraries—a library that exists wherever we have a computer terminal. Bill Gates, perhaps as a modern counterpart to Andrew Carnegie, has donated millions of dollars through Learning Foundation Grants to provide public libraries with Internet access. His goal is to wire the nation's libraries by the end of 2002.

And the Internet is transforming not only public libraries but the world of academics as well. Eventually, many journals may be published over the Internet, but even those that are now published in this way continue to demand high subscription costs. There are currently between 5,000 and 10,000 electronic journals today, compared with just over 300 three years ago. It is quite likely, the Internet and e-publishing will indeed change the way that academics conduct their business. But it is an unfortunate fact of academic life that new technology has often increased our costs. New technology is usually accompanied by the need for still more service and support as well as the required–often dedicated—hardware and the constant need to upgrade that hardware. And of course, there is the increased cost too of the electronic databases that any good library must now have. Some of these costs may be short term and transitional, but the very nature of the digital revolution is one of perpetual improvement.

It is now possible to access most literary classics online—the full editions of Shakespeare, the complete works of Emily Dickinson, the words of W. E. B. DuBois, of Huxley's *Brave New World*, and Orwell's *Animal Farm*, along with hundreds and hundreds of other classics. The *Encyclopaedia Britannica* and the *New York Times*, government documents including past censuses and annual immigration reports, key documents in American and world history, health care information, And the list goes on. A recent article in the *New York Times* (June 15, 2000) on libraries and the Internet told the story of a Harvard student who tried to do all her research online from her room. She said, "I hate the library, so I try to avoid it." Although it is hard to imagine that anyone would want to avoid your beautiful library, which is imaginative and charming in its design and feel, we have all probably run into such students. And we should recognize the practical basis for such an attitude. It is quick and convenient to be able to simply surf the net for the materials that you need for a particular essay or paper. But the student who relies on the Internet for all her research and would avoid the library worries me for a number of reasons. For one thing, there is so much more that is not available and perhaps will never be available over the World Wide Web. When I think of the research that I did for my book on New Hampshire politics—research at the State Library, the State Archives, the Boston Public Library, Widener Library at Harvard, the National Archives, the Library of Congress, along with Baker Library at Dartmouth—almost none of it is available online today. Nor is it likely it ever will be, as so much of it consisted of nineteenth-century materials and publications that probably no one had looked at for thirty years before me, if ever!

That student will also miss out on the serendipitous find in the stacks, the joy of the unexpected encounter, and the rich support system that is available. The Internet is a wonderfully democratic medium and is in many ways the culmination of the democratization of the library. It allows for the completely free exchange of information and ideas. Just about anyone can post information, and likewise, once posted, the information is accessible to just about anyone. In discussing the historical library we of course focused on books—and books traditionally have faced two tests that might determine their availability: the editorial and marketing calculations of publishers and the collection choices of librarians. To be sure, these powers are considerable and they have led too often to censorship of ideas. The American Library Association has unfortunately had the need to keep a list of the most banned books and have often led the fight to oppose such censorship. But generally speaking, the filters that are in place with printed matter, such as peer review and market potential, have provided one measure of quality control.

The information on the Internet is more often than not unfiltered, unreviewed, and has received little if any editing. Unfortunately, there is also a lot of inaccurate or misleading or simply silly information: sites that record Elvis sightings or that provide information on how to lose weight while you sleep. The Urban Legends site, maintained by the San Fernando Valley Folklore Society, keeps track of many of the most bizarre stories that can be found on the web. One of the urban legends that they recorded seemed particularly apt for tonight and involves libraries sinking into the ground because the architect failed to take into account the weight of the books when they designed the building. There is no basis for this widely repeated story. Still worse, are those sites that perpetuate malicious lies—that suggest, for example, that the Holocaust never happened or that the campaign against the flying of the confederate flag in the South is part of an ethnic cleansing campaign against white Southerners. A web site can look very professional and authoritative while its actual content is dubious at best. Readers and users will continue to have the responsibility that they have always had to validate their sources and to read critically and even skeptically. But cyber-librarians have a critical role to play here as well. As the sheer volume of information increases libraries can help students navigate through it and help them to discern truth from fiction. The library of the twenty-first century is an exciting place to be. The new information age includes a great deal that is digitized, but there remains much that is not and never will be. It is critical to sustain libraries staffed by professional librarians—a desktop is not, and never will be, a library.

In this information age, students and faculty alike need a facility that combines the functions and strengths of traditional libraries with the best of the new technologies. The new library must make available still more books and encourage and allow access to whole worlds of information. The new librarian must be an expert on information retrieval in a multitude of new formats—librarians and computer experts both. They must help students and faculty alike find their way through the increasingly complex world of information storage. Indeed, as the volume and complexity of information increases, it becomes more important than ever to have trained librarians who understand the multitude of different search engines. And regardless of these changes in concept and design, regardless of how virtual they become, one thing remains constant. Libraries need friends—defined comprehensively to include those who can make large and beneficent gestures of philanthropy as well as those who can engage in small acts of generosity. But finally libraries need ongoing encouragement and support from all of us. Who in this world would ever not be a "friend" of the library? The library today is indeed "a palace for the people." Sarah Ann Long, the president of the American Library Association, described our shared purposes in terms that bridge the history from Thomas Jefferson to our cyber and virtual world, she said that libraries today "connect even the smallest communities with the whole world of ideas and information and with each other." What a wonderful task we have to sustain this sort of vision.

GROWING AND PRESERVING: A MUTUAL
CHALLENGE, NOVEMBER 26, 2000

This opinion piece was originally published in the Valley News.

I had the opportunity recently to share my thoughts on the relationship between Town and College with members of the Howe Library Corporation. Those thoughts touched on over 230 years of interrelationship between Dartmouth and the wider community, as well as some of Dartmouth's plans as we look to the future. The histories of Hanover and Dartmouth have been intertwined since our earliest days. We grew up together, and for the most part we have got along very well. As one historian has said, "the connection of college and town was so intimate that the early history of one could not be written as separate from the other."

I first came to Hanover in 1969 as an assistant professor at Dartmouth, and I have lived in the town ever since, both in Etna and Hanover. My children went through the Hanover school system. I know and understand the importance of the relationship between Dartmouth and the community. Growth has marked both College and Town in the period since I arrived—as indeed it has since the 1770s when Dartmouth and Hanover were just a collection of buildings surrounding the green. An institution like Dartmouth can never be static. Change and growth are not only necessary but are inevitable. There are about 25 percent more students at Dartmouth now than there were in 1969, and there has been a similar increase in the numbers of faculty members. And over this period of time, more students have come to live in off-campus neighborhoods, and fewer faculty and staff live in Hanover. Dartmouth is now in a period of capital growth—we want to bring our students back onto the campus, and we want to provide more Hanover housing options for faculty and staff. We need to provide facilities that support our aspirations and assure our attractiveness as an institution of higher learning. These include additional academic buildings, residence halls, and enhanced social, athletic, and recreational spaces.

In the midst of this change and growth what remains constant is our understanding that no organization or individual in this town has a longer-term stake in the quality and strength of the Upper Valley community than does Dartmouth. Conversely, the community has a stake in Dartmouth—in making certain it is a strong, vibrant, attractive place. College towns have become some of the most popular places to live, and it's easy to see why. They are marked by intellectual vitality and suffused with the energy of scholarship. They feature some of the best libraries and research facilities in the world and, through academic teaching hospitals, provide some of the finest medical care available.

Many members of the community enjoy rewarding careers at the college, and we are enriched by the talents and abilities they bring. Local high school students participate in many of Dartmouth's courses, and our lectures and other programs are often open to the public free of charge. The Hood Museum and the Hopkins Center bring superb exhibitions and programming to the Upper Valley, and both have outreach programs; the Rockefeller Center and Montgomery Endowment bring exciting public figures to campus; and our athletic competitions and facilities are open to the local community. The Dartmouth Medical School offers all of us the latest developments in medical science through its Community Medical School forums, and Tuck and Thayer School students work with area businesses. Many of our graduates have remained here and started businesses of their own adding to the vitality of the Upper Valley that we all enjoy.

But with all this activity comes growth and change, and we know—particularly in the superb natural setting we are fortunate to share—that change can be unsettling and its consequences not always predictable. Throughout our intertwined histories, the college and Hanover have worked closely together to ensure that change is managed well. The college is interested in maintaining the natural beauty of the area and in maintaining a healthy and vital community that is itself a destination for nearby neighbors, as well as distant visitors. The quality of life here is not simply of value to the community but is critical to the college in terms of our ability to attract and retain the best faculty and employees. A large majority of our students see the rural nature of the Upper Valley as important in their decision to come to Dartmouth. Certainly our alumni return in large part because of the outstanding natural beauty and character of this area—and, as we all know, increasingly retirees and others with no college ties find Hanover an attractive place to live.

The college had the opportunity last year to acquire part of the downtown area called the Hanover Investment Corporation from an investor who wanted to sell his properties in a block. Dartmouth had an interest in this area because a large number of our students lived there. While no decisions have yet been made about how we will develop this property, there are principles by which we will be guided. We want to achieve our growth without overwhelming the town. We are not thinking about extending the campus into this area. If Hanover were essentially a Dartmouth campus we would all lose. We would like to preserve the vitality of Hanover as a village/town. While we would like to use some of this property to provide increased choice of housing for our students and faculty, we would also like to see more opportunities for retail outlets and commercial and professional spaces to the extent they would be viable. As we plan, we will also need to keep in mind pedestrian pathways, parking, open, and green spaces. We need quality, variety, and the idiosyncratic whimsy so characteristic of a classic New England town.

The college is also in the midst of discussions with the Dresden School Board regarding the possible relocation of the middle and high schools onto Dartmouth property and the sale of the current school sites to Dartmouth. These discussions are still preliminary although we are pleased to be able to participate in them. As Dartmouth's president, my charge and responsibility is to protect and enhance this college and its long-term competitive strength and excellence. But this cannot remain a singular focus. Strong schools, along with a strong town, are essential to Dartmouth's vitality.

These are exciting times for Dartmouth, as well as the community. A hundred years ago, when Emily Howe gave her home to the town for a library in 1900, she did so with the hope "that this library may prove a blessing to this community to the remotest generation." This is still a good summary of our legacy and our continuing responsibility—to protect the village of Hanover, and the college, "to the remotest generation."

REMARKS TO THE ALUMNI COUNCIL,
MAY 18, 2001

I am very pleased to be with you once again for this semi annual update on the state of the college. It is always a pleasure to welcome alumni—former students and long-time friends—back to Hanover. . . . This year marks the 200th anniversary of the graduation of Daniel Webster, and the 100th anniversary of the graduation of Ernest Martin Hopkins. These two men symbolize the loyalty and love demonstrated by so many Dartmouth alumni/ae.

When I welcome the parents of new students in the fall I often tell them the story of Daniel Webster's own journey to Dartmouth. He came from Salisbury, New Hampshire, where his parents owned 225 acres of poor farmland. Neither of his parents had any education but they knew that their son would not be a farmer, for he could never learn to hang a scythe. He could plow and rake and hoe, but he could not mow. And so his parents sent him to college. He was just fifteen years old. His brother Joe used to joke that "my father sent [him] to college in order to make [him] equal to the rest of the children."

Daniel Webster applied to Dartmouth at a time when applicants still needed to appear in person before the faculty to take examinations in English language, Latin (he needed to know Virgil and Cicero), the Greek testament, and arithmetic.

He came clad in a homespun suit that his neighbor had made for him and had dyed blue. Unfortunately, it rained that day and by the time he appeared before the faculty he was covered in blue dye from his suit. As he stood before them to take his examinations he said, "Thus you see me, as I am, if not entitled to your approbation, at least to your sympathy." Daniel barely passed his examination, but there was something about the young man that impressed the faculty, and they admitted him to the college.

Daniel and his family understood what a college education would provide for him. Indeed, Daniel was so convinced of this that he talked his parents into letting his brother Ezekiel come as well. "For myself, I saw my way to knowledge, respectability, and self protection, but as to him, all looked the other way." Ezekiel was expected to take over the running of the family farm, but Daniel argued that the opportunities that had been opened up to him should also be available to his brother. His parents had already fully mortgaged the farm to pay for Daniel's education, and Daniel himself worked to pay for Ezekiel's education.

One hundred years later, Ernest Martin Hopkins applied to Dartmouth. Born in 1877 in Dumbarton, New Hampshire, Hopkins was the son of a preacher. His family had saved a modest amount of money to send him to Phillips Academy but then needed that money to survive the depression of the 1890s. Hopkins went instead to Worcester Academy, where he paid his way by serving as the mail boy for his three years at the school. Before he could go on to Dartmouth, he needed to raise the necessary tuition and so took time off to work as a public school teacher and coached the high school football team.

Hopkins finally arrived at Dartmouth in 1897. The college offered him a scholarship, but he turned it down because of the requirement that he sign a statement saying that he would not swear, drink, or smoke. Although he was an upright young man, he was not sure that he could faithfully sign such a pledge. But he had not saved enough of his own money and needed to leave college half way through his first year. He went to work in the granite quarry. He returned to Dartmouth when a friend and former roommate worked out an arrangement that allowed him to live with a local family while working in one of the eating clubs. Hopkins later earned money by editing the *Aegis*, tutoring, and by writing editorials for the *Dartmouth*—the editor often got himself into a tight spot with deadlines and was happy to pay his talented fellow student to write his opinions for him. But because of the time lost when he dropped out Hopkins carried an extra course each semester.

Daniel Webster and Ernest Martin Hopkins had a great deal in common with each other. Both men struggled financially to be able to attend Dartmouth, both graduated with honors, and both went on to successful careers, albeit very different ones—one as a prominent lawyer and statesman, the other as a college president—and they both contributed in significant ways to their alma mater. Daniel Webster defended Dartmouth and President Francis Brown's administration before the Supreme Court protecting the college that he loved from the powers of the state. Webster sought to protect not just Dartmouth, but, in his own words, "every college, and all literary institutions of the country." What a thing to have done! Ernest Martin Hopkins served as Dartmouth's president for twenty-nine years. Under his administration Dartmouth developed a selective admissions process, expanded the campus by adding dormitories and Baker Library, and strengthened the quality of the faculty and students. He built on the legacy of William Jewett Tucker, and under his watch Dartmouth became a respected member of the Ivy League.

Together these two men represent several important aspects of the Dartmouth experience—the importance of remaining accessible to a wide range of students regardless of their financial circumstances; the quality of the education provided; the need to grow and change and adapt; and the loyalty of our alumni.

Dartmouth remains one of the few need blind institutions in the country and one of the few that meets a student's full need. In recent years, we have twice enhanced our scholarship program—two years ago we added $2.6 million, and this year we added a further $1.6 million to the financial aid budget. Our total financial aid budget is close to $30 million and is one of the most generous in the country. This program allows us to continue to attract talented students from across the country and from around the world. By attracting a diverse student body we strengthen the educational experience for our students. They are challenged by new ideas and new ways of looking at things. Financial aid students contribute significantly to the life of this college. Even though they comprise less than 50 percent of the student body, over the last ten years they have made up two-thirds of valedictorians, 54 percent of presidential scholars, and a significantly larger proportion of outside fellowship recipients such as Fulbrights and Rhodes.

Both Webster and Hopkins recognized the value of education, and they made the most of their time at Dartmouth. They received an education that had prepared them fully for the world in which they lived. Different educations to be sure. Webster received the traditional classical education of the eighteenth century while Hopkins studied in Mr. Tucker's Dartmouth—one that recognized the importance of social sciences and science on a humanities base, and most of all, one that recognized that knowledge is not a static thing.

Finally, Daniel Webster and Ernest Martin Hopkins represent the loyalty that Dartmouth alumni have for this great college. As John Dickey used to say, "in the Dartmouth fellowship there is no parting." Today, Dartmouth alumni are among the most loyal of any alumni of any college or university in the world. It is because of you that we can do so much. Your support of the Dartmouth College Fund allows us to support the financial aid program and to provide a residential liberal arts education to our undergraduates that is second to none. Through your participation in the Alumni Council and in local Dartmouth Clubs, through your work for admissions, and through the many others ways in which you provide advice, you help with the ongoing work of this college.

Dartmouth alumni take justifiable pride from having one of the highest annual fund participation rates in the country. But let us not rest on that! My challenge is that we should not be smug if one out of two alumni are not contributing every year. There is no excuse for this. None. But this is not about an unquestioning loyalty to an unchanging institution. Far from it. Dartmouth is not a museum. Both Daniel Webster and Ernest Martin Hopkins were committed to change and to making Dartmouth a stronger place for the next generation of students. Dartmouth has changed significantly in the past 200 years, but the idea of preparing students for the world in which they will live and work remains a central part of our mission. This is a place that values academic excellence. We take the most talented students in the country and provide them with a preeminent undergraduate experience. Our faculty are not only defining their fields through their research, but they are also enthusiastic and passionate teachers. They want to be at Dartmouth because of the way we value teaching and research, because of the way those two things come together here, and because of the opportunity to work with our students.

Dartmouth is a residential academic community that is second to none. The quality of the relationships that our students forge here—with their professors and with each other—last them a lifetime. I am confident that we are on the right track with the Student Life Initiative. We have additional programs in place, an improved orientation program for new students, additional personnel in the Deans Office as well as in residential life, more programming money, more facilities open later, and just more stuff happening. We also have moved along aggressively with plans for two new residence halls and a social and dining facility at the north end of the campus. I know that you received the latest brochure on the Student Life Initiative so I will not regale you with everything that is happening. But I would like to stress that we have made progress, we continue to make progress, and I am pleased with where we are.

This initiative is about much more than Coed, Fraternity, and Sorority (CFS) organizations. It is about providing more alternatives and developing a culture that is welcoming and supportive of the students we invite here and the academic experience that we offer. We have made it very clear to the CFS organizations that while the trustees have agreed that they may continue to play a role at Dartmouth, they must each meet our, as well as their own, standards of conduct. And we will hold them to this expectation. I for one am tired of the Animal House image. While it was a great movie—a cult classic of the 1970s—it is not an accurate portrayal of Dartmouth.

Dartmouth remains an exciting, intellectually vibrant, and diverse academic community. We have much to be proud of. You have helped to make all of this happen. There is a lot happening here—our aspirations are high but we are meeting them with confidence and joy. We are forever indebted to you for all that you do for Dartmouth. Thank you.

ADDRESS DELIVERED AT BEIJING NORMAL
UNIVERSITY, OCTOBER 10, 2002

I am deeply honored to be here today and to receive the award of Honorary Professor from such a distinguished university. It is a privilege for me to extend congratulations on behalf of Dartmouth College to Beijing Normal University (BNU) on your 100th anniversary. . . . This institution has educated thousands of teachers and has played a critical role in the important social and educational reforms of your nation. Consistent with your motto you have truly "studied to teach and have acted by example."

One of the examples that you have set is in your commitment to educational exchange and international understanding. As institutions of higher learning, Beijing Normal and Dartmouth College must foster the creative interchange of ideas. Our students and our faculty learn through their exposure to new ideas and new situations.

I am an American historian by training. My particular scholarly area of interest is the history of U.S. political parties and reform movements as well as the history of the American West. I have written on the Populists and the Progressives and have an abiding interest in the ways in which popular, grassroots movements have had an impact on the history of the U.S. Today, of course, I am an academic administrator, but I am also still a historian. My passion for the past continues, albeit with more of a focus on the history of my institution and the ways it has reflected national themes—and even helped to shape them.

Dartmouth and BNU, and indeed any institution of higher learning, do not exist in isolation from the history of their country; indeed they are very much of the world. President Zhong Binglin noted in his address at your centennial that "the one hundred year's history of Beijing Normal University not only epitomizes the development of Chinese contemporary higher education on teacher training, but also acts as a lively historical record of the ways which the Chinese have been exploring to modernize China by promoting education." For the past one hundred years, Beijing Normal, whatever its name has been, has focused on its purpose—the education of teachers, and this university has played a key role in providing academic leadership.

Let me tell you a little more about the history of my institution. Founded in 1769, on the eve of the American Revolution, the last colonial college, Dartmouth has grown alongside the nation for the past 233 years. As with BNU, the history of the college has helped to shape that of the U.S.; more often, the nation's history has shaped the college's trajectory.

Many of our graduates played a critical role in determining those histories. In the Dartmouth College Case of 1819, Daniel Webster, one of our most distinguished alumni, defended the school's independence against the state of New Hampshire. The case is considered one of the most important and formative in United States constitutional history because of the way it protected private contracts from the infringements of the state. Daniel Webster went on to become one of the foremost statesmen of his time.

During the American Civil War, hundreds of Dartmouth graduates (652) went off to fight for the Union in support of democratic republican government and in opposition to slavery, although the president of the college at that time, Nathan Lord, was a defender of slavery. Embarrassed by their president and his views, the trustees of the college finally forced Nathan Lord to resign his position in 1863.

The history of Dartmouth College, and indeed of American higher education in general, is about more than just the history of individual graduates. It is rather a story of expanding accessibility, of expanding opportunities. Dartmouth was founded as an institution to educate Native Americans and was one of the first to admit African Americans when Edward Mitchell was admitted in the 1820s. Daniel Webster was white, but he came from a poor farming family and his family made enormous sacrifices to send him to college.

In the late nineteenth century, Dartmouth began to admit students from across the country and even the world, including China—Lin-yi Ho from Shanghai arrived in 1907 and studied at Dartmouth for one year. Through the early twentieth century, the college expanded its scholarship programs to ensure that qualified students from poor families could attend. A generous scholarship program ensured that any qualified student could attend Dartmouth regardless of financial background, and today

Dartmouth remains one of only a handful of schools across the United States that admits students regardless of family income and then meets 100 percent of a student's need.

Education must be about more than enabling personal ambition and the education of individuals. Our students go out into the world carrying with them a commitment to education and to service. One purpose we have advanced at Dartmouth is internationalism, which is about thinking beyond the parochial and the personal. President Jiang Zemin said at your recent centenary celebration, "Educational innovation should be geared . . . toward the outside world and toward the future." And he went on to say that we must "keep an eye on the general trend of education throughout the world and draw upon the fruits of different civilizations and other countries' good experience." This is good advice for all of us.

Dartmouth's own history with China underlines this very theme. Charles Daniel Tenney graduated from Dartmouth in 1878, and in 1882 he came to China as a missionary with all of the preconceptions and misunderstandings of the West. But he quickly grew to love this country, and he decided to stay and to bring up his own children here. He proposed to devote himself to education. After just a couple of years, he left the mission and established a school for Chinese children. President Jiang said, "Teachers are important creators and disseminators of knowledge who bridge the past, present, and future." Charles Tenney was one such teacher. He soon came to the attention of Li Hung-chang and later still was appointed by the Chinese government as president of Peiyang University, a position he held for ten years. Peiyang, which later became Tianjin University, was the first modern university in China, founded in 1895. Dr. Tenney developed a great reverence for Chinese ideals and the Chinese people and always worked to further the education of the young.

Education must not only expand opportunity, it must also expand knowledge, and this process requires an openness to new ideas. While Dr. Tenney helped to carry western educational ideas to China, other scholars began to bring Asian ideas to Dartmouth. American colleges and universities began to introduce what today we call the social sciences— economics, modern history, anthropology, sociology, and political science—as well as modern languages into the curriculum in the late nineteenth century. The then president of Dartmouth, William Jewett Tucker, insisted that students needed to know more about the world they lived in, and he set out to broaden the educational experience for his students. As part of this plan, he introduced the study of Asian languages, literature, history, and philosophy, and by so doing Dartmouth became one of the first American institutions to have an Asian Studies program.

One of the new professors he hired was Kan'ichi Asakawa, himself a Dartmouth graduate. Born in Nihonmatsu, Asakawa was the first Japanese student to enroll at Dartmouth in 1895. An impressive scholar and a brilliant linguist, Asakawa followed his Dartmouth degree with a Ph.D. from Yale and then returned to Dartmouth to develop one of the first Asian Studies programs in the United States. He taught classes on East Asian civilizations including Chinese culture and history. Although Asakawa left to join Yale University, Dartmouth's commitment to Asian Studies remained. In 1921, Dartmouth hired David Lattimore, the brother of Owen Lattimore, the renowned scholar of Chinese and East Asian affairs. David Lattimore was a well-known Asian specialist in his own right and, twenty years later, was instrumental in bringing another noted Chinese scholar to Dartmouth, one who further strengthened the program and expanded knowledge in the United States.

In 1942 Dartmouth hired Professor Wing-tsit Chan. Born in Kwangtung, China, Professor Chan graduated from Lingnan University (one of the seventeen Christian universities founded at the beginning of the twentieth century) in 1924 and received his Ph.D. in philosophy and Chinese culture from Harvard University in 1929. He went back to Lingnan University where he served as the dean of the faculty from 1929 to 1936 and then taught in Hawaii before coming to Dartmouth in 1942 where he stayed until 1966. Professor Chan was an extremely important scholar and was one of the most respected and popular faculty members at the college. His classes were always heavily enrolled, and he helped Dartmouth to develop an extremely strong program in Asian Studies that remains one of our distinguished programs today. It was this program that assumed the leadership role in establishing our BNU initiative in 1982 and overseeing it since then. For twenty-four years as a professor of Chinese culture and philosophy at the college, Professor Chan published six books and numerous articles commenting on and translating important source materials and promoting the study of Chinese philosophy in the United States. His thoughtful comments on international relations and China did much to promote better understanding. His book, *A Source Book in*

Chinese Philosophy, continues to be one of the most used reference works in the West.

Charles Tenney and Wing-tsit Chan serve as models for our best aspirations—they traveled enormous distances in their quest for knowledge, and both became teachers who encouraged hundreds of other students to open their minds and hearts to different ideas and cultures. Their influence did not stop there. Both Tenney and Chan worked to encourage the development of educational institutions where they worked. While Dr. Tenney helped to found and encourage the modern university in China, Professor Chan helped to introduce the field of Chinese philosophy into the United States. Both encouraged greater understanding in their host country of their native countries. It is only through studying to understand different cultures that we begin to fully understand the issues that confront us.

This is a tradition that we are proud to continue today. This year marks the twentieth anniversary of collaboration between Dartmouth and BNU. In 1982, we began a program that brought a group of undergraduates from a single American college, led by a faculty member, to China to do on-campus study at BNU. This was one of the first such programs of its kind between an American institution and the People's Republic of China. I was pleased, as Dartmouth's dean for the social sciences, working with Professors Mowry and Blader, to assist in establishing the program in 1982. Over the past twenty years, Dartmouth has sent about four hundred of our own undergraduates to study on BNU campus via the college's summer Beijing Foreign Study Program. Since the mid-1980s, the college has also sent about a dozen recent graduates to teach English at BNU. We have also been privileged to have had thirteen visiting professors from BNU teach at Dartmouth. This year and last we are honored to have Professor Bai Quan with us

While our exchange program with BNU is thriving, so too is the scholarship in Asian Studies. As just one example, let me tell you about Professor Sarah Allan and Professor Robert Henricks who are collaborating with Chinese scholars, Professor Li Bo-qian and Professor Li Xue-qin, of the Chinese Academy of Social Sciences, Institute of History on the recently excavated ancient manuscripts from Guodian. As the first stage of this project, they held an international conference at Dartmouth that coincided with the release of a recently discovered text of the Laozi in May of 1998.

We must continue to give our young people the opportunity to visit and to study abroad, so that they can more fully appreciate other civilizations and cultures. Beijing Normal, like Dartmouth, has links with hundreds of other universities and institutions worldwide and welcomes scholars and students from all over the world. In addition to thirty-six faculty and researchers, Dartmouth currently has 117 students from China studying as either undergraduates or graduate students in the Medical School, the Engineering School, or in the arts and sciences. And while we provide these students with an excellent education, they enrich Dartmouth also. They add immeasurably to the educational experience of all the other students who are lucky enough to work with them or live with them or become friends with them.

When your faculty members return from a year at Dartmouth and when our students return from BNU, they have been enriched in many ways. They will have increased their knowledge; but more important still, they will have established personal friendships that will last a lifetime and will have a tremendous impact on the future of our two countries. As we enter the twenty-first century, this commitment to a wider world remains an even more critical part of Dartmouth and Beijing Normal. We must encourage the exchange of faculty and students and also the exchange of ideas.

International issues remain of central concern for our institutions and our graduates. We cannot afford to neglect this part of our students' education, and we must be aware of our responsibilities in this area. If our students are to become leaders in an increasingly global economy, we must provide them with the experiences that prepare them for this. What is more, as we seek to prepare graduates for careers in government, law, and business—to name just a few broad areas—the curriculum must introduce students to international issues and enable them to understand the world community. The most prominent institutions in this century will be those that are most heavily involved with the international exchange of both students and faculty members. Off campus study provides an important component of such an education. Such programs enable our students to appreciate different cultural settings, and few today would deny the importance of these experiences in furthering our students' understanding of the world. Any institution that is striving to play a leading role in education must also make a major commitment to internationalism. A school's reputation depends in part on having a faculty that is recognized not just nationally, but internationally.

The poet Robert Frost, who attended Dartmouth for a time in the 1890s, observed in his famous poem "Mending Wall," "Something there is that doesn't love a wall / That wants it down." He reminded us that before we build or fix a wall, we need to ask what we are "walling in" and what we are "walling out." Yesterday, we visited the Great Wall at Badaling that was constructed during the Ming dynasty to keep out invaders from the North. In New England we also have historic walls—stone walls constructed two or three hundred years ago by New England farmers to keep in their livestock. I know that we in New England treasure our historic walls and that the same is true for you in China. But perhaps, rather than walls, bridges would serve as a more appropriate metaphor of our relationship. We learned yesterday from our guide Xiao Kai that, in fact, walls like the one at Badaling did not simply serve as barriers but as meeting places for people on both sides to come together. We are very pleased that we have found a bridge to China, and we are proud of our affiliation with BNU. We hope that our relationship will continue for many years to come.

REMARKS TO THE ALUMNI COUNCIL,
MAY 2, 2003

There has been a custom at Dartmouth for presidents to make five-year reports, reflecting on the initial years of their presidency. In 1975 and again
in 1980 John Kemeny, for example, provided the Dartmouth community
with two comprehensive reviews of his presidency. President Kemeny, of
course, guided Dartmouth through coeducation and the introduction of
the year-round calendar. He rededicated the college to the recruitment
and education of Native Americans, and he pushed hard to make Dartmouth more diverse. He also dealt with the campus reaction to the Vietnam War, the bombing of Cambodia and the shootings at Kent State, and
with the budget shortfalls of the 1970s. He wrote in his ten-year report
that the economic downturn had reminded him of the line from Lewis
Carroll's *Through the Looking Glass*, where the Red Queen told Alice, "It
takes all the running you can do, to keep in the same place."

Over the last few months I have been thinking about my own five-year
report and will issue one later in the summer or early in the fall. I still
have trouble acknowledging that five years can possibly have passed so
quickly. Over this time we have set out to do some things of which I am
very proud—strengthening our financial aid program, addressing real
issues of lagging faculty compensation levels and of the size of the arts
and sciences faculty, remedying competitive disadvantages in some staff
salaries, enhancing budget support for the library, for computing, for faculty, for student life, including athletics, and renovating and expanding
existing facilities. None of these are one-time matters.

Thanks to generous alumni and friends, I have had the privilege of pre-
siding over dedication ceremonies celebrating Moore Hall, Berry Library,
Carson Hall, Rauner Special Collections Library, the renovation and expansion of Wilder Hall, McCulloch Hall, Whittemore Hall, the opening
of the McLane Family Ski Lodge, the renovation of the Golf Course, the
opening of Scully-Fahey field, the Blackman Fields, the Boss Tennis Center, and the Gordon Pavilion. We built faculty housing on Park and Wheelock streets and are nearing completion of graduate student housing on

Park Street. We have also renovated Baker Library, Silsby Hall, Steele Hall, Fairchild Hall, and Leverone Fieldhouse. Even while acknowledging some projects are still pending, we can catch our breath and take real pride in our campus.

Over these years we have also engaged in a series of discussions about the college and about our core values and our priorities. These efforts have included the reaccreditation review in 1999 and the strategic planning process. We have undertaken the complicated task of planning and organizing for a capital campaign. I have used the bully pulpit to stress, consistently, values of academic and scholarly strength, of diversity and inclusiveness, of our commitment to teaching, of collaboration between the college and the professional schools, of the historic strength of Dartmouth as a community that includes, enables, and encourages all of its members. I have sought regularly to affirm the high value of all of our employees. We would not be able to accomplish all that we do without them.

Early in my presidency I took full advantage of opportunities to complete some ongoing projects, to fulfill some dreams and ambitions, to address some challenges and needs identified by my predecessors, John Dickey, John Kemeny, David McLaughlin, and Jim Freedman. And we are not yet finished—and will never be finished. This is the 234th year of Dartmouth's history, and our legacy is also our obligation—each generation leaves the college a bit stronger. This is the Dartmouth story that has no end.

Surely any five-year period in our college's—our world's—history would be marked by highs and lows, by mourning and sadness, by hope and elation. There may not be many times, however, that could match this one in terms of the magnitude of these emotional fluctuations. It has been a five-year period full of consequential and intrusive events in the world beyond the campus, events that have had a full impact on us: war and terrible acts of terrorism, economic fluctuations with financial markets hitting the most bullish of times and plummeting to sustained bearishness. We have mourned and mourn still the senseless murder of two dear colleagues. We try hard to understand 9/11, that which cannot be understood. At a place devoted to learning and teaching, we know well uncertainty, even as we instinctively resist succumbing to it.

As a historian I always want to understand and discuss that which has gone before. But as president I need to focus on that which is yet to come.

And here my interests and my role converge, for any understanding of history suggests that those institutions that survive and thrive are not those that simply wait to take that which comes, but those who focus on who they are and what they seek to be. It is an appropriate time to share again my understanding of Dartmouth and my aspiration for our college.

Dartmouth is a $2.75 billion institution with a half a billion dollar annual operating budget. I function as CEO of the college, meaning that I am accountable to the Board of Trustees for all its operations. This includes oversight for matters ranging from union negotiations to insurance and retirement programs; to complicated federal requirements and regulations for the $160 million of our budget that comes from the government; to recognizing the increasingly consumerist and litigious nature of our society; to offering off-campus programs across a changing world; to managing an Inn and a skiway and a major piece of college property in northern New Hampshire. We engage in discussions regarding the development of property we hold in downtown Hanover, regarding our willingness to support the needs of the local schools, and our partnership with the largest health care provider and academic medical center in northern New England. Of course, these are all peripheral to my major focus—I worry first and foremost about protecting and enhancing the academic strength of Dartmouth in a competitive world with fewer resources, but to this end I also need worry too about foreign exchange rates, about financial markets, about immigration policy.

If all of this comes with the territory, there is an additional expectation that the president of Dartmouth be like a headmaster—visible and available for students and faculty alike. Of course my heart continues to identify with the faculty whose title and appointment I still hold, and I happily embrace this other role—both Susan and I take tremendous satisfaction from the time we can spend with students, and we are proud of their activities. The tension between the CEO and headmaster roles is more one of available time rather than any conflict in my interests. This balancing act is further complicated in that the culture of the college is one of an ongoing town meeting. This is a collegial environment. There are no command and control options for the president of Dartmouth College! I find great satisfaction in these roles, tensions and all. I recognized them well when I began my assignment. This is my culture.

This spring I set out to have a series of conversations, focusing essentially on the next five years. I realize now just how quickly five years can go. Surely our vision, our strategic plan, our campaign goals, address some longer-term objectives that remain critical, essential; but we cannot simply wait for longer term solutions to current challenges, we cannot defer some needs easily, and we cannot lose our special niche and competitive strength while waiting for a change in the economic climate. I have met with individuals and with groups, with faculty, with students, and with local alumni/ae. These have been substantive discussions, sometimes focusing on specific concerns and sometimes broader, more philosophical matters. But in all of these conversations I have been both struck and heartened by the commitment to and understanding about Dartmouth's special niche.

As we think about the near-term future let me say that we start from a position of incredible strength. It would be hard for me to imagine having a stronger, more energized and interesting, student body than the one we now have. It would be hard for me to imagine a faculty more energetic and more creative, more able to sustain the complicated and demanding commitment to teaching and to scholarship that marks this college. Nonetheless, Dartmouth did not become Dartmouth by standing pat! In this competitive world that is not an option.

Our goal quite simply is for Dartmouth to be the very best Dartmouth, to occupy energetically the special place we enjoy in higher education. I have no interest in conceding to other, larger, wealthier institutions a single student whom we want, a single faculty member whom we want. Neither will I concede the very special sort of educational experience that Dartmouth provides. Those who would want us to be less competitive should explain that to the men's and women's lacrosse teams, to the students who are winning scholarship competitions at historically high rates, to the faculty who are securing international recognition, and who are deeply committed to teaching. Explain to me, to the students who continue to rate the accessibility of Dartmouth faculty as among the very best anywhere—explain to all who, like me, find no tension between aspirations for excellence and the history and purpose of this place.

We cannot be all things; we cannot do all things. We need to stay focused on what we are about. I have been so impressed by the commitment of faculty and students, of administrators and alumni, to the idea of Dartmouth: Dartmouth College provides the best student experience, the best undergraduate education, in the country. This is our legacy, this is our strength, this is our shared obligation, and this is our future. I recognize the danger of hyperbole in these settings, in these sorts of discussions. And perhaps I can be forgiven some of this from time to time given my thirty-four-year-old deep and abiding affection for this place. I know an audience such as this one will be willing to tolerate, even encourage, some hyperbole about our college. But my assertion about our niche and our strength is not accompanied by a sheepish wink to suggest exaggeration. We know that there are different rankings shaped by different criteria, by different values, by different measurements and methods, rankings that describe the hierarchy of educational institutions. We also know where we are. Let me affirm as clearly as I can my belief that few can compete with Dartmouth in the quality of the student experience. Few can compete and none can exceed!

The Dartmouth of today is, on its face, different from the Dartmouth that I came to in 1969—that Dartmouth had 3,200 undergraduate students, all men, with probably 7 to 8 percent students of color, few off-campus programs, smaller professional schools—then called "affiliated schools." Much of my effort over the last five years has focused on embracing the changes that have marked the profile of Dartmouth, on making absolutely certain that all who are part of this community feel a full part of this community. This too is our legacy. But Dartmouth is not about only welcoming and including. These things are for a purpose. Now, as then, unambiguously and unequivocally, Dartmouth is committed to providing the strongest student experience in the country. And as strong as we were in 1969, today we surely do even better, even more clearly. This is as it should be. I would happily describe some of those qualities that I believe advance this commitment and underline our strength:

We are marked by a diverse student body that is intellectually strong
   and curious, that is marked by a sense of sharing and belonging,
   by friendships that are sustained for a lifetime.
We are shaped by faculty who are committed to discovery, to
   teaching, and to learning with students. They are the heart of
   our strength and the soul of our being. And they are committed
   to the college—to their college.
We protect an undergraduate liberal arts curriculum that encourages

learning as a life-long process rather than a product, that affirms the importance of critical thinking, of openness to new ideas, and tolerance for different opinions, and that provides opportunities for independent work of discovery and creativity within an environment that has state-of-the-art information systems, digital capacity, and international programs. At Dartmouth the arts and humanities are positioned as essential in an age of profound scientific discovery and expanding technology. Indeed, even more essential.

We embrace a true and shared sense of community that values independence of mind and generosity of spirit, responsibility for common interests and values, a commitment to integrity, mutual respect, and tolerance. Here we protect a scale and size that welcome the individual and respect the wider community. A Dartmouth degree should confirm a Dartmouth education and this signals a dedication to sharing and to service.

We value at Dartmouth a residential community that recognizes the importance of out-of-classroom experiences to the learning process, a place that values the special physical environment, the athletics and outdoor programs, that marks Dartmouth as an environment that resonates with a sense of history and of tradition even as it responds to new challenges and opportunities.

Dartmouth, of course, is more than a small undergraduate college. We are enriched so much as an institution by the strength of the professional schools and graduate programs. And we must remember that we have been enriched by these professional schools for decades, even centuries—they are very much part of Dartmouth's distinctive history as well as its promising future. The same qualities that define the undergraduate experience mark these schools: a scale that is personal, a sense of shared, collaborative learning, a faculty committed to teaching and to working with students. Dartmouth's goal for these programs is that they seek, within their areas of focus, to provide the finest medical student experience in the country, the finest business student experience in the country, the finest graduate engineering student experience in the country, and the finest graduate student experience in the country and to do this with faculties who are engaged in the work shaping their fields. While the undergraduate program is central to Dartmouth, together it and all of these programs derive strength from core values of sharing and collaboration that likely have no equal at other competitive institutions. Dartmouth is an exceptional community of learning.

Obviously the budget environment has changed over the last five years. We have completed some budget cuts over each of the last two years, and we face another round next year, a painful round. Dartmouth is not alone in this situation, some schools are in far more difficult situations and some are better off, but we all are facing the same fundamental conditions. Times such as these require a crisper sense of priority.

We have no interest in expanding our undergraduate student body—it is time, however, that we develop the facilities and the faculty size that meet the needs of our current students. Many of these needs date from the 1970s. Accordingly, I will attach a high priority over the next five years to underlining some clear purposes that are essential to protecting the strength of our undergraduate program. These are

1. Continuing to recruit a strong and diverse student body. Competitive financial aid support within a need-blind admissions program is critical to our purposes.
2. Maintaining and building upon the strength of the faculty through competitive recruiting, through aggressive retention, through supporting the work of the faculty, and through seeking, despite this economic environment, to continue to expand the faculty in order to meet the scholarly and teaching purposes of Dartmouth.
3. Strengthening the residential community through the construction of new residence halls. To advance this too-long deferred need, if we cannot now meet all of our objectives, we will move aggressively in the near term to build some substantial housing and to enrich the range of extra-curricular options by developing new dining and social spaces.

Each of the professional schools has been considering its near term priorities, and while they may differ somewhat in kind or in order, they are fundamentally similar: protecting the quality of students, enhancing the work of the faculty, and dealing with facilities needs on at least an interim basis. We all share in a commitment to meeting the goals described in the strategic plan; we cannot balk at accepting the cards that history has dealt us. Rather than wringing hands, we need to roll up our sleeves and confront the challenges before us.

Dartmouth did not become Dartmouth over the last two and one-third centuries by timidity, by complacency, by an absence of ambition. As I have said before, this lovely place is not a museum or an academic theme park; it is a place vitalized and continually revitalized by a sense of energy and of ambition. I invite you to share with me a tremendous sense of pride in this place and a renewed commitment to protect that which we do so well. Doing so is among the oldest and the most important of Dartmouth's traditions. I have told you before that there is no place I would rather be than in this position, at this place, at this time—and your good company, your support, your encouragement, have helped to make it so. Thank you for all you do.

UNLEASHED: MOBILE COMPUTING CONFERENCE, OCTOBER 8, 2003

Good afternoon. It is a great pleasure for me to welcome all of you to Dartmouth. We are delighted to host this summit on wireless and mobile computing. Yogi Berra once sagely noted, "The future ain't what it used to be." He was right, of course. In 1949, *Popular Mechanics* magazine felt safe to guess that computers in the future might need only 1,000 vacuum tubes and weigh as little as one or two tons. We know now that we cannot even begin to imagine all that lies ahead. Still, as new technologies—as wireless capabilities—begin to transform our vision of how we might work, learn, educate, and live, we are privileged to have an opportunity such as this one to think about the educational and organizational implications of the exciting possibilities before us . . . .

Universities have played such a leading role in developing the new technology that we are discussing—and new uses for it. Research, experimentation, innovation, these are things that our faculty do so well; things that are critical to the learning environment. It is also the case that students have pushed digital frontiers in ways they probably cannot do in most other fields of study. Watch them work and imagine around this campus. And I am sure around your own campuses. You all can relate stories—I would like to tell our story.

Dartmouth was founded in 1769, making it one of the oldest institutions of higher education in the United States. As you know, and can surely see, we enjoy a lovely setting. Paradoxically, this small, intimate community, rich with tradition and surrounded by woodlands and granite hills, has always been ahead of its time in the development and use of computer technology. We had a place in the earliest computer history. It was an 1879 graduate of our Thayer School of Engineering, Harry Bates, who designed a revolutionary apparatus combining electricity with holes punched in cards or tapes. Bates used this machine as the basis for the Tabulating Machine Company, which he left in 1911 before the business was renamed IBM. In 1940, George Stibitz, of Bell Laboratories, used a teletype console in McNutt Hall for a revolutionary demonstration of remote access to a digital computer through the use of standard phone lines. And a Dartmouth mathematician, John McCarthy, first coined the term "artificial intelligence," during a two-month conference here in 1956.

When I joined Dartmouth's faculty in 1969, the college was in the forefront of developments in computing. I arrived on campus with a heavy stack of computer punch cards, the ability to do some Fortran programming, and the patience to wait for batch processing. John Kemeny, a brilliant mathematician who had previously worked with Albert Einstein, was already here, and he was well on his way to transforming the use and role of the computer for me, Dartmouth, and for workers and students in schools and corporations far beyond our boundaries. John Kemeny and his colleague, Thomas Kurtz, bought Dartmouth's first computer in 1959—an LGP-30 that Kemeny later remembered fondly as beautifully designed, "with a slow drum and paper tape input." From that moment on, as a faculty member and, later, as Dartmouth's president, John Kemeny never wavered from his conviction that computers could and should serve as widely accessible, central tools in teaching, research, and learning. In the early 1960s, he already understood that computer centers had as central an importance in universities as libraries and arts centers. And he believed that students could play a critical role in the work to create new technology. "If you only open up computing to students, they're going to do incredible things," he said.

Kemeny was a pioneer who laid the foundations for the accessibility and ubiquity that computers enjoy today. As many of you know, he and Tom Kurtz, developed a system for time-sharing that revolutionized the usefulness of the machine itself. The Dartmouth Time Sharing System (DTSS) began in 1964 by executing two identical programs from two teletypes. Within ten years, the system was able to handle two hundred users. And critically for its success, Kemeny, Kurtz, and several Dartmouth undergraduate students also developed an interfacing language, BASIC, that was simple enough for nonspecialists to master. Kemeny was later to say that the small group of Dartmouth student programmers who helped with the earliest work accomplished things that looked impossible—even to him. I have often thought that the basement of our Kiewit Computation Center thirty to thirty-five years ago was an academic equivalent of the famed garages of Menlo Park.

By 1970, when John Kemeny was inaugurated as president, computers had already radically altered the work and culture of our campus—from the biomedical library to the hospital, and from swimming meets (where Dartmouth students created programs to tabulate results) to community service projects (in 1969, two engineering students developed a computer system for two high schools, city hall, and a hospital in Jersey City). Innovations continued during the Kemeny presidency and in the years that have followed. Dartmouth became a pace setter in academic computing. We automated our library acquisition system and networked it with the Kiewit Computation Center in 1972. In 1984, we became the first college or university in the country to strongly suggest that matriculating students buy and bring to campus a personal computer. (We made the suggestion a requirement seven years later, offering help through financial aid whenever needed.) Early on, thanks to a gift from Apple, we also made computers (Mac 128s) available to all faculty. By 1985, the entire college was hardwired. One year later, the combined efforts of staff, faculty, and students led to the remarkably successful deployment of a campus-wide email system, a version of which we still use today. BlitzMail ("Blitz") is such a part of life here that all of us routinely use the word throughout the day as a noun, a verb, and an adjective. Building upon our past, we have also continued to extend our services to our neighbors: in 1994, Dartmouth developed a stand-alone, nonprofit ISP for use by people throughout the Upper Valley.

The pace and breadth of change at Dartmouth is astounding. We benefit, always, from the strength of our Computer Science Department, where faculty members push the boundaries of their discipline and continue to move our entire institution forward. The Institute for Security and Technology Studies, founded in 2000, serves as a center for cyber-security and counterterrorism research, development, and analysis—a nationally defined and coordinated focus.

And we are particularly proud of the Baker-Berry Library, which we formally dedicated last year. Under the leadership of College Librarian, Richard Lucier, this facility builds upon a thirty-year commitment to marry the old with the new by providing an "information place" for printed and archival materials, and an "information space" for our digital collections and initiatives. In addition to making more than 10,000 electronic journals immediately accessible, the library is supporting the development of new forms of scholarly "publication." Our first digital journal—*Linguistic Discovery*—edited by Professors Lenore Grenoble and Lindsay Whaley focuses on little-known languages that are in many cases endangered. The journal's inclusion of sound and video vastly increases the possibilities for research, documentation, and understanding.

Dartmouth has attracted wide attention for the inauguration of a wireless network, but, as I hope my remarks have made clear, we do see this—and the unveiling of Voice over IP last month—as parts of an almost fifty-year trajectory of innovation by faculty, students, and staff. Today, as in Kemeny's time, faculty members have been centrally involved, students are creatively pushing the technology and its applications forward, and we are benefiting from the collaborative support of partners from the corporate world. Generous alumni/ae at Cisco were instrumental in our ability to make the transition to a wireless environment.

Where will all of this take us? We can each guess, or hope, but none of us can predict (a fact which I find more exciting than troubling). But we do well to pause, as we are doing here for these few days, to benefit from our collective experience and thinking. . . .

REMARKS TO CLASS OFFICERS,
SEPTEMBER 16, 2004

Thank you, and let me add my welcome to those of others. . . .

It is a busy time. It is always a busy time at this dynamic and energetic place. As I begin the seventh year of my administration, it is easy to get caught up in the complexities of a complicated place. So I remind myself to stay focused on our core purpose. My goal has been and continues to be to have the strongest undergraduate program in the country. Let me repeat that. This is not complicated to state or to understand. We want to have, and I intend to ensure that we continue to have here at Dartmouth, the best undergraduate program in the country and in the world.

I am aware of the voices of concern that you hear and will hear tomorrow at the association meeting. There are some who would suggest that Dartmouth is on the wrong track. Let me tell you where I think we are going because other people are not always as clear as they might be in describing what we are doing. Dartmouth has no secret plans, no plans to do away with the Greek system, to devalue teaching. Indeed, we have strengthened both. I have not devoted my life to this place to make it something else. I have devoted my life to making it a better Dartmouth. I am proud of Dartmouth, what it has been and what it is. I am enthused about our future, and I am honored to be president of this college. Dartmouth does not seek to be like any other institution. Dartmouth has a special place in American higher education, and I intend to protect that place.

Let me tell you where I think we are going and why I think that this is the right direction for Dartmouth. When I say that I intend to ensure that we have the best undergraduate experience in the country, what does this mean?

It means bright and energetic students studying with faculty engaged in the research and creative work of their fields and enthused about teaching students.

It means having here facilities and programs that advance our vision and enrich our soul.

It means protecting a true sense of community, one that enables and sustains our students and graduates for a lifetime.

It means having here graduate programs that meet the same standards of excellence and enrich, rather than compete with, our vision and purpose for the undergraduate college. Tuck and Thayer, the Dartmouth Medical School, and the graduate programs in the arts and sciences are small but they are strong. They stand alone as programs from which we can all take pride, and they complement and add to the best undergraduate program in the country.

How do we advance this vision? It begins with students—we need always a strong admissions and financial aid program. Last week, I sent out my semiannual letter to the community. I hope that you received it. It is always gratifying to get back responses. Several of the correspondents picked up on my commitment to keep Dartmouth accessible to a broad range of students.

One alumnus who is now a high school teacher wrote: "We are sending our top two students from last year's graduating class. I know that one of them, one of the most talented and giving people I have ever encountered, would not have been able to attend without generous support from financial aid. Thanks for keeping Dartmouth a place which is open to all who are deserving of its opportunities."

Another graduate who was on financial aid wrote: "Thank you so much for giving me that chance. Thank you so much for that opportunity. What Dartmouth has invested in me I plan to pay back to society. I just wanted to express to you my gratitude for what Dartmouth has done. Dartmouth is one of only a handful of institutions that is need blind in its admissions program and that meets 100 percent of an admitted student's need. Alumni generosity through the annual fund helps to make this possible."

The faculty are also at the core. We advance our vision through faculty recruitment and support for scholarly and teaching initiatives. We need to continue to attract faculty who are excited to be at a place like Dartmouth. Because of its size and its incredible sense of community, this college encourages collaboration between faculty and students. I am always pleased when I read surveys of Dartmouth students to see how satisfied they are with the accessibility of the Dartmouth faculty. We lead our peers in this measure. One young woman wrote to me in response to my community letter to say that she is currently a graduate student at another Ivy League institution. She went on to say: "As a graduate student, I've had the opportunity to speak with fellow graduate students from many of the top universities in the U.S. and around the world. From these conversations, I am even more convinced that Dartmouth offers one of the very best undergraduate programs anywhere. The faculty are truly excellent and the emphasis on undergraduate education is unique in an institution of Dartmouth's caliber." Dartmouth faculty are truly excellent. I am sure that you remember many excellent professors who made a difference in your lives. The college has prided itself on its faculty—faculty who are on the cutting edge of their discipline and who are committed passionate teachers. This is the Dartmouth model. Our faculty are devoted to providing the best liberal arts education.

The best teachers are those who are current in their field—this brings an excitement and rigor to their teaching. Here the term "teacher scholar" is not a hyphenated label for discrete responsibilities. Rather, it is a description of a singular commitment and strength. The frontier between the known and the unknown is never fixed. For this reason, research and other creative and scholarly work are essential for a vibrant faculty. Last year, we took a number of measures to build on the faculty commitment to teaching. In response to student requests, we improved the advising system, we have instituted a new writing program, and we have opened a Center for the Advancement of Learning to provide our faculty with more support for their teaching. And, finally, we provided an additional increment to the faculty compensation pool specifically earmarked to recognize excellent teaching. And we will do this again this year.

How do we know if we have accomplished this vision for Dartmouth as the preeminent liberal arts institution in the country? *U.S. News & World Report* ranked Dartmouth ninth in the country. Dartmouth is also listed ninth among the "Great Schools, Great Values." Kaplan/*Newsweek* named Dartmouth the hottest "tech-savvy" school and ranked the college fifth for "happy students." The Templeton Foundation named Dartmouth as one of the top one hundred character-building institutions in the country. Now, I am uncomfortable with many aspects of these ranking systems. They are certainly one measure of our strength, but as I said in my letter, I am skeptical of their methodology. I would rank our undergraduate program, which is what the *U.S. News & World Report* ranking purports to measure, even higher—much higher. But there are other, perhaps more reliable, measures.

> *Admissions*: We already have an excellent pool of students to choose from; more students than ever are applying to Dartmouth, and every indication suggests that these students are as strong as ever. Last year, eleven students applied for every one that matriculated. Now I am not suggesting that we simply increase our pool so that we can reject more students, but the size of our applicant pool is an indication of just how attractive Dartmouth is to young people today. A lot of students want to come here.

> *Student satisfaction*: Dartmouth students are very satisfied with their overall educational experience, with the courses in their major, with the accessibility of the faculty, with their residential experience. We compare very favorably with our peer institutions on all of these measures. Ninety-one percent of students are satisfied or very satisfied with the quality of their education.

> *Faculty recruitment and retention*: We already get our top choice of faculty, but we must ensure that we continue to attract those special faculty who are as enthusiastic about their teaching as they are about their scholarship.

> *Financial data*: We have balanced the budget over the past few years, and we have weathered some difficult financial times to emerge in a very strong position. If we look at schools that rank above Dartmouth, they have larger endowments and more financial resources. (Harvard's endowment is $22.6 billion. Princeton has a much higher endowment per student than does Dartmouth. Princeton ranked second among a group of national universities on this measure, Harvard fourth, and Dartmouth twenty-fourth.) We do more with less because we are focused on our purpose, but we need to remain clear about our priorities.

> *Alumni engagement*: Last year, 35,845 alumni, parents, friends, foundations and corporations gave to Dartmouth and through that action they affirmed their confidence in the institution and in the direction we are headed.

Moreover, thousands of you, literally, volunteered for Dartmouth as interviewers for the admissions process, as career and placement mentors, as officers in clubs and friends groups, as members of the Alumni Council and Association, and as class officers. You know what that means, and I know how important it is and how demanding it can be. Last year 47.4 percent of alumni participated in the annual fund. This was better than the previous year, which in turn, was better than its previous year. Thank you for all that you did to make this possible. We are not yet finished or satisfied. I know that you work hard to encourage your classmates to participate. We focus so often, and appropriately on our large gifts. But every gift makes a difference; in this way you affirm your commitment to this generation of students. As Ernest Martin Hopkins said, "You are the living endowment of the college." We need to reach for historic levels of participation and then exceed them.

One hundred years ago, in 1904 Dartmouth Hall burned to the ground. Completed in 1791 and built from the trees felled to clear the green, it was the college for forty years, before the building of Wentworth, Thornton, and Reed Halls. Daniel Webster had roomed there. Word of the fire spread as quickly as had the fire. Francis Lane Childs, a member of the Class of 1906 and later a professor of English here, wrote in a letter home in 1904, "It speaks well for the loyalty of Dartmouth alumni," he wrote, "when you consider that the fire only broke out at 8 o'clock Thursday morning, and at 10:10, before the end walls and part of the back had fallen, a hall in Boston had been obtained and a meeting of the alumni of Boston and vicinity had been called for Saturday afternoon." Because of that outpouring of alumni support, Dartmouth Hall reopened for classes two years later. I told this story to the incoming students on Tuesday to underline for them the community that they now join. This fall we plan to launch an aggressive but essential capital campaign that will enable Dartmouth to build upon our strengths and our best qualities. The focus will be on financial aid, faculty support, student life, and facilities. Your support and engagement as always will be critical to that. We will set an aggressive goal and with your involvement I look forward to exceeding that goal.

Let us be frank, we clearly do have some issues that we need to address, and I plan to do just that this coming year. We need to improve the way we work with students. Our data tells us that Dartmouth students love their experience here. They are among the most satisfied students among our peer institutions. But we also know that there have been some missteps, and they are often frustrated with their interaction with administrators. Jim Larimore plans to tackle this issue very directly this year by meeting with students, and my colleagues are committed to reduce some of the irritants in this relationship. Last year we worked hard to bring in the CFS leadership and made some important progress. Those discussions were very helpful, and the resolution of the issue satisfactory to both the students and the administration. We need to find more opportunities for such common ground. And we will.

I also think we could do better engaging with our alumni. Last year when I issued my Five Year Report, I wrote there that one of my priorities going forward was to improve communications with alumni. You play an awfully important role here by how you communicate and what you communicate with your classmates. But I am not sure that we always give you all the information that you need. And communication is a two-way process. We need to give you the information you need, and we need to develop a greater level of trust with the material coming from the administration. And you need to share better with us your ideas and input. The Annual Fund is one indicator of this—but this is about engagement more than dollars. I am aware of your concerns regarding class dues, the magazine, and our support for your work. Let us work on these matters.

We discussed this issue of alumni communications at our recent meeting of the Board of Trustees. And the board has agreed to set up a trustee working group to look into the whole issue of alumni relations. Karen Francis will chair the group, and Trustees Bill Neukom, John Donahoe, Michael Chu, Brad Evans, Ed Haldeman, T. J. Rodgers, and I will all participate. We will solicit your advice and feedback. This group will report back within the next year with some recommendations. Joe Stevenson's group on alumni governance is also a great example of a group that is working to bring people together. I spoke with Joe this morning and told him how much I value what he is doing to bridge the differences among alumni. I am prepared to help with this task. We need to come together; our shared interest in this College on the Hill is too strong for us not to work together. Alumni are not adversaries of the college; we are in this good and historic work together. Let us revel in our strength and in our shared purpose and work together to solve our problems. This is Dartmouth. We have a big tent; come on in. Let us quit the sniping and fighting.

In his inaugural address, David McLaughlin described Dartmouth as "rich in heritage and strong in purpose." In 2004 the heritage is even richer; the strength of our commitment is even greater. I am excited to be here, to be Dartmouth's president, and to be launching this campaign. I have taught you, and I have welcomed your children for thirty-five years (at least eleven students in the current class are the sons or daughters of students I taught). I have visited you in your clubs and at your reunions. We have had good times and occasional debates. But we share in an important work in keeping Dartmouth as good as it is, as good as it can be. This is my life work, and this is your ongoing commitment. I look forward to your participation and to your support. Let us now come together. The Hill winds call your names. Thank you.

REMARKS IN MEMORY OF
DAVID T. MCLAUGHLIN '54 TU '55,
PRESIDENT EMERITUS OF THE
COLLEGE, OCTOBER 4, 2004

This morning we have remembered David McLaughlin as husband, as father and grandfather, as friend, and as businessman and public servant. Even though his family was the most important part of his life and even though those other roles consumed greater parts of his life, one cannot know David McLaughlin without also knowing his fifty-four-year relationship with Dartmouth.

Great and enduring institutions do not just happen. They are protected and nurtured and extended by the individuals committed to advancing their institutional purposes. As president, David McLaughlin said, "This is a place where you put your arms around it, and you care for it." In the long history of this college there surely have been some who cared for it as deeply as David. But it is hard to imagine any who cared more than he did.

Mrs. McLaughlin—Judy—Susan, Wendy, Bill, Jay, all of the McLaughlin grandchildren, and other family members, today we put our arms around you, and together we join you in missing and grieving—but also celebrating, for this good man's good marks are all around us. Milton wrote,

Nothing is here for tears, nothing to wail
Or knock the breast, no weakness, no contempt,
Dispraise or blame, nothing but well and fair, . . .

When David McLaughlin was an East Grand Rapids high school football star, Gerald Ford, then a first-term congressman from Michigan, tried to persuade him to go to the University of Michigan, but David was drawn to Dartmouth. He described his relationship with the college as "a kind of love affair at first sight." It was a love affair that was to last well over a half century to the very end of his life.

At his matriculation in 1950 David met President John Sloan Dickey and quickly became friends with him. They would in later years go walking together in the woods or fishing, and always, as trustee and later as president, David would visit with and seek guidance from Mr. Dickey. And he looked out for Mr. Dickey during Mr. Dickey's final years, in ways that few would know. At convocation in the fall of 1950, David's freshman year, President Dickey challenged the incoming students to "be worthy of the privilege of being judged as a Dartmouth man." David McLaughlin surely met this challenge.

A financial aid student, he excelled in every regard. A Phi Beta Kappa major in International Studies, he was president of the Undergraduate Council and led students in opposing restrictive clauses in Dartmouth organizations. He received the Barrett Cup, given annually by faculty and students in recognition of his all-round achievement and worthiness as an individual. A star football player, he was the top receiver in the Ivy League and in the Eastern Intercollegiate Football Association, and the Philadelphia Eagles drafted him to play professionally. But he figured that he was not going to play football for the rest of his life, and so turned down the offer and went instead to the Tuck School, and from there to an illustrious business career. But success in business was never enough for David McLaughlin. He was not yet finished.

Through all his busy days, with his work and family, he never lost touch with his college. He served as president of his class for four years, president of the Dartmouth Alumni Association of Chicago in 1968, member of the Tuck School's Board of Overseers, and member of the committee for the college's Third Century Fund. And in 1971 he became a member of the Board of Trustees, chairing the board between 1977 and 1981.

It was during one of his very first meetings as a trustee that the board voted in favor of coeducation. David was an ardent supporter of coeducation as his daughter, of the class of 1981, and his granddaughter, of the class of 2007, here today can attest. At the end of his service as a trustee, upon his election as president of the college in 1981, the board credited him as one "whose work will create the Dartmouth College of the twenty-first century." It did, but he was not yet finished.

His legacy as the fourteenth president of the college is clear. He revitalized student life, increased significantly faculty salaries, protected and extended need-blind admissions, dramatically grew the endowment, oversaw the expansion of the physical campus with the construction of three new residence halls, as well as the Hood Museum and the John Berry Sports Center.

And, in perhaps the most long-lasting accomplishment, he helped to move the Medical Center from Hanover to Lebanon, opening up the north part of the campus for the college. I said to David many times—and told his classmates so at their fiftieth reunion in June—that the decision to relocate and reconstitute the Medical Center, audacious and even controversial though it was, was both right and courageous. It stands only behind coeducation in shaping the modern Dartmouth and the future of this college. The poet Thomas Gray wrote, "Large was his bounty, and his soul sincere."

For David McLaughlin, the most gratifying aspect of being president was the dimension directly involving students. He once said, "The highlight of my whole experience here has always been commencement. You see students come into this college, different sizes and shapes as freshmen, and then four years later you see a transformation go on that is pretty important . . . there is an ongoing process here that goes well beyond any individual." I had the privilege of saluting David at commencement this past June and had the thrill of seeing students and faculty accord him a warm greeting—a resounding welcome home.

He was a mentor and a friend to me. I first met him when he was board chair and I chaired a major faculty committee reviewing the curriculum. He made clear that he would do whatever he could to advance this work and he did. For me—and for Susan—he was always a friend and a colleague, through the bad times and the good. I never asked him for a thing that he didn't respond quickly and affirmatively.

We had a quiet lunch this past April at which I told him that I wanted to do something to recognize him on the occasion of his fiftieth reunion. He modestly demurred and said we had plenty of time to think about such things in the years ahead. Of course it proved to be, tragically, time that we were not to have. I believe, however, that he would be pleased with the board's decision that I announced last week to name the student facilities we are building on the old hospital property in honor of David McLaughlin. It is appropriate and symbolic.

For over half a century, David T. McLaughlin helped to shape and guide this college. Dartmouth is a more inclusive place and a stronger place because of his contributions. As Ralph Waldo Emerson wrote, "He builded better than he knew. . . ." We knew though, and we hope that he did. I salute here my predecessor and my friend. We grieve, knowing that his passing was premature—he was not yet finished. But builded in our hearts is the knowledge that we were privileged to have known him and to be the beneficiaries of his legacy. And for as long as there is a Dartmouth, the college that he loved, and that loved him back, will cherish his loyalty and will be the richer for his contributions.

THE LESLIE CONFERENCE ON THE FUTURE
OF THE LIBERAL ARTS, NOVEMBER 6, 2004

I have in the last quarter century chaired two comprehensive curriculum review committees at Dartmouth—at least one more than any person should take on in a lifetime. In the late 1970s I served as chair of the committee that brought in recommendations to adjust the general distribution requirements, and in 1991 I chaired the committee that recommended more fundamental restructuring of the curriculum. These experiences, as well as my work as an American historian, and, for the last six years, president, have given me some insights that I would now share with you. They have to do with the historical context of where we are today in this conversation about the curriculum and the academy and where we are headed, but represent my reflections rather than any scholarly focus I have had.

The curriculum on any college campus is the concrete representation of the educational philosophy and academic priorities of the faculty, and it is not easily changed. Over the years as our basic philosophy of education has changed, as, in some fundamental ways, the purpose of higher education has evolved and so too have the curriculum and graduation requirements. Those American colleges and universities like Dartmouth chartered in the colonial or early national periods had a quite specific purpose: to transmit that which was known rather than to expand knowledge. Their focus was on the discipline of learning and reciting and the total course of study was classical—narrowly so. The first schools were private and their mission was to pass along received traditions, to train ministers and thoughtful graduates. Degrees were less important than education. And there was a presumption of homogeneity—even at a place like Dartmouth that was founded in part to education Native Americans and was among the first colleges to admit African American students. There was not much debate about the nature of the curriculum and probably even less about how to read and interpret and understand the texts that were part of it.

In the late eighteenth and early nineteenth centuries the classical curriculum had a heavy emphasis on Greek and Latin grammar and the development of mental discipline. Modern languages, history outside of Greek and Roman history, and science, these had no place in the curriculum of early American colleges. All students took the same courses at the same time. This curriculum held sway in the world of American higher education into the mid-nineteenth century and suggested revisions met with general resistance and skepticism. President Charles Hodge of the Princeton Theological Seminary proudly claimed that "a new idea never originated in this seminary." In the mid 1840s Professor Evert Topping of Princeton tried to change the way in which he taught his classes. He said that his students had reacted to his classes taught in the traditional manner with groans and "other willful noises." So he tried to use Greek literature to engage his students' interest in the subject matter. But when the president of the university found out about this innovation, he asked Professor Topping to resign his position. When John Maclean became president of Princeton in 1854 he proudly declared, "We shall not aim at innovations . . . no chimerical experiments in education have ever had the least countenance here."

In addition to the undergraduate courses of study, a few universities also had professional schools. Dartmouth established its medical school in 1797—the fourth such school in the country—and the first engineering school in 1867. But even here the emphasis was on rote learning and not discovery. . . .

In the mid-nineteenth century, two new university models began to emerge. The first was the state universities like the Universities of Illinois and Wisconsin. These were funded by the states, and by the federal government following the passage of the Morrill Act in 1862, the legislation that established land-grant universities. These universities provided a more practical education. Or as the president of the University of Illinois put it, "utilitarian education for the producing classes." Vermont Senator Justin Morrill did not want to simply establish more of the same—universities and colleges that taught the classical curriculum. Instead, in keeping with his democratic ideals, he wanted a system of higher education that would serve the national welfare by disseminating the latest scientific research, particularly in the area of agriculture but also the industrial arts. The land grant universities would teach some traditional classical studies, but they would also teach more practical applied knowledge: "such branches of

learning as are related to agriculture and the mechanic arts." This curriculum, unlike the classical curriculum, Morrill believed would have a
direct relevance to the lives of students and would serve the public who
supported these institutions. Justin Morrill hoped that the new universities would be more accessible to a broader cross section of students.
They were to "promote the liberal and practical education of the industrial classes"—farmers, laborers, skilled artisans, and their children.

Although the land grant institutions were state institutions, many private universities also opened more practical branches. Ezra Cornell married a private academy with a land-grant college and proclaimed that he
wanted to found a university "where any person can find instruction in
any study." Similarly, Yale had its Sheffield Scientific School, Harvard its
Lawrence Scientific School, and Dartmouth had the Chandler School of
Science and the Arts. Admission standards for these schools were lower,
and the degree granted not as prestigious. At Dartmouth the Chandler
School provided an alternative to the classical curriculum and included a
mix of the practical (bookkeeping, graphics, carpentry, masonry, and the
use of instruments for example) with more modern academic subjects
not included within the Classical curriculum (English Literature, physical
geography, and physiology among others).

The second major influence on American universities in the mid- to
late nineteenth century was that of the German universities, which em-
phasized the idea of the university as a place to expand that which is
known. This encouraged the founding of several universities in the United
States with a primary purpose of research—Johns Hopkins 1876, Chicago
1890, Clark 1887, and Stanford 1891—and the invigoration of many older
institutions with a focus on discovery, systematic research, and graduate
education.

Together these influences—the more practical even utilitarian education provided by the land-grant colleges and the emphasis on the creation of new knowledge by the German and new research universities—
challenged the traditional course of study offered at older universities.
The presidents of these institutions (Charles Eliot, Woodrow Wilson, and
at Dartmouth William Jewett Tucker and Ernest Fox Nichols) responded
by expanding their curriculums, encouraging their faculties to participate
in research, and providing for more electives. By the late nineteenth cen-

tury, research was clearly accepted at the country's major universities, with many of them now encouraging their faculty to study for advanced degrees. In 1900, the Association of American Universities formed as a means of discussing policies surrounding graduate education. Universities became less the transmitters of received knowledge and more places of inquiry.

At Dartmouth, President Tucker wrote, "A college stands in relation to the society at large," and he set out to thoroughly reform the classical curriculum that still sat at the heart of a Dartmouth education. In his inaugural address he said, "If by a liberal education we mean the introduction to the broader ranges of thought, we cannot leave out the study of nature (and) or man as a part of nature." He overhauled the curriculum and introduced new disciplines in the social sciences, and he established the first in the world school of business with the Tuck School of Business Administration in 1900. The first new professorships were in history, sociology, and biology with later additions of French and German, economics, and astronomy and physics. He introduced the teaching of evolution and laboratory science.

In the 1920s, Dartmouth President Ernest Martin Hopkins called for a general review of the educational requirements, and he appointed Professor Leon Burr Richardson as head of the review committee. Richardson visited nineteen other colleges and universities in the United States and another fourteen in Canada, England, and Scotland. He noted that the previous seventy years (those years since 1850) had seen a "deluge of new ideas, of new methods," in higher education. He went on to note, "If we examine the whole history of education it will not be easy to find a period so brief in which so complete a change of educational outlook and so sharp a modification of method has taken place as has been witnessed in the United States." Richardson then posited that the purpose of the university was "the stimulation and development of those gifts of intellect with which nature has endowed the student, so that he becomes, first, a better companion to himself through life, and, second, a more efficient force in his contacts with his fellow men." Students needed to both understand the received knowledge of the time but also be able to think for themselves. Thus, the basic model of leading American universities during the first half of the twentieth century combined several strands:

a faculty dedicated to research, a much expanded curriculum that combined both utilitarian and classical knowledge, and a desire to teach students to think critically.

The mid-twentieth century was also the period of the core curriculum
based on western civilization and the idea of the "canon," first developed
at places like the University of Chicago under President Robert Maynard
Hutchins. Harvard University under President James Bryant Conant in
1945 issued its report *General Education in a Free Society*, in which they
suggested that all students needed to take a course on Great Texts of Literature and another on Western Thoughts and Institutions.

The period following World War II saw another wave of fundamental
change in colleges and universities, one that would more directly shape
our world today. The G.I. Bill expanded significantly those who might
aspire to higher education. This and the great expansion of opportunity
that marked the civil rights movement led to the remarkable expansion
of students enrolled in colleges and universities. Today, we celebrate our
heterogeneity and pluralism and have even defended them before the
Supreme Court as essential to the educational experience that we offer to
students.

Concomitant with the expansion of American higher education was a
growing expectation that a college degree is essential. It was a practical
and necessary step to a life of opportunity. The Horatio Alger story now required a college degree — and indeed, even today, as we open our doors to
a more socioeconomically diverse student body, the demand for a "practical" education has increased. Unlike during the early national period,
now the degree as credential has come to be the focus of our work and the
course of study generally has become less material. The degree validates
the worth of the individual.

Also following the war, as a result of military exigencies from both the
war itself and the Cold War, the government accelerated its involvement
in research and public health, initiating tremendous investments in university research programs — in infrastructure and in projects of individual
faculty. Stanford, for example, grew from being a regional university into
a major national, indeed international, research university with federal
research dollars being a significant factor in their growth.

Today, universities have embraced a dual mission: the education of talented students through a combination of utilitarian programs and liberal arts, and the creation of new knowledge through extensive research programs. The idea of received knowledge has receded still further—indeed, the nature of research and inquiry assume a healthy intellectual skepticism toward received knowledge.

What are the consequences of these themes and patterns for us today? Are the liberal arts still relevant? I would say yes—an unequivocal yes. In the last half a century we have also seen a wonderful expansion of the nature of research and of subject matter in the humanities, including my own field of history. There surely is no longer a core or shared curriculum. Whenever either of the two committees on which I served discussed common core courses any agreement in principal shattered as anyone tried to be specific. This ongoing intellectual foment is an exciting part of our work. It is complicated by another trend: our entering students, brighter than ever, have little common academic core themselves as high schools have gone through a similar expansion of curriculum. We continue to expect our students to take a full range of courses from across the curriculum if they are to present themselves as liberally educated, but the last nineteenth-century elective system may sit less well in a world where there is no shared knowledge.

We know that more students come to Dartmouth wanting to major in the sciences—perhaps a result of the growing value of science and technology in our lives. It is also the case that first-generation college students, those whose presence we value, often have a very focused sense of the practical value of education. Thomas Jefferson once wrote, "I am a farmer so that my son can be a lawyer so that my grandson can be a poet." But as a liberal arts institution, we continue to insist that our students take many courses outside of their area of interest including literature, and art, and history, and on and on. I have told our students, "You need while here to continue the process of understanding these things as best we can now understand them—and some of you will begin a lifetime of expanding our understandings. None of you should leave Dartmouth without engaging with the work that defines modern science and technology." I have also encouraged students not to look to their education here "for practical guidance, for instruction, or for recipes for life. History, together with the liberal arts more generally, assist us in knowing that the human experience is a complicated and rich continuum and that ours is not a world that we can model and predict."

The question then is really how we construct that education, what degree requirements we insist on, and how we structure the curriculum. There are several different models on how to do this among our peer institutions. Brown and Amherst have a minimum set of requirements and encourage their students to simply choose among a very broad range of courses. At the other extreme, are those institutions like St. Johns that provide a highly structured core curriculum centered on the great books of western civilization. The Universities of Chicago and Columbia have both retained the notion of a core curriculum. At Dartmouth, as a result of the last curriculum review in the early 1990s, we chose to focus less on distributive courses and more on a set of skills and areas of knowledge that we thought were essential—our students must take courses in the arts, literature, philosophy, religion, and history, as well as those that include a comparative or international focus. They must take courses that encourage social analysis, quantitative or deductive thinking, and courses in technology and applied science. They must take a science class including one with a laboratory, field, or experimental component. Richardson's focus on teaching students to think critically remains a central priority. But how well do we do this. That, it seems to me, is the question before us. Could we do this better?

We have continued to refine the curriculum, and we continue to face some difficult and important questions. Currently every course counts toward something—should this be the case? Would we think about our curriculum differently if we needed to identify just a handful of courses that were best suited for nonmajor and introductory students? I have previously challenged our academic departments to think more about how they teach nonmajors. The wonderful explosion of research and discovery needs to be distilled better for those who seek an introduction to a field. I think perhaps that the sciences do this most clearly with their separate tracks, and departments in the social sciences and humanities might learn from that model and that we could all usefully think about how to teach to nonmajors. As we shy away from canonical requirements, is the only option a sort of intellectual relativism where every idea and approach has merit?

I worry a bit about our ability to set priorities and to offer a curriculum that reflects those priorities. In a world that is pushing for more practical and professional education, we must ensure that the liberal arts curriculum remains vital and relevant to our students, that it challenges them to reach their fullest potential, and that it continues to provide us with the next generation of leaders.

DARTMOUTH LAWYERS ASSOCIATION, OCTOBER 11, 2003

The American system of higher education is the envy of the world, and this is in part a result of how accessible and free our universities and colleges are. Since World War II we have seen a real democratization of education so that virtually any prepared student, regardless of their background or their financial circumstances, can attend some school. We are committed to make certain that their choices may include Dartmouth, a place that surely provides one of the strongest undergraduate programs in the country. Dartmouth is extremely proud to be one of only a handful of institutions that is need blind in its applications process and that provides 100 percent of a student's demonstrated need. Our ability to continue to admit a diverse student body was threatened last year by the cases brought against the University of Michigan regarding admissions practices in both the undergraduate university and the Law School. We were very pleased with the decision in the *Grutter v. Bollinger* law school case.

Dartmouth, along with our peer institutions in the Ivy League, follows an admissions process that uses a flexible individualized assessment of each candidate, taking into account a student's range of accomplishments, interests, and backgrounds. We have no set formula for admission. A candidate's racial or ethnic background is only one of a wide range of factors bearing on his or her potential to contribute to the college community, and only then in the context of their other academic and personal qualifications. In the *Grutter* decision, the court preserved the flexibility of universities to pursue admissions policies that promote student diversity and the vital educational benefits that flow from that diversity. The court recognized the compelling interest that we have in encouraging diversity.

We all recognize that the Michigan affirmative action cases were the sequel to the Supreme Court's decision in the *Bakke* case, issued twenty-five years earlier. What is less well known, is that both the Michigan decisions and *Bakke* were rooted in part in principles of educational autonomy and academic freedom announced by the Supreme Court in two

New Hampshire cases—one involving Dartmouth, the other the University of New Hampshire.

The first of these was the famous Dartmouth College case—*Trustees of Dartmouth College v. Woodward*—decided by the Supreme Court in 1819. The court case was the culmination of a fight that lasted from 1815 to 1819. It was a battle between Presbyterians and Republicans, on the one side, led by President John Wheelock, the son of the founder who was also tied to some dominant state political interests, and the Congregationalists and Federalists on the other, represented by the Board of Trustees. The trustees and faculty (there were just three faculty then), or the "College" faction as they were called, fought President Wheelock and the state, or the "University" faction over control of the institution. Ultimately, the trustees decided to dismiss John Wheelock as president and appointed Francis Brown in his stead. This decision aroused the ire of both the state legislature and the newly elected governor, John Plumer, who had campaigned on the platform that, if elected, he would have the legislature assert authority over Dartmouth and mandate a more secular curriculum at the college.

In 1816, the legislature did indeed extend its authority by passing a series of laws that aimed to take control of the college. Among other things, these laws changed the name of the college to Dartmouth University, increased the number of trustees from twelve to twenty-one, gave the governor the power to appoint the new trustees and future replacements, and created a board of overseers appointed by the governor to exercise most of the powers formerly held by the trustees, including the power to appoint and remove the president and other officers of the institution. For a time, Dartmouth College and Dartmouth University operated in tandem with rival students and faculty (the University faction had to hire additional faculty) and even libraries. But faced with the power of the state, the faculty agreed to hand over the college buildings if necessary because they would make "no forcible resistance, it not being a part of their policy to repel violence by violence." (Although in fact, the opposing factions did come to blows when two faculty of the University side rounded up some "village roughs" and attempted to take possession of the college library. Students led by Rufus Choate barricaded themselves in the library as the university faction attempted to break down the door with an ax! Eventually enough college students turned out that the professors and roughs were quickly outnumbered and fled.)

The changes passed by the legislature directly contradicted the terms of the college's Charter, which Eleazar Wheelock had secured from the British Crown in 1769, with the help of the Royal Governor of the Province of New Hampshire. Among other things, the Charter from Great Britain gave Eleazar Wheelock the authority to name his successor, with the concurrence of the trustees, and gave the trustees sole authority to elect all subsequent presidents, and to appoint or remove any officer, teacher, or employee of the college. In addition, the Charter established that the Trustees of Dartmouth College existed as an independent corporation, not requiring any further "license, grant, or confirmation," in order to maintain its independence in the future.

The college's trustees met in August of 1816 to decide how to respond to the new legislation. Litigation was one option. As John Sterling recounts in his book, *Daniel Webster and a Small College*, "[t]he atmosphere for successful legal action was very bad." Popular sentiment, secular, anti-elitist and anti-special privilege, was running in favor of state control, and the idea of self-perpetuating religious schools was falling out of favor. The legislatures of New York, Kentucky, Massachusetts, and Connecticut had already asserted control over some private colleges in those states, and in each instance several schools had acceded to the legislature. Ex-President Thomas Jefferson, hearing of the Dartmouth dispute, captured the view of his followers when he wrote, "The idea of a self-perpetuating board of trustees assumed that 'the earth belonged to the dead, and not to the living.'"

Nevertheless, despite the national mood, the trustees sued, and retained alumnus Daniel Webster (Class of 1801) to represent them. Thirty-six years old, Webster was already a renowned constitutional lawyer, having argued before the Supreme Court for nearly five years. The college lost the first round in the New Hampshire Supreme Court, but the trustees appealed to the United States Supreme Court, where, following three days of oral argument Chief Justice John Marshall framed the issue as follows:

> That education is an object of national concern, and a proper subject of legislation, all admit. That there may be an institution, founded

by government and placed entirely under its immediate control, the officers of which would be public officers, amenable exclusively to the government, none will deny.

But is Dartmouth College such an institution? Is education altogether in the hands of government? Does every teacher of youth become a public officer, and do donations for the purpose of education necessarily become public property, so far that the will of the legislature, not the will of the donor, becomes the law of the donation?

The Court answered "No" to all three questions. And the basis for the court's decision was that private colleges were autonomous legal entities. As such, their charters represented contracts with the state, protected from unilateral amendment by the government under Article I, Section 10 of the Constitution—the contracts clause. Of course, it is the broader affirmation of contracts that made the case an important constitutional landmark—and was likely the context in which you studied this in law school. (And in Dartmouth lore, Webster's peroration, "it is a small college, but there are those that love it," became an important tradition and slogan in Dartmouth's history—even if Webster's reference was not to "small" relative to the other colleges, but rather "small" relative to the state. Dartmouth was at that time in fact one of the larger colleges in the United States. Nonetheless, his statement continues to resonate today.)

Although Chief Justice Marshall did not mention the concept of academic freedom as such in the Dartmouth College case, the implicit message that society was served by insulating the academy from government control provided the foundation for the eventual judicial recognition of academic freedom in another case from the Granite State: *Sweezy v. New Hampshire*. In the early 1950s the Attorney General of New Hampshire was investigating subversive persons and asked Paul Sweezy, a Marxist economist, some questions about a guest lecture he had given in a humanities class at the University of New Hampshire. When he refused to answer, he was convicted of contempt.

The case went to the Supreme Court, where the conviction was overturned on a technicality. But the case became famous for Justice Felix Frankfurter's concurring opinion arguing that the conviction was unconstitutional because it violated academic freedom, which Frankfurter said was protected by the First Amendment. Frankfurter's opinion warned of

155

the "grave harm resulting from governmental intrusion into the intellectual life of a university" and the need for First Amendment protection to assure "the exclusion of [such] governmental intervention." In its most illustrious passage, the opinion quoted with approval from a statement issued by the two "open" universities of South Africa—the University of Cape Town and the University of Witwatersrand—that accepted both white and nonwhite students. The open universities' statement was drafted in 1957, in response to apartheid laws enforcing segregation in South Africa's universities. Such laws, the statement declared, represented "an unwarranted interference with university autonomy and academic freedom." The particular passage quoted by Justice Frankfurter in *Sweezy* stated: "It is the business of a university to provide that atmosphere which is most conducive to speculation, experiment and creation. It is an atmosphere in which there prevail 'the four essential freedoms' of a university—to determine for itself on academic grounds who may teach, what may be taught, how it shall be taught, and who may be admitted to study." Twenty-one years later, Justice Lewis Powell, in his tie-breaking opinion in the *Bakke* case, invoked Justice Frankfurter's concurrence in *Sweezy v. New Hampshire*, and the definition of academic freedom contained in the statement of South Africa's open universities, to uphold the right of colleges and universities to consider diversity as a factor in admissions decisions. Quoting the language that "who may be admitted to study" is one of the four essential freedoms of a university, Justice Powell wrote, "Academic freedom, though not a specifically enumerated constitutional right, long has been viewed as a special concern of the First Amendment. The freedom of a university to make its own judgments as to education includes the selection of its student body." On this basis, Justice Powell concluded that race could constitutionally be considered as one factor in the admissions process, alongside other factors, in order to achieve the atmosphere of speculation, experiment and creativity that enriches the educational experience for all students.

Twenty-five years after *Bakke*, the Supreme Court revisited the issue of diversity in admissions in the two University of Michigan cases—one involving Michigan's undergraduate college, the other involving its law school. And again, Justice Frankfurter's teaching in *Sweezy v. New Hampshire*, emphasizing the autonomy of universities in the core areas of academic decision making, played a critical role in influencing the court's thinking. By a 5–4 majority, the court in the Michigan cases essentially adopted Justice Powell's reasoning in *Bakke*, holding that colleges could lawfully consider race as one factor in admissions decisions, as long as they engaged in an individualized, holistic review of each applicant's file, did not use quotas, and did not use race in a mechanical way. Citing *Sweezy*, Justice Sandra Day O'Connor wrote in her majority opinion:

> Today, we hold that the Law School has a compelling interest in attaining a diverse student body.
>
> The Law School's educational judgment that such diversity is essential to its educational mission is one to which we defer. . . . Our holding today is in keeping with our tradition of giving a degree of deference to a university's academic decisions, within constitutionally prescribed limits.
>
> We have long recognized that, given the . . . expansive freedoms of speech and thought associated with the university environment, universities occupy a special niche in our constitutional tradition. In announcing the principle of student body diversity as a compelling state interest, Justice Powell invoked our cases recognizing a constitutional dimension, grounded in the First Amendment, of educational autonomy: "The freedom of a university to make its own judgments as to education includes the selection of its student body."

The deference to the judgment of educators reflected in *Bakke* and the Michigan cases has not been confined to the admissions area. With few exceptions, courts have followed the same approach in dealing with university decisions about disciplinary proceedings, including student dismissal, and faculty tenure assessments.

To be sure, the nearly two hundred years since the Dartmouth College case—and especially the years since the end of the Second World War—have seen a considerable narrowing of the autonomy accorded colleges and universities in this country. Dartmouth is a highly regulated enterprise, subject to a dizzying array of laws concerning employment, taxation, immigration, privacy, health and safety, environmental protection, animal welfare, Internet access, technology transfer, research misconduct and a score of other subjects.

In a study that is now several years old, the Institute for Higher Education Policy calculated that the federal student aid regulations alone consume more than 7,000 sections of the Code of Federal Regulations. Part of this circumstance relates to the fact that we do receive federal funds for any number of our programs. But even if we did not take any money, we would still face a number of regulatory controls. This is largely as it should be. Universities should not expect to be immune from legitimate government regulation. When universities operate power plants that release emissions into the air, they should expect to be subject to the same clean air regulations as industry. When universities employ people to engage in maintenance work, they should expect to be subject to the same occupational safety and health regulations as industry.

The question is how to strike the right balance between the public's interests and academic autonomy. This finely tuned state will often be difficult to achieve. But the fundamental integrity of our institutions asserted in the Dartmouth College case and the four freedoms identified by Justice Frankfurter in *Sweezy* and applied by Justice O'Connor in the Michigan cases provide valuable guidance concerning those areas where the public interest is generally best served by permitting educators to make academic judgments free of governmental control.

If today we are not as small as we were in the early nineteenth century, nor as unfettered as we were in the early twentieth century, we nonetheless do enjoy essential independence, which of course puts the burden on us to use our position responsibly. Thank you for encouraging and supporting us in this role.

REMARKS AT THE MEMORIAL SERVICE FOR JAMES O. FREEDMAN, FIFTEENTH PRESIDENT OF DARTMOUTH COLLEGE, MAY 15, 2006

Today represents one of those symbolic occasions when the good work of learning pauses in order to remember and to celebrate an important figure in Dartmouth's history. Jim Freedman's contributions, to us and our world, are forever. Today is a time for friends to stop and reflect about someone whose memory will be for our lifetimes and an opportunity for us all to extend to Sheba, Deborah, and Jared Freedman our condolences and affection. Susan and I do so. And, more personally, this moment provides me a chance to say something about my predecessor in the Wheelock succession.

James Oliver Freedman was a wonderful colleague, friend, and mentor who taught by example and who enabled by encouraging. I spent so much time with him, and I remember our times together with a fondness and deep respect that help ease the sadness I also feel today. He had an astonishing intellect, a deep humanity, courage in the face of adversity, and a great sense of humor. And we surely shared a passion for the Boston Red Sox!

Jim died on March 21, and I was deeply honored when he asked me a few weeks earlier if I would speak at the funeral service at his temple Congregation Kehillath Israel in Brookline, Massachusetts. On that occasion, I shared my reflections on Jim Freedman as a person and as a man who was remarkably well read. (When he left Iowa City in 1987, people claimed, the revenue of the Prairie Lights Bookstore went down by five percent! The Dartmouth Bookstore certainly counted him as their best individual customer during his Dartmouth years.) But my theme at his funeral was not about his learning or even his obvious intellect—but his wisdom, which is what set him apart.

I also reflected then upon his courage—his intellectual courage to stand for principles and purposes despite criticism. And his personal courage in the face of repeated assaults from his cancer over twelve difficult years. If this disease managed to lessen his body it never lessened his spirits. He inspired many. Who can ever forget his remarks here at commencement in 1994, his bald head shining from the ravages of chemotherapy, where he reminded us all that liberal education is finally the best preparation for the worst that life can deliver. He said, "It does enable us to make sense of the events that either break over us, like a wave, or quietly envelop us before we know it, like a drifting fog."

I also talked about his Jewish identity and how increasingly important that became to him. Jim once wrote: "Growing up . . . I often wondered . . . what it meant to be a Jew. I gradually came to understand that a devotion to learning was at the center of Jewish identity. My parents were both readers. Our house abounded with books and conversations about ideas. And so, as I matured, my search for my most authentic self was ineluctably linked to my identity as an intellectual, and that identity was inextricably linked to my sense of myself as a Jew."

We mourn a friend who inspired, one who could elicit a smile in the down times, celebrate warmly in the good times, and who encouraged our aspirations to be higher for all times.

Today, I would like to focus more on Jim Freedman as president, what Jim meant to Dartmouth. Dartmouth, at its historic best, has drawn outsiders and free spirits, welcomed the loners and made them, on their own terms, part of this community. The fifteenth president in the Wheelock succession, the first in over 150 years to have had no prior connection to the college, Jim Freedman encouraged us to celebrate this legacy even as he expanded it. He reminded us that in the academy, ideas count for more than does place of birth, of education, or of appointment.

With Jim there was no disconnect between the personal and the public. The man he was, the friend he was, the teacher he was, these made him the president that he was. The board elected him in 1987 to strengthen Dartmouth academically and to engage the community intellectually — goals that he embraced and set out to fulfill. Jim Freedman's administration at its core was deeply affirming and resolutely ambitious. And this college is the better as a result. There is little that happens at Dartmouth today that is not somehow rooted in what he did and his vision. I had the privilege of serving him in his last nine presidential years as dean of faculty and as provost. He was a mentor who surely influenced my vision for Dartmouth.

His presidency amounted to a celebration of intellectual life. Quite simply he wanted Dartmouth to be confident and proud of its academic accomplishments, a Dartmouth that lived up to its best promises. He wanted to recruit and retain the best faculty and to pair them with the most talented students we could find. He wanted learning to be joyful, discovery to be exhilarating, the academic life to be passionate. He insisted always on excellence, and he brought to his administration colleagues who understood and worked toward these common goals. And he was personally engaged in making all of this happen, whether it meant talking about new curriculum requirements or how to hire the best faculty or valuing the positive impact that we derive from the strength and the diversity of the student body. Jim promoted always the essential importance of liberal learning.

It is not possible to consider the Freedman presidency without recognizing the partnership that it represented. Sheba Freedman was fully a part of and a partner in all that Jim Freedman valued and advanced. As a member of this community, a colleague in the Psychology Department, an informed advocate of the arts, and as someone who shared Jim's passion for literature, for public affairs and politics, and for the Boston Red Sox, she too raised our sights and warmed our hearts. The modern Dartmouth owes much to Sheba Freedman.

Lee Pelton, the current president of Willamette University served President Freedman as dean of the college between 1991 and 1998. Lee wanted to be here today, but needed to be at the commencement exercises at Willamette. I would like to share with you some of his reflections on a friend whom he and I both served and who served us so well:

He knew that education at liberal arts colleges was deeply rooted in and connected to human experience and human endeavor.

He wished for the sons and daughters of Dartmouth that the process by which they deepened their connection to the living world would excite, inspire, delight, and confound them every day of their lives.

Above all, he would have said that our students are educated to serve humanity.

161

If President Pelton summarizes well President Freedman's academic ambitions, those ambitions also provide a good assessment of what Dartmouth does and represents today. When Susan and I visited him last at Massachusetts General Hospital a few weeks before his death, I told Jim that we would at the appropriate time have a service here to remember him as an important historic figure whose ambitions for Dartmouth were now woven into the fabric of who we are and what we seek.

Those of you who knew Jim well will not be surprised that he had thought about this day. In recent months he had guided plans for his funeral at his temple, who would speak and what would happen. Back in 1994 when he first learned he had cancer, he thought about a Dartmouth service. (As he would describe it at the 1994 Commencement, "Hearing a physician say the dread word 'cancer' has the uncanny capacity to concentrate the mind.") He wanted someone to read Psalm 121, and he selected the recessional music (the "Battle Hymn of the Republic"). He also hoped to have a reference made to William Faulkner's acceptance speech when he was awarded the Nobel Prize for Literature in 1950. Jim loved writers—his public addresses attested to the wisdom and insights and guidance he received from the best among them. Faulkner was probably his favorite. When he received the Nobel Prize, William Faulkner told the assembled audience,

> I believe that man will not merely endure: he will prevail. He is immortal, not because he alone among creatures has an inexhaustible voice, but because he has a soul, a spirit capable of compassion and sacrifice and endurance. The poet's, the writer's, duty is to write about these things. It is his privilege to help man endure by lifting his heart, by reminding him of the courage and honor and hope and pride and compassion and pity and sacrifice which have been the glory of his past.

It is not surprising that President Freedman was drawn repeatedly to this statement. And it is not surprising to know Jim articulated these values for Dartmouth. If he was not from Dartmouth, he was from New Hampshire, and the granite of integrity and of courage was part of his character and of his legacy. He was an adopted son of this college—the Class of 1957 formally adopted him—who gave us pride and earned our love and respect. He reflected himself on his legacy at Dartmouth in this typically modest way,

> As I conclude my eleven-year tenure as president of Dartmouth, I cannot help but wonder how my stewardship will be judged. . . . I can do no more than to adopt the words of my mentor Justice Thurgood Marshall, who hoped that history would remember him as one who "did the best he could with what he had." . . . I shall step down from the presidency of Dartmouth with a deep love for its people, a great respect for its mission, and a high confidence that it will forever remain a beacon of intellectual excellence and a commonwealth of liberal learning.

A commonwealth of liberal learning: Dartmouth proudly embraces and lives this vision, and we give thanks to Jim Freedman, the fifteenth president of Dartmouth College, for everything he did to ensure that we realized it. He surely did the "best he could," a considerable asset, to make us the best we could be. His success shouts from the soul of the Dartmouth campus. Courage and honor, hope and pride, compassion and pity and sacrifice, Faulkner's values, have been the glory of our past and, through our faculty and our students, through Jim Freedman's vision and values and examples, they live today and shape our future. So here we say farewell but with the grateful knowledge and firm resolve that the Freedman legacy will continue to enrich the Dartmouth experience.

ATHLETICS AND LIFE: ESSAY FOR THE CLASS
OF 1964, ON ITS FIFTIETH REUNION, 2007

I grew up in a small town, Galena, Illinois, a river town, in the post–World War II era. There were a large number of Irish and German families there, farmers and miners and factory workers. Sports were very much a part of the culture, albeit in a very traditional way. College football was then more popular than professional football—the Lombardi era would change that for many of us—and in my community, with a large Catholic population, Notre Dame was king. Leon Hart was one of my early heroes, and I remember attending my first college game at the University of Iowa when Notre Dame's Johnny Lattner ran a punt back for a touchdown. High school basketball and football were important community gatherings. When there was a heavyweight championship fight, everyone was glued to their radios, and later to the small black and white television sets. Despite it being a community that had only a few black families, Joe Louis was popular. But baseball dominated—major league baseball. Most people, including my family, were Cubs fans—and the radio was always on for a game. I still remember the sound of Burt Wilson's voice. I was something of an outlier as a White Sox fan. Minnie Minoso was my favorite player. I can still go through the lineup of the early 50s, names like Pierce and Fox and Carrasquel and Lollar and Rivera and Robinson. I remember going to Comiskey Park several times—my grandfather took me on the Illinois Central "Land of Corn" train where we connected on the bus or the "El" to go to a game.

Baseball was the game everyone played. During the war women's softball was the local substitute, and I recall going to see my mother play. I was very proud of her. At family picnics at my uncle's farm, we would always have a pickup game in the pasture. I remember the "chatter" that everyone engaged in. There were also town teams that played each other in summer leagues—men that never wanted to quit playing. They worked all week on farms or in the mines or mills and then would play each other on Sundays, organized in teams by towns and rural crossroad areas. They took it seriously. One time at a Sunday game a foul ball rolled under a car—the players looked for it, as they always did and couldn't find it. I later went looking and picked it up and took it home to proudly show it to my father. He scolded me for doing such a thing, reminding me that these teams had to pay hard money for these balls. I returned it.

One image, now sixty years old, I will never forget—I can play it in my mind as clear as life. My grandfather and I were watching the Benton, Wisconsin, team play a team from Truman—a rural township. My grandparents lived in Benton, a very small mining town. The Benton pitcher was in control and in the eighth inning, and—this is the image that is fixed—he threw a pitch and went forward on his face. He didn't move and after people gathered around him the word buzzed through the crowd that he was dead. He was a young twenty-seven-year-old World War II veteran who worked in the mines and had a small child and another on the way. Someday I want to research more about him and to understand better what happened to Dick McRae that July afternoon in 1947 and to reflect on how a seven-year-old boy reacted to it.

I never played that much myself—or that well. On the playground at St. Michael's school, a small concrete space, we used to play "stocking-ball" as kids—literally with socks sewn together in a tight ball that we hit with our hand. It worked in a small place surrounded by many windows. One time we were playing football on the playground and someone kicked the ball up toward the Sister Superior, Sister Henriette. She apparently thought it was done on purpose—and it well may have been. So she kept the ball. We, at age ten or eleven, decided to challenge this injustice with a rebellion, chanting, "No football, no school." She was not amused—and we were caught up enough in our cause that we decided to march down the block to the rectory where we would tell Father Guccione, the parish priest, what had happened. Surely he would be sympathetic—he regularly invited groups of us to watch the World Series games—daytime games, which meant we were excused from school. We were confident that he would support us—and learned a good lesson. He was not amused and chased us down the street where we faced our punishment from Sister Henriette!

I was not bad in pickup baseball games. There was nothing like Little League then, in my part of the world. I hit with great power, but I struck out a lot more. I played center on the high school football team and played J.V. basketball. When I was in the Marines, I played a lot of pick-up basketball and learned to use my elbows and size better. (I had a brief interlude in Balboa Naval Hospital in San Diego with a broken nose!) I always thought about playing football in college after the Marines, but, alas, I was working several jobs and did not have time for games. My last football game was in an intramural league of touch football at the University of Wisconsin. The law school team, with a number of former college players, creamed the history department team, and I retired. (In the 1970s I played on the history department baseball team at Dartmouth, and the economics department beat us. I was so frustrated at losing to them that I retired from that game as well—you will be forgiven for judging me a sore loser! I prefer to think of it as a competitor who knows when to retire!)

When I came to Dartmouth in 1969, I encountered a wonderful range of teams, of very good teams. I saw Bob Blackman's football and Tony Lupien's baseball teams, enjoyed hockey at Davis rink (I had been introduced to hockey at the University of Wisconsin when they again organized the sport in the middle 1960s). I enjoyed basketball and was introduced to sports that were unfamiliar to me—lacrosse and rugby and soccer.

I have had the privilege of watching many student athletes over these thirty-eight years, a number of them students in my history classes whom I always tried to watch. My interests now range widely—Susan and I try to see every Dartmouth team play during their season. It is fun to be in Thompson arena when the crowd is roaring with a hockey game—but it is also a treat to go to women's volleyball, smaller and quieter crowds watching contests of remarkable athleticism. I do try to go to some of the practices as well, never wanting to intrude but often having a moment to talk to a few of the players when they are not in the scrimmage or the work out. My two sons introduced me to rugby—my older son played here at Tuck and continued for several years after that. I think it would have been the game I would have taken up if it had been an option.

Moving to New England introduced me to Red Sox nation—and started my own obsession with the Red Sox. I became a fan in 1975 and haven't let up at all since. (As a White Sox fan in the 1950s, my dislike of the Yankees transferred here easily.) Susan and I were there for the first game of the World Series against St. Louis in 2004. And I have my unused tickets for games six and seven on my desk. (Susan did get a ball at the Yankee playoff game three in 2004. She lets me display it with my signed baseballs— and there was no guilty feeling that caused her to return this one!) I am a

James and Susan Wright with the Dartmouth Aires when he threw the first pitch at Fenway, June 2009. Photo by Joe Mehling.

Celtics fan and have been, actually, since Bill Russell joined that team a half century ago. But New England hasn't totally won me over: I am still a Packer fan! (It would be far more satisfying to be a Patriot fan at this time—but loyalty is a stubborn, even perverse thing.)

I enjoy athletics immensely. Those qualities that I promote as being key to a Dartmouth education, things such as teamwork, responsibility, leadership, these are taught well in athletics. I regularly remind the coaches that they too are teachers. And we are blessed with some very good ones. A few years ago I served on the NCAA Division I Board of Directors. It was an interesting experience. Of the eighteen Division I presidents serving as directors, I was the only one from a place called a "college." While I was involved, we took on some real issues in intercollegiate athletics, notably the embarrassing graduation rate in some sports at a number of schools. I was on the reform task force of eight presidents that brought in some recommendations that seem to be having an impact. It was an experience that reinforced for me the value of the Ivy model of athletics. And I particularly was proud of Dartmouth's accomplishments within that model—relatively small, with not quite the wealth of some of our competitors.

We compete very well—and as I am writing this I take real pride in our ski team winning the NCAA championship. I hope everyone realizes what an accomplishment this is for a relatively small school that has no athletic scholarships and whose students meet and excel in a place with high academic standards—just as it was for women's lacrosse to play Northwestern for that national championship last year and for our figure skating team to have three consecutive national championships and to be hosting the nationals this year and seeking their fourth.

I do have a few practices that I follow as a spectator at Dartmouth athletic contests. I never leave early if we are losing. (I told the football team regarding this one time when I sat pretty lonely in the stands in a freezing rain: they never quit, so I wouldn't quit either.) I never show any frustration with the performance of our players or our teams; I know how hard they work and how much they care. (I have shot reprimanding glances to some of our "fans" who actually booed a failed Dartmouth play!) Finally, it is true that losing can be a great learning experience—but it is best that it should not become habitual. Remember that I am the guy who retired from two sports because losing was too frustrating! Moreover I am the guy who last played golf in 1964 when I threw a five iron across a stream and walked up the hill to the clubhouse! It is the case that winning, beating a strong opponent in a fair competition, is just a lot more fun and satisfying! But I have also learned not to take sports too seriously. As the sixty-year old haunting image of Dick McRae reminds me: enjoy it fully for every minute, but it really is just a game.

HONORING VETERANS, OCTOBER 6, 2007

This opinion piece was first published in the Boston Globe.

Last week, the new Ken Burns series on World War II aired on public television around the country. As we remember that generation and all it accomplished, let us not forget our current generation of veterans from the conflicts in Iraq and Afghanistan. I fear, in the midst of the debate over troop levels, exit strategies, and assessment of the war's progress, we have lost sight of the men and women who are fighting this war. To be sure, there is deference to them, but too often they are seen as abstractions, as numbers and not individuals, as heroes or helpless pawns. Those who gave their lives are remembered for but a moment, except in their hometowns. Those who have been seriously injured seldom even have the moment.

In early August I visited Balboa Naval Hospital in San Diego. Fifty years ago, as a seventeen-year-old Marine, I had suffered a minor injury during boot camp and spent a few days at Balboa. Nothing looked familiar but the overall experience was similar to the ones I had a few weeks earlier at Walter Reed and Bethesda hospitals: experiences that were both inspiring and overwhelming. Over the last two years I have made multiple visits to military hospitals to talk to wounded veterans about their experiences and hopes.

So as we talk about exit strategies, let's be sure that we address in a far more engaged way those whose exits will be aboard medical evacuation aircraft. Predictably we will forget about them soon after the war is over — most will slip back into the anonymity of their lives, and, as far as many are concerned, happily so. However, the education and rehabilitation programs provided by the government to enable veterans to make that transition need to be enhanced significantly. It is time for a new G.I. Bill. This is a national debt — and a wise national investment.

The difficulties and conditions at Walter Reed stem from a simple set of facts: We misjudged the duration of the conflict and the number of troops it would require, and the extent of the casualties we would sustain. While debate about who voted how four years ago and projections about who would withdraw at what pace are important, they surely have little impact on the treatment of veterans. The medical and military officials at the hospitals I have visited care deeply about their patients, but they are overwhelmed by the numbers of casualties and are struggling to address the shortcomings highlighted last year. The Dole-Shalala Committee recommended much-needed changes in veterans' treatment. But problems remain. I spoke to a young Marine several days ago who is waiting for a wheelchair.

Improvements in body armor have ensured that more casualties survive. However, though vital organs are protected, limbs are vulnerable and head injuries are nearly epidemic. I have listened to young soldiers and Marines, as fluids seeped through their stumps of limbs, explain how they first learned their leg or arm was not there; to a National Guard single mother with cognitive impairment who missed her three children; to a mother wiping the head of a son who could not respond even as she assured him he would be fine; to a father, with his hand on the shoulder of his son in a wheelchair, who acknowledged that the family had lost everything to Katrina, "but my boy is alive, and I now know what is important in life."

The wounded veterans are real people — not objects of condescending sympathy or abstracted heroes. They don't consider themselves heroic. (For the most part, they simply want to get on with their lives.) I have rarely heard them express anger or blame. Clinically, many will suffer from Post-Traumatic Stress Disorder, but young men in the military are not likely to admit to being depressed, nervous, or scared. As one young man who had lost both legs up to his torso said with an embarrassed grin, "I was depressed for a while, but now I have got over it." He said he had suffered his injuries ten days before.

Remember that the G.I. Bill at the conclusion of World War II enabled that generation to contribute to society. Let us focus as well on the sacrifices, needs, and the remarkable potential of this generation of veterans.

ELEVENTH ANNUAL REPORT TO THE GENERAL FACULTY, OCTOBER 27, 2008

For the last decade I have immensely enjoyed this occasion. It provides the opportunity for me to gather with colleagues, friends for many years, and to reflect upon some of the major developments at Dartmouth and my perspective on matters that affect us. Even though we have had some difficult circumstances in recent years, the trend has clearly been a positive one. That continues to be the case, even as we convene in the midst of a major international financial crisis. No institution and none of us is unaffected by this. But the good work goes on. What I will call our true endowment is focused and healthy. This culture of faculty doing exceptional work and enthusiastically advancing an intimate learning environment marked by student-faculty collaboration resists all challenges. As a historian and as a participant in forty years of Dartmouth's history, I have a particular perspective on this.

Let us understand up front that the state of the college is good and strong. Dartmouth is dependent upon the quality and the intellectual energy of faculty and students. Each day your accomplishments and those of our students—undergraduate, professional, and graduate—affirm that the enterprise is on course. To be sure, current economic conditions make our course a bit stormy right now. But strong and enduring institutions are accustomed to weathering stormy conditions.

Let me summarize some of the major accomplishments and goals of the faculties. In the arts and sciences it has been my privilege to work with Dean Carol Folt. She has engaged with faculty and her team in strategic planning that raises our ambitions and has been an indefatigable fund-raiser who represents Dartmouth's academic values well. Over the last decade we have undertaken a period of unparalleled faculty and program growth. I have read every promotion, tenure, reappointment, and endowed professor recommendation from arts and sciences for twenty years. I have met most of the new faculty who have joined us, at whatever level, and I can affirm that the faculty has never been stronger. I am pleased with the intellectually exciting initiatives in digital humani-

James Wright at his last faculty meeting as president, May 2009. Photo by Joe Mehling.

ties, sustainability, computation, international and global studies, and ethics, among others that have emerged from the faculty in the last few years and which cut across departments and divisions. We also have seen a major growth in the social sciences and other departments that have dealt with the greatest enrollment pressures. These departments have become world-class in their academic reputations. We are looking to initiate new off-campus programs in India, Tibet, and Central America and to strengthen our work in Africa. The off-campus programs are an essential part of the Dartmouth educational experience. None of our competitors is even in our league in this regard.

As one who reads student surveys and receives quite a bit of student and parent feedback, I would simply like to thank the faculty for their work. The commitment you have to working with students one-on-one, meeting with them out of the classroom, and caring about their growth as individuals, defines Dartmouth. By every metric, the number of independent credits, theses completed, and returns on student and faculty surveys, student-faculty collaboration is only getting stronger. Your students value you.

Dean Paul Danos has provided exceptional leadership at the Tuck School since 1995. Over the past few years, Tuck has set records on most factors we measure: the quality and diversity of applicants and the entering student body, employment opportunities and starting compensation for graduates, publications by faculty in refereed journals and leadership in their fields, annual and capital giving, and wide recognition of the excellence of our MBA program. We achieved our initial $110 million goal for Tuck in the capital campaign and are now expanding our effort to raise funds to support a further expansion of the size of the Tuck faculty. Expanding the faculty without increasing the size of the student body is one of the goals laid out in the five-year strategic plan that was approved by the Tuck faculty in June 2008. In December we will open and dedicate our new living and learning facilities (Achtmeyer, Raether, and Pineau-Valencienne Halls), and we will soon renovate Buchanan Hall for use by faculty and for executive education programs.

Dean Joe Helble hit the ground running—and he hasn't stopped a bit. He and the Thayer School faculty have settled into new facilities and have worked hard to develop some exciting strategic initiatives. I am delighted that they have moved ahead with a new exchange program for A.B. students with Chulalongkorn University in Bangkok. This represents the first foreign study opportunity in engineering for undergraduates. Thayer has completed new faculty appointments in the key area of engineering in medicine. Now Dean Helble and the Thayer faculty are focusing on hiring in the area of energy, which will be a field of strategic growth. The school has seen record numbers of applications to the Master's of Engineering Management and the M.S./Ph.D. programs. This past summer Thayer initiated an Innovation Track within its Ph.D. program, with an enrollment of four talented students in its first class. We believe this is the first explicit program of its kind in the country. We were delighted to learn that we have just been awarded a Luce Foundation award in support of Ph.D. fellowships for this program.

I want to thank Dean William Green for stepping up to assume leadership at the Dartmouth Medical School. This is a difficult time for medical research because of the decline in NIH funding. Nonetheless, the medical school faculty continues to compete with exciting initiatives that help to drive the growth of interdisciplinary science at Dartmouth. I would like to congratulate Dean Green and his colleagues for the major effort that has now resulted in a Clinical Translational Science Award proposal to the NIH that will fund efforts cutting across DMS, Dartmouth College, the Hospital, the V.A., as well as other locations. If the grant is funded, it will have a significant effect on the medical center and its future directions. The DMS faculty is moving ahead with plans for improvements to the medical student curriculum—specifically in clerkship offerings for year three of medical school by the recent affiliation with California Pacific Medical Center, and new elective offerings in the third and fourth years.

Dean Folt has recently appointed Professor Brian Pogue of the Thayer School as dean of graduate studies, and we are delighted that he has taken on this responsibility. He succeeds Professor Charles Barlowe of the medical school, and their leadership in this role underlines that the Office of Graduate Studies at Dartmouth has responsibility for all of the nonprofessional master's and Ph.D. degree programs in Thayer and DMS, in addition to those in arts and sciences. These programs have grown significantly in the last decade, with the largest growth occurring in DMS and Thayer and in interdisciplinary programs linked with arts and sciences.

The total and the quality of the applicant pool continue to improve, and international students are critical participants in several of the programs. Last year Dartmouth awarded eighty-one Ph.D.'s, the largest number ever.

The strength of the faculty and the programs summarized above give me tremendous confidence in the future of the college and allow me, despite some economic pressures, to affirm that the state of the college is strong. The academic leadership, the deans and their associates, and Provost Barry Scherr and his colleagues, enable the strength of the faculty.

Before commenting on the economic situation, let us acknowledge and then move beyond the fact that the college is in a period of presidential transition. Transitions can be unsettling times, marked by both uncertainty and the excitement of anticipation. My best advice is not to dwell too much on the uncertainty but to enjoy the excitement. I have been through this before: I have seen four presidents complete their service, and when I was full time in the faculty, as I was for the first three transitions, I can't say that it had any immediate impact upon my work. The good work of the academic enterprise continued and thrived, despite comings and goings in Parkhurst. And so it shall in this period.

Let me share a few personal reflections. I came to Dartmouth as an assistant professor of history in 1969, with a new Ph.D. President John Dickey was completing his twenty-five years as president, and the search for his successor was well under way. Dartmouth faced some profound questions: When and how would Dartmouth become a coeducational institution? How could we welcome more students of color (then a concept that was not much broader than African American students)? How could we insure that the faculty and the staff mirrored our ambitions for the diversity of the student body? Could we expand and strengthen the faculty? How could we incorporate our historic professional schools—then still called "associated schools"—more directly into the academic life of Dartmouth?

The Dartmouth that I came to in 1969 was a school with 3,200 male undergraduates, with probably fewer than 10 percent students of color and some ninety international students, the majority from Canada and Western Europe. Dartmouth was on a conventional nine-month calendar, with Saturday classes. There were a few off-campus language programs. Tuck still counted among its students many Dartmouth graduates. Thayer was a small program that essentially focused on undergraduate engineering majors, and the medical school was a two-year school, also dependent upon Dartmouth undergraduate applicants. Most of the faculty lived in Hanover.

It was a time of cultural and political change, marked by great protests against the war in Vietnam. When I drove out from Madison, Wisconsin to Hanover in mid-summer 1969, I saw hitchhikers going to the concert at Woodstock in New York. It was a time of U.S. hegemony. World currencies were fixed on the dollar, which was in turn fixed on gold. Petroleum was cheap, and energy was inexpensive. With the civil rights and the women's rights movements, American society was confronting the gap between the promise of American life and the reality of the experience for many. Massive anti-war demonstrations rocked U.S. campuses. Following protests here, Dartmouth suspended classes and largely closed down for the last month of my first year at the college.

The legal drinking age in 1969 ranged from eighteen to twenty-one (depending on the state), and in any event the social attitude toward alcohol—and in some ways even drug-consumption—was casual and permissive. Colleges, including Dartmouth, had recently suspended parietal rules; in loco parentis was shelved. There was little discussion here or on any campus about accommodating physical disabilities or emotional problems, and there was not much counseling to assist students dealing with issues of addiction, depression, sexuality, and sexual orientation. Few had even thought about learning disabilities and eating disorders, and there was little sense of institutional responsibility at Dartmouth or anywhere else for assisting students with these issues. Faculty largely spent the day in their offices or laboratories and were avuncular advisers to students on all matters, academic and personal. Computing was in its infancy, and digital security was not even part of science fiction vocabulary.

What I did not realize at the time was that the college was in a difficult economic situation. Dartmouth experienced its first deficit in twenty years in 1967–68. The gap between revenue and expense grew over the next several years. Partially this was the result of a decision in 1967 to provide more financial aid support for students and a commitment to improve compensation for faculty and staff. Perhaps most importantly, the deficit resulted from a downturn in the value of the endowment, following a significant decline in the equities market. The college met the budget deficit by allocating "quasi-endowment" principal to meet the needs of the operating budget. This all provides support for an observation of mine: In the history of American higher education, lean years have been the norm more than years of growth.

I will not belabor the obvious contrasts between the college and the world in 1969 and our situation today. I would simply observe that Dartmouth is a far richer, less homogeneous place, one that operates around the year and around the world, and one whose affiliated schools have become exceptional professional schools. Dartmouth functions now in a world that is far more laden with governmental regulations and demands, with a range of compliance restrictions, with governmental oversight defining some basic relationships between the college and its students. The long list of compliance and reporting requirements included in the Higher Education Reauthorization Act is just the most recent example. Increasingly, individuals consider litigation as a natural remedy for disagreement. We are part of a global society and are subject to the patterns of a global economy. Information technology has transformed how we work and communicate with each other. We live in an exciting time, and we must not allow the problems of our generation to impede the education of the next.

Over the last forty years we have seen the endowment grow significantly so that it provides support for an increasing proportion of the budget. This has been the result of remarkable generosity from graduates and friends and from professional management of the endowment so as to maximize returns. Over the last ten years our endowment performance has been among the top quartile of comparable schools. This past year, although we still had top-quartile performance, was not as good as we had hoped: We were marginally positive in the fiscal year ending June 30, and in the quarter following that we have been down several points. The immediate impact here is that under our endowment distribution formula, we have less revenue than we projected this year and are likely to have still less next year—and this despite the fact that we do have a comparatively aggressive endowment spending formula.

We will discuss this situation with the Board of Trustees at its upcoming November meeting and following that we will initiate measures to reduce expenses. We will consult with the Faculty Committee on Priorities, with the Student Budget Advisory Committee, and with other groups and individuals about the potential steps we will take. As we begin this process I would like to make clear my view that Dartmouth does not have patterns of discretionary spending that can easily or harmlessly be ratcheted back to meet new budget goals. We will take the steps that are necessary, but it might be useful first to take a step back in order to assess those things that define and enable the college.

Over the last decade I have spoken on a few occasions about my concept of the Dartmouth endowment and made clear that I thought of myself as a teacher, an educator, and not an investment banker. I noted at the outset of my administration that I would not assess the accomplishments of my service as president based simply on how large the endowment became. Clearly we all want a larger endowment—that is a good thing. But a larger endowment is not an abstract benchmark, but rather it is a means to advance priorities and purposes. The financial endowment, the bank account, is a remarkable asset that must serve both the current work of the college and provide a trust fund for future generations. We have at times spent it more aggressively than at other times. And we have often tipped more in favor of accumulating assets for future generations—as all growth returned to endowment beyond the rate of inflation does.

I have supported the board's recent move to an increased level of spending, because I define Dartmouth's true "endowment" more broadly than this wonderful financial resource. As we consider our responses to the economic downturn, I would urge everyone to remember that the true endowment of Dartmouth, the legacy for which we are all responsible and accountable, has to do with the overall strength of the college and its capacity to meet the changing needs of a changing world. This is a far richer and more complicated asset than the size of our bank account. At the core of this true and comprehensive endowment is the quality of the faculty. We need to protect Dartmouth's ability to recruit, retain, and enable the work of faculty. The formula to protect the faculty as Dartmouth's endowment is really quite simple: First, provide competitive compensation, and I include with this the support that enables excellence in scholarship and in teaching. Second, work to grow a diverse faculty that will always position us on the boundary of new fields of study that are critical to our academic interests. Finally, provide our students with opportunities to study their areas of interest with faculty who care about them. This is the Dartmouth story.

Over the last ten years we have been resolute in growing the faculty and in bringing our compensation up to a competitive level with our peers. We have done this through a recruiting policy that seeks to appoint the very best young faculty and a judicious recruitment of senior faculty to provide ballast and leadership in selected areas. Doing both of these things simultaneously, expanding the faculty and increasing average compensation, is difficult and expensive, and we need take pride in the accomplishment. But the most compelling is the quality of the faculty. You are the individuals who are defining your fields, and you have maintained Dartmouth's clear commitment to strong teaching and mentoring. This quality, it should be clear, marks the graduate schools as it does the undergraduate programs.

Over the past decade we have grown the arts and sciences faculty from 380 to 439 FTEs, and in the same period have moved the undergraduate student-faculty ratio from 10 to 1 down to 8 to 1. Over the course of the campaign, generous donors have endowed nineteen new professorships and established sixty-six new endowment funds in the arts and sciences. Since 1998, Tuck has increased its faculty lines from thirty-seven to fifty-five. Thayer has also expanded its faculty, from thirty-six in 1998 to forty-six, in keeping with new strategic areas of focus. And DMS has undertaken a period of selected growth in emerging areas of medicine, notably in genetics, molecular and cellular biology, cardiology, and in cancer research and treatment.

The companion piece of the faculty as endowment at Dartmouth is the quality of the student body. I can affirm that Dartmouth has always attracted students who are among the most accomplished academically and the most creative and interesting of their generation. These qualities are each important in providing a Dartmouth education. In order to attract our first choice of students we need to provide financial aid that is both competitive and enables all students to enjoy the full range of opportunities that are part of the Dartmouth educational experience. During my time as president we have announced three separate initiatives to enhance our financial aid program. The latest, announced earlier this year, eliminates tuition for students whose families earn less than $75,000 annually, substitutes grants for loans as part of the financial aid package, introduces need-blind admissions for all international students, and provides additional funds to relieve one summer's earning expectation. In the current year, Dartmouth will provide $65 million dollars in scholarship aid, more than double the amount we funded in 1998.

The board and I also made a commitment to invest in the out-of-classroom experience for students. We sought to provide more on-campus housing and dining options and to increase the range of social and recreational opportunities. We have built nine new undergraduate residence halls and renovated several others, expanded late-night programming options and leadership development programs, subsidized student tickets for Hopkins Center performances, supported a growing club sports program, and made student admission to athletic events free. Additionally, in the last decade we have either replaced or extensively renovated almost every athletic facility, providing greater access for club sports and recreational fitness. I have affirmed our clear commitment to competitive intercollegiate programs within the Ivy model and to the broader role of athletics and the out-of-doors experience in advancing a Dartmouth education. We all will celebrate the upcoming centennial of the Dartmouth Outing Club. Finally, the college has worked closely and positively with the coed/fraternity/sorority leadership so that today their role in the community is far stronger and more positive than it has been in the time I have been here. We have worked with them and with other student leaders to create a stronger and more inclusive community. We have a wonderful student body at Dartmouth. They are committed to learning; they assume responsibility for the college; and they will make a difference in the world. Early returns suggest that applications for the Class of 2013 are running ahead of last year's record numbers. The economic situation will make this a complicated year in admissions.

Students and faculty are the energy that powers the true Dartmouth endowment. Any steps backward from our commitment to recruit, retain, and enable the very best students and faculty would present a far harder problem to correct than a market downturn. The competitive world of recruiting the very best students and faculty is hard on those places that have faltered. The diversity of this community enhances the energy and excitement that mark our work.

There is a third element in the endowment of Dartmouth that I would mention here—our graduates. President Ernest Martin Hopkins referred to alumni as the "living endowment" of the college. They still are. The $42 million they provided last year in the Dartmouth College Fund represents the equivalent of $800 million of unrestricted endowment. Alumni/ae are the key contributors to the $1.1 billion we have raised so far in the capital campaign. Some 67 percent of living alumni/ae have participated. This is a wonderful story, but there is more to this living endowment than simply contributing money. Alumni volunteers are critical to recruitment of students and to working to support our graduates. They provide service and advice to a range of our programs, academic and extra-curricular, and they keep the Dartmouth brand alive and well in the broader world.

We need to acknowledge that many alumni have been concerned about the board's governance decision a year ago. I respect that, as I repeat that I believe the board did the right thing. Even if there is disagreement on board action, a strong majority of alumni who participated in the election last spring did not support a lawsuit against the college. We need to work hard to reaffirm and rebuild our relationship, and faculty are critical to this. These are your former students, and they take confidence from knowing that you are here doing the good work of Dartmouth.

There are other elements that comprise the true endowment of Dartmouth that I would like to include in this conversation. One has to do with the physical endowment. This is a lovely campus, one that is inviting and human in scale and one that seeks to have facilities that enable the strongest faculty and the strongest students to do the strongest work. We are careful here to address deferred maintenance needs, even if we sometimes are more patient than we wish to be with deferred renovation. We have engaged in a significant period of construction over the last several years, and in doing this have met some needs that were identified years ago. In the last ten years we have invested over $1 billion in facilities. In addition to the student life improvements mentioned earlier, the greater investments have been in academic facilities, both new construction and substantial renovation. They have enriched your work and enlarged our capacity. We have also completed a number of projects at the hospital campus and in Centerra Park, and have renovated and added faculty and graduate student housing.

Finally, the true and comprehensive endowment of Dartmouth includes a remarkably committed administrative team. The officers and staff who serve Dartmouth protect and advance the other components of the endowment: the students, faculty, alumni services and development, plant, and the financial support system. They provide an operations and service culture that cares deeply about Dartmouth. They reach out to a diverse student body in a complicated world. As I have said on other occasions, it is most unfortunate that they have sometimes collectively become targets of uninformed critics. We are, in fact, thinly staffed for our commitment to quality of service, our expectations for the quality of the physical environment, and the systems management, compliance, and monitoring demands that mark Dartmouth today. I am proud to serve with this group of colleagues.

The traditional endowment as bank account may provide the lubricant for the larger true endowment. We cannot sustain operations without the financial support it provides. But we should never confuse it with our purpose or imagine that it defines our values.

Last year at this meeting I outlined for you several objectives that I hoped to reach in the remainder of my term as president. I proposed that we enhance the financial aid system to make certain that a family's economic situation was not a barrier to student enrollment at Dartmouth. I promised to continue the growth of the faculty. I endorsed the plan of the arts and sciences faculty to establish a program in writing and rhetoric. I urged the development of a program to enable Tuck School faculty to offer some selected courses for undergraduates. I advocated a discussion of ways we could enhance the summer term academically. I made clear my hope to move ahead with some of the major facilities projects that were still pending. Finally, I promised to help conclude the Campaign for the Dartmouth Experience.

One year later we have accomplished most of these goals: The financial aid program, the writing and rhetoric program, and the Tuck teaching program are all under way. We broke ground on the Class of 1978 Life Sciences Center. Dean Folt and a faculty committee are reviewing summer term academic initiatives, and Provost Barry Scherr and the directors of the academic centers and institutes are considering some summer activities.

The capital campaign needs $171 million to reach its $1.3 billion goal. This is a remarkable accomplishment, and we need to recognize that raising the remainder will be difficult. We surely will do it, but perhaps not as quickly as we had hoped. In the near term many of our generous donors will not be able to provide financial support as much as they wish to do. This will result in the delay of some of capital projects previously announced and in the planning stages. Consistent with our past policies we will not authorize projects that do not have a full funding plan established. In these economic conditions, putting these funding plans in place will simply be more challenging. We will review with the board controlling additional debt except for advantageous refinancing of current obligations and for projects under way or for those required for basic renovation and for safety and code issues.

Over the next several months we will need to reduce significantly the growth in expenses. I will want the senior officer budget group to consult widely and develop recommendations to bring to me. At the outset I wish to make clear my priority is to protect our financial aid program and our competitive faculty compensation objective. We will need to reduce payroll projections, but I hope that the need for reduction in force will be accomplished through attrition.

I surely had not wanted to spend my last year overseeing expense reductions! There is, however, a certain symmetry to this—when I entered the senior administrative ranks twenty years ago as dean of faculty, we early on faced budget shortfalls. I also appreciate now that this is a periodic, even cyclical, thing—not intending by this description to minimize the serious economic circumstances today, which do have few historical precedents. Great and enduring institutions, as we are, survive these downturns better than most, as we shall. We will do this by remembering the component parts of the true endowment of Dartmouth. These are what we must protect.

I will probably not meet again with you in this forum, as the General Faculty, and if we do it will not be for me to make an annual report. So let me simply say that it has been a privilege and a personal pleasure to preside over this body. My annual reports have essentially involved affirming your strength and your good work. This has been easy!

We have several months to work together and then Susan and I do not intend ever to be too far away. Thank you for your friendship and support. And thank you for all you do for Dartmouth.

THE YELLOW RIBBON PROGRAM AND
PRIVATE COLLEGES, FEBRUARY 2, 2009

James Wright delivered these remarks at the 2009 Annual Meeting
of the National Association of Independent Colleges and Universities
(NAICU) in Washington, D.C.

. . . . Two weeks ago many of us sat mesmerized before our televisions as we watched the inauguration of the United States' forty-fourth president, Barack Obama. Regardless of individual politics, it was a moving occasion—the sight of the first African-American taking the presidential oath just a few decades after blacks won the right to vote in this country. I told some students that I was not so sure that their generation could fully appreciate what this moment symbolized. I had spent a winter in Mississippi fifty years ago when I was an eighteen-year-old Marine from a small town in the Midwest and was shocked by what I encountered. President Obama's inauguration indeed marked a different world in ways that most of us could not have predicted then. The substantive work of extending to all equality and opportunity is surely not finished, but the symbolism as well as the accomplishment this occasion represented should cause us to pause in shared pride.

While watching I reflected on what a privilege it is to be a part of a nation capable of redressing injustice within its own borders and unafraid of adapting to meet the challenges of a global economy. We are fortunate to live in a place that holds freedom of thought and speech among its core values—two values central to the lives of academics—and a country with an unparalleled tradition of intellectual leadership. As you well know, with privilege comes responsibility. Higher education remains one of the most important paths to individual success and a critical means for national achievement and the attainment of global understanding. If our country is to succeed and to play a positive role in an international context, we must ensure access to postsecondary education for all our citizens. Accomplishing this will be both one of the greatest opportunities and the biggest challenges we will face in the twenty-first century.

My focus today is on but one of the tools and the means to move us to our goal of expanding access and opportunity. It is my hope, and indeed my expectation, that we will meet this challenge and that the Post-9/11 Veterans Educational Assistance Act of 2008, including the Yellow Ribbon Program, will play a significant role in this endeavor, as did the 1944 Servicemen's Readjustment Act (or G.I. Bill) for previous generations. As a historian, I cannot resist the opportunity to speak about the 1944 G.I. Bill. I want to talk about its consequences for the veterans who received benefits and to consider the impact it had on higher education institutions and our country as a whole. The broad positive impact of the bill makes a compelling case in support of the current G.I. Bill and the Yellow Ribbon Program.

From 1942 to 1944, the years of the G.I. Bill's development, President Roosevelt's attention was largely on wartime strategy but he could never drift too far from thinking about the postwar economy. The great depression was still fresh in the minds of many Americans, and most anticipated that when the war ended the country would again be plunged into a financial crisis. The Serviceman's Readjustment Act was among the many proposals developed.

It called for the development and expansion of educational and training opportunities for veterans. While Roosevelt and others recognized that the Readjustment Act would help veterans resume educations disrupted by the war and serve as a means to thank them for their service, they primarily viewed it as a means to strengthen our economy. The author Keith Olson wrote, "To prop up the postwar economy Congress could have poured money into corporations, as it did in the 1930s . . . ; it could have created jobs, as it did during the New Deal . . . ; it could have curtailed the profit motive and moved toward a planned economy. . . . Instead, Congress chose . . . the veterans." It was, by today's terminology, a stimulus plan!

Regardless of the initial intent, the results went far beyond what anyone could have predicted. Thousands, then millions, of men and women suddenly had the financial means to attend any institution that would admit them on their academic record. For the first time, education was no longer for the wealthy and white alone. Institutions once considered off-limits to all but the elite were open to all, for few institutions could refuse qualified students when the government guaranteed payment of their bills!

Unsure of the reception awaiting them upon their return from war, African-American vets found that they had more options than ever before, although surely not enough. Many schools relinquished their quotas on Jews, although not always without additional pressure to do so. While increased access did not end discrimination in all areas of life, it did alter the social climate on and off campus. It paved the way for our current understanding of the important role access and diversity have in the learning environment and for the heterogeneity and pluralism that we celebrate and defend today. What we have described as the greatest generation did not earn that distinction simply by their role in a difficult and costly war. They were more than warriors. That generation fundamentally came home from the war and set about to shape American life—economically, culturally, politically, and intellectually.

Initially, the numbers using the educational benefit were small—about 8,000 in the first year of the program—but by the fall of 1946, as a result of significant demobilization of the military, over a million veterans were enrolled at a college. During the next ten years, veterans continued to enroll in high numbers, and as a result the number of total college enrollments, including veterans, increased by 75 percent. Unprepared for the massive numbers of veterans enrolling, many colleges and universities rushed to hire faculty and expand facilities. In a number of states, new institutions and consortiums were formed in order to meet the demand.

Among its significant achievements, the original G.I. Bill helped usher in what has often been called the knowledge society. It was a process that had been under way, but slowly and without a clear vision. Down through the late nineteenth century, American colleges and universities had largely served to transmit received wisdom and classical knowledge. A college degree had limited practical meaning but a college education was a mark of culture. Beginning with the Land Grant College Act—the Morrill Act—of 1862, this changed, and often dramatically. And public institutions began to assert leadership roles in asserting the role of research and creating knowledge as a core purpose of the university. In the nineteenth century, private institutions, including my own, were slower to value curiosity and to encourage faculty and students to challenge received wisdom. Perhaps down through the depression, private education still focused primarily on transmitting knowledge to those who would constitute the cultured class.

By the end of the Second World War in 1945, just as veterans were pouring onto our campuses, government sponsorship of research and interest in public health greatly increased. Regional universities, such as Stanford, grew into major national and international research universities with the aid of federal research dollars. Innovation, creativity, and the abilities to analyze were of paramount importance, not only for faculty work, but also for a student's success in the job market. Work as we knew it changed, and as a result, the four-year degree became an essential tool for individual access—and we became certifiers as well as educators.

Of course, there were other forces influencing the shape of our society at the time the G.I. Bill was expanding the student population—and causing students to have an expanded set of ambitions. The civil rights movement and the women's rights movement, scientific and technological advances, and ever-changing international relationships helped to direct growth in higher education and this country's future. But we cannot underestimate the contributions made by the veterans. Enabled and encouraged by the G.I. Bill, they made this a stronger and more inclusive society.

Some sixty years later, we stand at another critical moment in our history. The worldwide financial crisis has affected every aspect of our lives. I am sure all of us feel the reverberations on our campuses. State and national support for higher education has been declining as a percent of revenue for years. Society depends on our schools for advancements in knowledge, for practical contributions to economic innovation, and for credentialing and enabling our young people—and society supports this essential work less generously. Our private schools may have different revenue sources, but the changing demand and our capacity to meet it have changed. And our society is losing the race to maintain our competitive edge in many arenas.

In his inaugural remarks, President Obama noted: "Our time of standing pat, of protecting narrow interests and putting off unpleasant decisions—that time has surely passed. . . . [W]e must pick ourselves up, dust ourselves off, and begin again the work of remaking America." His plan for this remaking includes an investment in science, healthcare, technology, and a rebuilding of our infrastructure, both physically and intellectually. To do this, the United States will need increased numbers of citizens with a post-secondary education. Unfortunately, today there are many signs that the pipeline for educated workers is broken. Today, only about 67 percent of students graduate from high school, and college completion rates have also declined. Thirty-five years ago the United States ranked second internationally in terms of workers with a college education. Now we are eleventh. In December 2008, the College Board Commission on Access, Admissions, and Success in Higher Education, of which I was a member, released its report: "Coming to Our Senses: Education and the American Future." In it, we asserted that to reclaim our position as a leader in education we must make sure that 55 percent of young Americans complete a two-year degree or higher by 2025.

To achieve this, we need to find ways to help the estimated 1.7 million to 3.2 million academically qualified students who will not earn a four-year degree this decade because they cannot meet the financial costs—or even when financial support is available, who have never been *encouraged to believe* they can secure a college education, and those who simply do not have the counseling and information needed to make informed decisions about applying and enrolling in a degree program. Fortunately, through the Post-9/11 Veterans Educational Assistance Act of 2008 (the new G.I. Bill), we have the capacity to bring a significant subset of both populations into our institutions.

I have taken an active interest in the educational needs of our veterans for several years. Having enlisted in the Marines when I was seventeen, I felt, and still feel, a strong connection with the young women and men serving this country. Most of them are the same age as Dartmouth's undergraduates, and as the Iraq War unfolded my impulse to reach out to them grew. Since 2005 I have made seventeen visits to the National Naval Medical Center in Bethesda, or Walter Reed Army Medical Center, or Balboa Naval Medical Center in San Diego. During these visits, I met with young men and women whose injuries were serious and, at first, shocking. I talked with them about my own experiences as a veteran and as the first member of my family to go to college, and I found that many were excited about pursuing a college education. They were also daunted by the prospect of finding information, presenting themselves as applicants, and finding schools where their severe injuries could be accommodated. Unlike other veterans, their disability benefits would likely provide full funding for their attendance at almost any institution, but they needed help to begin their educational journey.

I began working with David Ward, then-president of the American Council on Education, and later, Jim Selbe, director of Program Evaluations at ACE, to develop an educational counseling program for injured veterans who were still in hospitals. ACE launched its Severely Injured Military Veterans Program in early 2007, and it has since helped several hundred students enroll in colleges and universities. I made my most recent visit this morning when I spent a couple of hours out at Walter Reed hospital. I talked to young men about the opportunity provided by education and assured them that they can do anything they want to do.

As I became more involved in issues related to veterans' education, I also came to understand how desperately we needed a new G.I. Bill for all veterans. The Montgomery G.I. Bill did not provide adequate support for the cost of higher education. A year ago, in February 2008, I spent an afternoon with Senator Jim Webb of Virginia, who had introduced legislation for a new G.I. Bill when he first joined the Senate a year earlier. He arranged for us to talk with Senator Chuck Hagel of Nebraska and for a meeting with Senator John Warner of Virginia to discuss a new G.I. Bill. Senator Webb believed that Senator Warner, as a senior Republican and former Secretary of the Navy was critical to passage of the legislation. The three of us, old Marines all, talked at length about congressional concerns regarding the costs of a new G.I. Bill that would cover tuition, fees, and other expenses, given the variances in charges between institutions. The Grassley effect complicated any plan that might provide more federal support for private institutions that appeared to be comfortably wealthy and still charged very high tuition. As a result of this attitude, there was significant congressional sentiment to cap G.I. Bill support at the level of the highest public tuition charged in the veteran's home state. In fact the February 2008 draft language for the legislation would include such a limit. We felt it important to put in place some measure that would provide sufficient funding to enable veterans to consider private colleges and universities as well as out of state charges at public institutions. We wanted to give them as many options as possible, just as the 1944 G.I. Bill and the Vietnam-era bill did for those veterans. Senator Warner had used the G.I. Bill to attend Washington and Lee and Senator Webb, a Naval Academy graduate, used the G.I. Bill to attend Georgetown Law School.

They amended the original bill to include language that we had developed in which institutions that charged more than the cost of the highest public tuition in the state could share equally with the government in covering the difference, the "delta" as Senator Warner called it. The higher education community, led by NAICU and ACE, worked with veterans' groups and many other individuals and organizations to secure passage of the legislation. There was significant resistance from the administration at first. But in June of 2008 President Bush signed the new legislation, including what was called the Yellow Ribbon section whereby institutions with tuition rates higher than the state cap can look to share some or all of the incremental cost with the V.A. Beginning this next August, most continuing students who are veterans will seek to transition their benefits from the Montgomery G.I. Bill to the Post-9/11 Bill, and others will take advantage of their educational benefits for the first time through the new G.I. Bill. There could be a twenty to twenty-five percent increase in the number of enrolled veterans—currently there are 350,000 enrolled under existing V.A. programs—and this could be greater, and almost surely will be in the future.

The bill covers the cost of any public institution's undergraduate program and provides a monthly housing allowance and book stipend for all veterans. However, the institutions most of us in this room represent charge undergraduate and graduate tuition rates higher than the tuition benefit cap, leaving a balance for veterans to pay or for colleges to cover through institutional aid in partnership with the V.A. As college and university endowments continue to suffer during the current financial crisis, the number of schools that are comfortable signing onto the Yellow Ribbon program may be decreasing. None of us are comfortable with incremental expenses at a time when we need to cut costs substantially. If many of us do not participate this places a greater burden on veterans who wish to attend more expensive schools, a burden that most of them cannot meet. Let me urge you all to join in this program.

The Yellow Ribbon Program provides more flexibility for institutional participants than is immediately obvious. Signing onto this does not obligate your school to contribute the maximum amount, half of the difference, to all veterans who enroll. It provides a dollar for dollar match of *up to* 50 percent of the difference between the highest undergraduate tuition at a public institution in its own state and its own tuition. Your campus can choose at what level you will participate—what percentage of the cost difference you will cover and you may choose the number of veterans you will enroll under this program. Colleges must enroll annually and can change their level of participation and the number of veterans accommodated.

For those institutions that are concerned about participating in the full 50 percent match, I would urge you to run the numbers with care. There is in this program the possibility of federal support for up to 75 percent of the tuition cost of the veteran—your obligation would be the remainder. And these students would bring support for additional expenses with them. I would urge you to join in the program and to limit the numbers if you are apprehensive rather than limiting the amount of support for each student. The latter puts the burden on the student. Your participation underscores support for veterans and affirms that they are welcome on your campus.

As I have learned over the last several years, it is not enough to sit back passively and expect veterans to come to us. It is my observation after several years of talking to veterans—largely wounded veterans, to be sure, but I think they are pretty representative in this regard—that the financial barrier is only part of what is keeping them from thinking about higher education. They have in some cases never been encouraged to think about this, and they have often come to believe they would not be welcome. We need to step up to remedy this. This requires us to remember that these are not conventional students being encouraged and supported by high school guidance counselors, teachers, and parents. They need encouragement. They need information. They need help in applying. And they need us to be flexible.

I do think we have an opportunity to think carefully about how our practices and policies either deter or encourage veterans to join us on our campuses. We have done no less for other underrepresented groups as we have sought to fulfill our educational missions, and I believe it will take less work than some fear to make a similar effort for veterans: Posting information in a central location on your website; identification of a coordinator or contact person who can address specific needs of veterans; development of workshops to help students, faculty, and staff understand the experiences of veterans; accommodating the needs of these particular students; and possible partnerships with your closest V.A. hospital or other veterans' organization. These are all manageable steps we can take

James Wright with a group of undergraduate veterans enrolled at Dartmouth, September 2008. Photo by Joe Mehling.

toward creating an inclusive environment for veterans, as is enrolling in the Yellow Ribbon Program.

I understand that each of your schools will have to come to its own decision about participation and that for those of you with graduate programs or differing tuition levels, there may be different levels of participation. Last week I read some of the public comments posted in January about the proposed regulations, and I know that there remain unanswered questions related to the administrative work they will require, both for the Department of Veterans Affairs and for institutions. Among other questions, there are concerns about what fees will be covered, about how need-based financial aid can relate to this program, about the current requirement that schools waive tuition rather than use scholarship programs, and about the ways in which multiple schools within a single institution can have different plans.

These are all important issues to consider, and over the next several months these will have to be addressed. Even then, it is likely that there will still be concerns to be worked out over the first year of the program. Last week I had the opportunity to talk to Keith Wilson who is the director of education benefits at the Veterans Administration and is responsible for developing the regulations for administration of the new program. He will join us tomorrow for a session on the Yellow Ribbon program. I am impressed by his commitment to find a way to make this work for the veterans and for the schools.

All of our schools are privileged, to be sure some more than others, but we are all enabled by government grants and protection and by the tax-advantaged support of individuals. With privilege goes obligation—and we do here have an obligation to recognize those who have stepped forward and have served the country. But there is more than that, beyond privilege and obligation, we all surely do feel a commitment to make our school the better and the experience of our students the stronger.

That need introduces one additional reason for participating in the Yellow Ribbon Program that I have not yet addressed, and it is perhaps the most compelling of all—the students themselves. At Dartmouth we have several Iraq and Afghanistan veterans who have joined us in the last two years—they now number nine. Probably six of them have purple hearts and three or four had major injuries. I counseled a few of them before they applied, and one of them I first met when he was in a hospital bed suffering from gunshot wounds suffered in a firefight in the battle of Fallujah. These students are exceptionally bright and engaging young people. If they stand apart from their peers in any way it is to their credit: their GPAs are at or above the average. Several have already earned honors. Their professors report they rarely miss class and are diligent and timely in the completion of all work. They have tended to take many history and government classes and are particularly interested in international affairs and languages. They are active in all aspects of campus life, and last year they formed their own student veterans association. Other students have enjoyed having them as classmates. They are a wonderful addition to our classroom discussions and to the campus environment. We expect several more veterans will matriculate at Dartmouth next fall. These students have and will continue to enrich our campus, as did the veterans who came to Hanover before them, dating back to the fall of 1945.

There are many compelling reasons for us to proactively support access to higher education for our country's veterans. I would argue it is the right thing to do for them, an important thing for us to do for our nation, and the wise thing to do for our institutions. This is a wonderful opportunity, a trifecta you should not let pass you by!

VETERANS DAY AT THE VIETNAM MEMORIAL WALL, WASHINGTON, D.C., NOVEMBER 11, 2009

The Vietnam Veterans Memorial Fund published this speech in 2010 in Dreams Unfulfilled: Stories of the Men and Women on the Vietnam Veterans Memorial, *compiled by Jan C. Scruggs. A generous grant from General Electric enabled the book to be distributed to 40,000 schools across the country.*

. . . . For the past few years I have worked with veterans wounded in Iraq or Afghanistan to encourage and enable them to pursue their dreams through education. Today we remember those who did not have an opportunity to pursue their dreams.

I grew up in a mining town, Galena, Illinois. With four friends I joined the Marines in 1957 at the age of seventeen—to keep me out of the mines for at least a few years. When I returned in 1960 I decided to go to college—but I needed to work in the mines while in school. My boss when I worked underground was Clarence Lyden. He was a good boss, a good man, who had received a Purple Heart while serving in the Army in World War II. He encouraged me to become a powder man, setting dynamite charges, in order to earn twenty cents more an hour. I did take on this assignment and continued to study—and was a student teacher back in my old high school. One of my students was Clarence Lyden's son, Michael. I remember him as an energetic, pleasant, hard working young man. A few years later he was drafted and went into the Army where he became a sergeant in the 101st Airborne. Already holding a purple heart, Michael died on May 15, 1969 in Operation Apache Snow at a place we remember as Hamburger Hill.

This Wall records the sons—and daughters—of many miners, factory workers, and farmers. And so many others. The Wall contains the names of fifteen graduates of Dartmouth. I did not know any of them. But I came to know well the father, the sister, the brother, the classmates, the coach and teammates of one. Bill Smoyer grew up in comfortable circumstances in New Jersey. At Dartmouth he was an All-Ivy soccer player and a star hockey player. He was by all accounts a gracious and generous young man, a gentleman. And he joined the Marines in order to go to Vietnam because he believed that wars should not be fought only by the sons of the miners, farmers, and factory workers. He was in Vietnam for only two weeks on July 28, 1968, when his platoon was caught in an ambush while crossing a rice paddy at An Hoa. 2nd Lieutenant Smoyer and eighteen other members of Kilo company, 3rd Battalion Seventh Marines were killed that Sunday.

Who knows what Billy Smoyer and Mike Lyden would have done with their lives? Mike may have gone back to work at the Kraft Foods plant in Galena—he did not want to follow his dad into the mines. His old teacher here believes that whatever he did he would have done well. Billy Smoyer was a history major who may have gone into business—but all attest that whatever he did he would have tried to make a difference for others.

Late this past summer my wife, Susan, and I visited Normandy where we spent a lot of time walking through the American cemetery at Colleville. The white marble crosses and Stars of David filled the hillside with a sense of order and tranquility—and whispered of lives lost. We walked among the graves for some time, reading the names, observing where they were from and how old they were. We thought of lives cut short and of dreams unrealized and wanted to know more about them. Casualties of war cry out to be known—as persons, not as abstractions called casualties nor as numbers entered into the books, and not only as names chiseled into marble or granite. We have carried in our memories the stories of those recorded here. But memories fade—as do those who remember. We are graying. After all of us who knew them are gone, the names on this Wall will endure.

It is essential that the Education Center planned for this site sparkle with the human records of those whose sacrifice was forever. We need to ensure that here, in this place of memory, lives as well as names are recorded. Lives with smiling human faces, remarkable accomplishments, engaging personalities, and with dreams to pursue. We do this for them, for history, and for those in the future who will send the young to war.

4

COMMENCEMENT ADDRESSES,
1999–2009

Following once again in the tradition of President Dickey,
President Wright used the same opening and closing remarks
for each of his commencement addresses.

I extend my hearty congratulations to you, the graduates of the Class of.... This place today resonates with your accomplishments; this is your special day. Your memory will forever cherish this occasion. And there will surely be few times in your lives when you will be surrounded by so many who care so much about you—family and faculty, alumni and administrators, classmates and friends.

Your hearts, I know, are filled with many things on this day, and I would be pleased to participate with you in acknowledging one of them: a sense of gratitude. I join you in thanking the faculty who taught you, as well as learned with you, the families who sacrificed for you, and the friends who sustained you. And I also would like to extend a special salute to all who received graduate and professional degrees. We celebrate your accomplishments, and we are enriched by your contributions to this community of learning. We have full confidence in you and all that you will accomplish.

[Body of individual commencement address]

Now we come to this moment, to the time for leave taking, for you to commence the rest of your lives. Go catch the wind in your sails. We have left much for you to do. "The strongest and sweetest songs yet remain to be sung," wrote Walt Whitman near the end of the last century. We leave them still, for your voices. But know too as you leave today that the door here is always open for you. You are ever a part of Dartmouth undying as Dartmouth is forever a part of you.

JUNE 13, 1999

. . . . Whatever your individual capacities and energies may be—and we here attest that they are indeed considerable—others enabled you and your accomplishments. But let us acknowledge also that the gratitude you feel leads to an important obligation you now assume: that of assisting others, so you can glow in the warmth of their accomplishments, as they in turn extend to you gratitude for what you have given them. Those whom we have celebrated today with honorary degrees can affirm that behind any life or deed of honor there is an implicit awareness of those who supported, taught, and sustained. And who is to deny that perhaps the best measure of a life well lived is less a tally of our own record and more a pride in what we have encouraged in others. Surely, this commitment to empowerment shapes an institution like Dartmouth, and it enriches those of us privileged to do the good work of this good place.

All of this points to one of those transitions that is marked today. You will now ceremonially march away from this important part of your life and move on to engage the rest of it. Life transitions are personal, their meanings subjective, and their recognitions typically delayed. The fact that this public transition of yours occurs on the cusp of a new millennium may attach even greater symbolism to it. You are the last Dartmouth class to graduate in the twentieth century. (And we won't forget, either, that you were the first Dartmouth class to have a majority of women.) You have accomplished much in your four years here. You are the worthy conclusion of a long line of distinguished Dartmouth classes in this century. But today you look ahead, rather than backward. We ask only a few things of you as you move forward. Never lose your appreciation for the richness and diversity of the human experience. Never lose your sense of curiosity or enthusiasm for learning. Your education does not end here today; it continues. This is not a time of conclusion, but of commencement. As you progress on your journey you will find that some of the things learned at Dartmouth will need to be unlearned in the future and replaced with new understandings. That is part of the continuing marvel of human imagination and discovery. Emily Dickinson wrote, "I dwell in Possibility." And so do you.

Leave here too with a sense of belonging, with an understanding of the importance of community and of the obligation of sharing. These things will be especially important for you to hold onto in a world increasingly marked by the anonymity of cyberspace and the increased fragmentation of life's activities and personal connections. As our society becomes busier and more complicated, it can also become lonelier. The random violence we have seen of late in our society does not necessarily reflect a lack of learning, but rather an absence of belonging. Recognize and celebrate difference, but define your lives and your communities as inclusive. You leave here knowing the value of community and of sharing; carry that knowledge with you always.

We wish we could alert you more precisely to what lies ahead, but we are unable to do that. Just in the last few days our community has been jolted by unexpected loss and trauma. The Class of 1949, joining you today in their reunion and in their own reaffirmation, can attest as well to the impossibility of anyone predicting life patterns and the turns of history. As Robert Frost wrote:

> The tree the tempest with a crash of wood
> Throws down in front of us is not to bar
> Our passage to our journey's end for good,
> But just to ask us who we think we are
> Insisting always on our own way so.

Fifty years ago, on a quiet Hanover day, the Class of 1949 received their degrees, and they shared in the same feelings you have: a mixed sense of excitement and anticipation tempered by the bittersweet sensation that all this is happening too quickly. Since their graduation, members of the Class of 1949 have witnessed the expansion of the nuclear age, wars both hot and cold, declared and undeclared. They have seen the long-overdue recognition that minorities and women need to be in the mainstream life of our nation and our world. They have witnessed the exploration of outer space and the unfolding wonder of cyberspace. The Class of 1949 has observed and has participated in many things. They have witnessed human cynicism, despair, and suffering; they have also seen, time after time, a reaffirmation of the creative wonder of the human imagination and the generosity of the human spirit.

Oliver Wendell Holmes, the great nineteenth-century man of letters, once wrote, "I find the great thing in this world is not so much where we stand as in what direction we are moving . . . we must sail sometimes with the wind and sometimes against it. But we must sail, and not drift, nor lie at anchor." Members of the Class of 1999 do not be afraid to test yourself in uncharted waters. . . .

JUNE 11, 2000

. . . . The year 2000 has finally arrived. You have named your class the "Zeros," "double zeros," "oughts," and even "ought nots." But if these terms identify you, they surely do not describe you. Ahead of you now is a new century—and the rest of your lives.

If you think that this moment has come too soon, I urge you not to worry. Our ceremony today attests that you are ready. I have great confidence in your ability to dream big dreams, to challenge your limits, to make those dreams come true, and to continue to ask much of yourselves.

Many of you now expect fame and fortune, and there is little doubt that if you pursue such goals, you will likely attain both things. You graduate into a world in which the concept of fortune has taken on additional digits—and has done this just in your lifetimes. Remember, though, that success is finally a personal thing, defined against your own aspirations and expectations.

The Class of 1950 joins you in celebration here today—a fiftieth anniversary moment that has undoubtedly come upon them sooner than they ever imagined it could. If you were to ask them about success, few if any of them would, I am sure, describe their satisfactions merely in terms of how many digits were associated with the money they have earned or accumulated. They would talk to you about family and friends, about personal challenges met, about sharing with others, about music and art and letters, about stunning examples of human creativity. Some would talk about faith, about quiet times on the side of a mountain or on a shore. All would agree with Wordsworth that the best portion of a good life was marked by: "the little, nameless, unremembered acts of kindness and of love." The fifty-year class would tell you, as do I, that these little things are the better appreciated the sooner they are recognized.

The women and men who have stood before us today and received honorary degrees from the college provide us with models of full and rich lives. Each of these individuals has been measurably successful. All have excelled in the face of challenges, some of which we may not even know about. They have redefined the markers and the measurements of success. And they have also made the lives of others better, fuller, and happier. And so can you.

Few people have enjoyed the privileges of the sort of education you have had. Accordingly, we urge you now to assume a special and lifetime obligation to assist and to enable others. We know you well enough to understand that at this time you fully intend to do these things. You have already demonstrated in so many ways your generosity of spirit. But as you become absorbed in the mechanics of the rest of your lives, remember that defining who you are is a lifetime task and one that is far more complicated than is determining what it is you will do. Georgia O'Keefe said, "Where I was born and where and how I have lived is unimportant. It is what I have done with where I have been that should be of interest."

For many, the task of defining who they are is complicated even more by categories imposed and stereotypes presumed. At the beginning of the twentieth century, W. E. B. DuBois confidently predicted that the "problem of the twentieth century is the problem of the color line." From the vantage of this century, we need to acknowledge the accuracy of that prediction.

The twentieth century was marked by many problems, but certainly color and race ran through the history of the last hundred years, and not always showing the human condition at its best. Now, we start a new century, and rather than prophesize, let us resolve: It is time for race—and, more broadly, for difference—to cease being a problem and to be, instead, a source of celebration.

In a world that values diversity there should be no dominant majority; there should be only a recognition of mutual interdependence. The richness and vitality of American life stem from this and not from our homogeneous sameness. Our strength depends upon our capacity to transcend our differences—of race, surely and most obviously, but also of gender, of intellect, of religion, of background, of sexual orientation—to transcend them and to share a commitment to core values such as equality and freedom. Remember the importance of this task—and your personal responsibility for it. As Dr. Seuss has said: "Unless someone like you cares a whole awful lot, nothing is going to get better. It's not."

There is an immediate way in which you can move out from the self-absorption that getting on with your lives necessarily will require. The year 2000 is, of course, a national election year in this republic. Some of you may have participated in various campaigns this past winter. Our democracy depends upon participation, and I urge you to continue joining in its processes, revitalizing it by your idealism and by the questions you can bring to the process.

American democracy must be more than a process for aggregating individual interests into a working majority. It also needs to promote a sense of civic responsibility that transcends the self and that recognizes our shared obligation to promote the common good. Barbara Jordan once said, "A spirit of harmony can only survive if each of us remembers, when bitterness and self-interest seem to prevail, that we share a common destiny." Such recognition is consistent with the best of our history, the strongest of our values, and the highest of our aspirations. . . .

. . . . You may wonder if graduation has really come so quickly. We look out at you and ask the same question. Time may be constant by the measurement of the great clock of the universe, but its passage is quite uneven in the timepieces of our hearts. Moments to be savored move far too swiftly. Members of the Class of 1951, whom we honor today, can tell you about the pace of time for I am sure it seems to them but a finger snap ago that they had their own commencement. On that occasion they watched the Class of '01—1901, that is—celebrate its fiftieth reunion. That was the Class of Ernest Martin Hopkins. And, indeed, a century earlier still, Daniel Webster graduated, as a member of the Class of 1801. Such overlaps mark every commencement and remind us of both our history and of our obligations to those who will follow us.

When we are young our lives are much devoted to planning, to concern for what is to be done in the future. When we are older, our lives focus more on things remembered, on what was done in our past. But life is neither a state of becoming nor one of memory. Life is a condition of being, and we must celebrate and cherish what we have. President Hopkins occasionally quoted from Robert Louis Stevenson that "those who miss the joy miss all." The Class of 1951, in their wisdom, will I know wish to shout that to you on this occasion.

At Dartmouth we talk a lot about our special sense of community—not as a physical neighborhood, although surely it is that, but as a gathering of people with a shared commitment to the life of the mind and to the work of enabling one another to aspire and to achieve. This is a place that at its best encourages curiosity and a willingness to take intellectual risks, while evoking a sense of friendship and of belonging. Together we have had times of learning, of laughter, of sharing, of becoming, and—this year, too often—times of grieving. In recent months we have lost friends and colleagues. Time moved too quickly and reminded us too late of the need to stretch out our hands and welcome every opportunity to meet and to know those whose lives intersect with our own—to say the things that should be said to those about whom we care.

We know all too well that no community is apart from the intrusion of tragedy. No peaceable kingdom is immune from violence. But the test of a community is not whether it is protected from bad and evil, but rather how it responds to these things when they come upon us without warning or reason. By this test, we can, in the midst of our pain, take pride. This community has responded well whenever challenged. The worst among us can never prevail so long as the best among us do not allow this to happen. I salute you, graduating seniors, for helping us to affirm this obligation. This Dartmouth tradition has resonated in the lives and deeds of graduates throughout this college's existence.

This day is marked by anticipation, as well as by reflection. Myrlie Evers-Williams once said, "I have reached a point in my life where I understand the pain and the challenges; and my attitude is one of standing up with open arms to meet them all." I hope that you, too, will meet the challenges ahead with open arms and a loving heart. At Dartmouth you have had opportunities to encounter and to reflect upon the best that has been thought and done. This campus resonates with optimism and with challenges to be met. So do and must the lives to which you now turn.

As you move ahead each of you will need to define what constitutes a full and a rewarding life for you. At your convocation in 1997, President James Freedman suggested that the question "How should I live my life?" is at the center of a liberal arts education. Now, four years later—four brisk years—you are ready to put your Dartmouth experience to the test. You are ready to dare yourself. Learning and knowledge are not, by and of themselves, sufficient elements of a good life. While they may be necessary conditions for human societies to flourish, they are neutral factors in shaping a life well led. Intelligence and learning can coexist—often too comfortably—with selfishness, with greed and, even with malice.

The Sabbath morning service includes the invocation, "Teach us to number our days, that we may attain a heart of wisdom." Learning needs finally to work with a heart that is generous and full of love, as well as one that is wise. When he conferred an honorary degree on Robert Frost, President John Sloan Dickey said, "The hardest part of getting wise is being always just a little otherwise." Some commentators have suggested that your generation is one that values accomplishment over virtue. I would not say this of you whom I have been privileged to know. In any good life achievement and goodness are not disparate, much less mutually exclusive, things. If the former comes at the price of the latter, the cost is far too high. As we now move into your century, remember that virtue and accomplishment sustain each other and that virtue has little to do with what we think about ourselves and has everything to do with how we relate to others. . . .

JUNE 9, 2002

. . . . Members of the Class of 2002: We started our assignment together on a soft September day in 1998, your first convocation and my inauguration becoming a singular moment—happily so in my view and as such forevermore in my memory.

On that day I shared with you these few lines from Emily Dickinson:

We never know how high we are
Till we are asked to rise
And then if we are true to plan
Our statures touch the skies.

I affirm here today, with the endorsement of the faculty and in the company of your families and friends, that you are a group that has soared to impressive heights.

Back in the fall of 1998 you each entered into this community with certain understandings about yourself and, most likely, with certain assumptions about what you would do here, as well as how you might lead your lives after June of 2002. It has been the college's purpose over these four years to encourage you to test those things you thought you knew about yourself and to expand the context for this lifetime process.

Because your own understandings of who you are and what you are about are individual ones, profoundly personal and subjective matters, I would not presume to assess your progress in reflecting upon them. I hope, though, that you have found here a place where you were challenged by the faculty and your classmates and where you could test your own assumptions and values.

Lives are not programmed things simply to be lived out according to plan or design. Ability, will, purpose, hard work, discipline—these surely are determinants of the directions of our lives. But so too is luck; and so also are the actions of others and those historical forces that are beyond our control. The events of the last four years have significantly altered the context for your self-discovery and your articulated ambitions. The world may appear a different place today from the one you looked to four years

211

ago. In these years you have seen times of tragedy, of cruelty, and of war. You have seen our political system embroiled in battles over impeachment and in contests over the outcome of a presidential election. You have seen significant economic fluctuations, from heady highs to disconcerting lows. You have celebrated a new millennium and have seen the unlocking of the genomic code—and you now know that understanding this basic biochemical cornerstone of our lives does not alleviate tensions over race, religion, and boundaries.

We have together been eyewitnesses to horror and hatred: from the Middle East to lower Manhattan, from the Pentagon to the quiet Pennsylvania countryside, from a school in suburban Denver to back roads in Texas and the high plains of Wyoming. And our own peaceable kingdom here has been stunned by inexplicable tragedy and choked in grief.

It is hard to mourn the innocent on the scale that we have had to mourn and also to maintain our own sense of innocence. Nonetheless your lessons here and your lives before you must not be ones of fear, apprehension, suspicion, pessimism, and cynicism. Knowledge of who we are, of our own values and priorities; understanding the ways in which our background, our race and gender shape us and perhaps privilege us—these are important things. But we also need to know, really know, who others are.

Our self-knowledge is wholly inadequate if others become a focus of our fear or our hatred or our dismissal. Hatred can never win unless we allow it to win. Confronting it is never simply a passive exercise. You must never allow the worst among us to represent you or your time; you simply must not. And I have seen enough of you to know that you will not. Despite the unexpected and unwanted turns of history, despite the tragedies that have screamed out for our attention and commanded our tears, your four years here have also been marked by a world filled with love and caring, with poetry and music, with curiosity and discovery, with hope and encouragement—with people daily doing the small things to make the world a better and a more humane place.

Our task is to make certain that these things continue to dominate. The most successful among you—defining success in your own personal ways—will be those who continue to learn, to adapt, to deal with those things you have to deal with; those who never confuse independence of thought with selfishness of action. Never forget who you are and what is important to you. Encourage and nurture your best instincts. Olympic

212

hero Jesse Owens said, "The battles that count aren't the ones for gold medals. The struggles within yourself—the invisible, inevitable battles inside all of us—that's where it's at."

So your work, your assignment, is not ended today. This is indeed commencement, not conclusion. Rest assured, you are prepared for the sequel. Learning about yourself; relating to the human, the cultural, the physical world around you; adapting to the changes that mark history and shape lives; facing tragedy and acknowledging setbacks—at this point you know these are not only assignments of the academy, but are also your responsibilities for a lifetime. Do not ever doubt your capacity to take on these matters. Whatever the challenge, your stature will continue to reach the skies. . . .

. . . . Goodness, this day has come upon us quickly. I recall greeting you in the fall of 1999, when the world seemed to be your oyster, to be opened and enjoyed. The past four years have not followed script. They have been marked by economic dislocation, by the anxiety of war, and by the fear of terrorism. And our own community has been jarred by loss and tested by tragedy.

Joining you here this morning, are members of the Class of 1953, returning for their fiftieth reunion. On the weekend of their graduation, a member of the Class of 1903 passed along greetings that members of the Class of 1853 had, a half-century earlier, asked them to transmit! Having shared this salutation, he in turn asked the Class of 1953 to remember the '03s "the 1903s" to you. The consecutive bearers of those greetings, spanning a century and a half, represent enduring values and traditions of Dartmouth.

While such links connect you to Dartmouth's past, and while your recollections of your college years pull at you today, this is fundamentally a time to look ahead. Of course, we should learn from our history. We build upon our experiences and are enriched by our memories, each providing us with important guidance. But these are never predictors for the future or recipes for life. Members of the Class of 1953 can tell you about occasions coming on too quickly and of the continuing need to improvise on the plan of life.

The world is still your oyster. It may seem a little scratched and discolored, a little dented perhaps, spinning a bit off the course you had projected; but none of us who are older would hesitate to travel with you through the uncertain times you face. Although life is not scripted, it can be led; and your lives will be shaped by your capacity to respond to changed circumstances, by the values you hold most deeply and tenaciously, and by the ambitions you set for yourselves.

In one of his poems, William Merwin wrote about the image of the physical world that endures despite the onset of blindness. "It is all awake in the darkness," he declared. So need be your principles and values, and the liberal education that informs them. Today, you are ready for the twists and turns of life; and no darkness can extinguish the light that is in you.

In 1953 President John Sloan Dickey invited President Dwight D. Eisenhower to receive an honorary degree at that year's commencement exercises. In an historic, well-publicized statement, President Eisenhower urged the graduates not to join "the book burners," an obvious and pointed challenge to the excesses of McCarthyism and a remarkably clear call for openness to ideas and tolerance towards those with whom we might disagree. President Eisenhower's comments that day offered much more than the criticism of the book burners, which produced the headlines across the nation. He also told the graduates here that there were two qualities he wished them to embrace: joy and courage. Joy, that which makes for a happy life, is obviously personal, but it is critical. And President Eisenhower thought courage equally important. He described honesty and integrity as manifestations of courage—the honesty to look closely at ourselves and what we do, the resolution to face those broader matters that seem to be simply wrong, the courage to confront them.

A year before *Brown v. Board of Education*, the president, in front of Baker Library, challenged "the disgrace of racial discrimination." The old war hero went on to say it was good, but not sufficient, to salute the flag and to sing "The Star-Spangled Banner." Individuals also needed, he suggested, the courage and the resolution to make their country better. "It is not yet done," he said to the Class of 1953. "You must add to it."

So, now we stand here today reminded of a sense of history and tradition, a recognition of connection to the Class of 1853, participating in a ritual that dates back to the founding of the college. We raise our hands to you not only in farewell salutation, but also as an embrace—a sign of our commitment to stand by you. I will not seek to improve upon President Eisenhower's formulation in my charge to you. Life is to be enjoyed; don't try to follow a path that does not permit you to be true to yourself. How you live your life is up to you. Our hope is that you will do so thoughtfully, generously to others, and fairly to yourselves led by ambitions that respond to circumstance and are shaped by values that transcend circumstance.

The fulfillment that marks a good life requires integrity and honesty and sharing and giving. It also requires recognition that full and satisfying lives finally are not measured by what you do for yourselves but by what you do for others and for the natural world that is your legacy—and your responsibility. "It is not yet done" remains your life assignment.

My bet is on you—and I say this with an assurance that comes from my experience with you and from knowing the faculty's regard for you and for what you have done. These provide the best base we have for the wager of life. You have strengthened your college; you are fully ready to take on what comes next—and to help shape, for the better, what that is. You slip away from the Hanover plain in the year when the Old Man fell off the mountain. But as that symbol survives, fixed in our memories, so your experiences here will remain in your hearts. You are prepared for the "girdled earth" before you. And '03s, the world had best be ready for you! . . .

. . . . Members of the Class of 2004, you have the special privilege today of graduating in the company of a former president of the college who is here for his fiftieth reunion. David T. McLaughlin as student, as graduate, as trustee, as Dartmouth president, as man of business, and as world citizen has devoted a lifetime to making this a better and a stronger place. Mr. President-Emeritus, welcome back to campus—and thank you for all you have contributed to your college as well as to our world.

The Class of 1954 joins you today as they commemorate the fiftieth anniversary of their graduation. The Korean War marked their time at Dartmouth, and they could, I know, share with you many stories of hope prevailing over fear despite the twists and turns that occur in life. They took seriously the task that each generation of Dartmouth graduates assumes. They have done much to make the world better, and they have done much to make Dartmouth stronger.

This morning you have walked onto the college green for the final time as undergraduate students. Theodor Geisel of the Dartmouth Class of 1925 had a friend, Dr. Seuss, who described well what I know you must now be feeling:

My goodness how the time has flewn.
How did it get so late so soon?

We come together here for a ceremony marked by tradition and shaped by ritual; one that aims to celebrate your accomplishments. Embrace this day for it symbolically and substantively affirms your place in the Dartmouth legacy. Today, you participate in a ritual rooted in our past; you are at a place where the buildings around you have absorbed the echo of your voices and those of generations before you; and you are part of the company of friends who will stand by you for a lifetime. Tradition, place, friends—and a faculty committed to working with you in learning and expanding that which is known. This is Dartmouth.

But as we celebrate your class, we also recognize each of you. I wish I could sit down with you individually—to tell you how much we regard you, to ask about your personal dreams and to encourage you to pursue them, and to assure you of our confidence in you. Most importantly, given such an opportunity, I would tell you why you should have confidence in yourself. It is easy to get caught up in the anonymity of crowd, to be swept along by the pace of life, to be shaped by the unexpected patterns of history. But you did not spend four years here to allow these things to happen. Have confidence in yourself and in what you stand for.

You have learned here as part of your liberal education to be wary of generalizing about others. I hope you have also learned not to generalize about yourself. You are not defined by your surroundings, captured by your history, or encouraged to be a follower of the crowd. I have been inspired and impressed over the past four years by your accomplishments — and by your stories.

I told you at your convocation ceremony on September 19, 2000 that "every one of you is here this morning because of who you are. We selected and invited you individually—with attention to your accomplishments, your personal potential, your capacity to make this a stronger and more interesting place, your own promise to live lives that will make those of others fuller, richer, more informed. We expect much of you, as you have already demanded much of yourselves." Now, four fleeting years later, you have surely met our expectations and what constituted Dartmouth's challenge. You leave us the better. We could ask no more — or less — of anyone. Your learning, your service, your sharing, your generosity, these are your record and our inspiration. At this point you move on to a world that needs you — dearly needs you. It is a world that seems too often to reverberate with shouts of hatred, one that cries out with sorrow and that is punctuated too often with the tragic silence of the innocent. Margaret Atwood gave us this advice: "This is the world, which is fuller/and more difficult to learn than I have said."

Know well your capacity and your power to shape your lives, your communities, and your world. Humankind, this world, is far better than our fears. But it can only be as good as our dreams when our efforts would have it be. For all who scream to the worst of our instincts, there are many, many more who live to the best of our hopes, who hug and comfort a child, who love and encourage a friend, who sustain those upon whom fortune has inadequately — or never — smiled.

No sounds of violence or hatred should prevail over quiet expressions of human faith. Langston Hughes urged us to "let America be the dream the dreamers dreamed." With the privilege of your education and with spiritual and other values to provide direction, you can foster that American dream and encourage whispers of hope. . . .

JUNE 12, 2005

. . . . Among those who join us today are members of the Class of 1955. They share with you the distinction of having matriculated as the largest class in Dartmouth's history. They also share with you, I am sure, the sensation that this day has come on quickly—very quickly. If they were to advise you now, I suspect that among other things they would say is that life cannot be counted on as living out according to plans. Adjusting to the twists and turns that will abruptly confront you is the sign of a good education—and such adjustment is something the better and the more pleasant when aided by those who care for you and when in the company of those for whom you profoundly care.

You matriculated shortly after 9/11—a day that the poet Lucille Clifton described as, "thunder and lightning / and our world is another place." At the 2001 Convocation, I related to this community that you were joining into the world of which we are a part. I said to you then: "There are those who suggest that the world of higher education is an ivory tower set apart from some "real" world. Let me say that this world—this so-called ivory tower, this world of ideas, of possibility, of wonder and discovery, of embracing difference and of celebrating accomplishment—that this world is indeed more real than are worlds marked by hatred, violence, and cruelty. Do not permit the cynics and the fearful to insist otherwise. Your task is to make the realities that are the everyday stuff of Dartmouth more common in the world at large. And, so, here we come to your assignment—not simply your first assignment at Dartmouth, but your assignment for a lifetime.

Now, four years later, that remains your task as you now move on from Dartmouth. My hope for you is that with the values that you have lived and learned and taught here, that you will advance the best of your dreams. You will be distracted to be sure, but never be deterred.

In *The Greatest Generation*, Tom Brokaw reminded us of the sacrifices that the World War II generation made for this country. I, too, remember them coming back from the war—so young still and, yet, the innocence of youth was gone from them prematurely. Their legacy, though, may be less a result of their remarkable courage and sacrifice and more that they did not respond to history's heavy demand upon them by subsequently withdrawing into lives of cynicism and bitterness. They surely did not seek the task that they had taken on, but they did not turn away from it. And that, finally, is all that we can ask of any generation.

On a starry night, September 12, 2001, members of this community gathered here on the green, where we assemble today. They were holding candles and surrounded by light softly reflecting from the facades of Dartmouth Row and of Baker Library. We gathered to grieve and to resolve together, and a number of you were there that night. That evening, I quoted Robert Frost, who had walked across those same paths around this green so many times. Mr. Frost wrote in "Birches": "I'd like to get away from earth awhile / And then come back to it and begin over." While many of us would have been forgiven then for thinking that such a withdrawal from the world might have been a fine option, you never took that route. You know just how much you can do. You have no limits. But our work together here will have been incomplete if you think all accomplishments can be measured and counted. I hope you have learned here, too, the value of contemplative absorption in a good book, an inspiring performance, a stunning work of art, a quiet sunset, and simply good moments with good friends. I know that you have learned about service to others because we have observed the good works that you have done.

Over the last thirty-six years I have seen a lot of classes pass across the Hanover plain, and it is impossible—and surely would be foolhardy to attempt—to make comparisons among them. But I can say to you, Class of 2005, that you are an impressive group. You leave your college the stronger and you have emphatically affirmed your intent always to make certain that it is. My farewell to you is tinged with regret that you leave too soon—but it is warmed by tremendous gratitude for what you have done and confidence in what it is you will do.

. . . . The Class of 1956 gathers with us today to renew their friendships, to share with one another the paths they have taken, and to salute your accomplishments and to send you warmly on to the next phases of your lives. We celebrate them for what they have done and for the continuity they bring to this gathering.

The world that waits to welcome you seems different from the world that greeted them a half century ago. But this would be true in any half century of history. The world does not stand still, nor, indeed, do we. As was true with the Class of 1956, your education will see you through a life filled with change. As they have, you will take on the world's problems and will maximize life's opportunities.

President John Sloan Dickey told the Class of 1956, that the world will be better only if we assume responsibilities for the challenges we face. And our commencement speaker, Elie Wiesel, has said, "the opposite of love is not hate, the opposite of love is indifference." The world will be better only if those who are motivated by hatred and cruelty, and a lust for power are challenged by those who are not. The world will be better only if those who are privileged by life and history accept that life and history have not really been constructed simply to privilege them. It will be better only when we recognize those things that are truly important and know they cannot easily be counted or measured.

Last October at a military hospital, I talked to a young soldier who had been seriously wounded in Iraq. He had lost one limb and had other serious injuries, including terrible physical disfigurement, especially of his face. My heart went out to him as he described how an explosion had shattered his Humvee and his body. Confined to a wheelchair, he was eager to get on with his life. He hoped first to return to his unit, and then he would think of returning to school. I turned from the young soldier to speak to his father, who was standing close to him. I asked where they were from, and he said the Gulf Coast. This was a month after Hurricane Katrina, so I expressed to them the hope that they had come through the storm okay. The father replied that they had lost everything they had, everything. But then he put a hand affectionately on his son's shoulder, saying, "But that is okay. My boy is alive, and I now know what is important in life."

We all need, instinctively and surely without such harsh lessons, to know what is important in life, and it must be more than what we possess. It is the love and well being of family and friends. It is caring for those who do not share our good fortune. You have cared, members of the Class of 2006, you have reached out often and unselfishly—to Tanzania, and Darfur, and Southeast Asia, and Pakistan, and to the Gulf Coast. And you have extended a hand to our own neighbors here in the North Country. You have affirmed that you assume responsibility both for your world—and for your natural environment—and also for your college.

Four years ago, at your convocation, I asked you to take on one of the fundamental tasks of our time: learning to navigate those categorizations such as race and ethnicity that can divide us. You took on the challenge, and I salute you. We surely have work yet to do, but we here are the better because of your efforts. You now need to embrace the fact that this is a lifetime assignment—for Dartmouth always, but also for you as individuals, as you move on from this place. And how well you handle this challenge will shape your world.

Many of the world's tragedies have come from natural disaster, but those shaped by human cruelty are in so many ways the greater. So many of the tensions of our time flow from suspicion, hatred, or arrogance derived from constructs that are set by race, religion, national origin, gender, or sexual orientation.

These categories need to be embraced as descriptions that enlarge and enrich the human condition, rather than as ones that divide and confine. Our fundamental and shared humanness should never accept fear or hatred as being inevitable parts of our condition.

I have confidence in you, and I have faith in the liberal arts education that you have received. It is an education for a lifetime. But it must be used to be of value. Remember that learning is forever—the capacity to take on the new and the unexpected, for relearning and unlearning, these are essential components of your education. Knowing how you relate to the physical, the natural, the historical, the human world gives you a context for all that you do. Appreciating the richness and the range of human creativity can brighten our darkest times. And knowing your own values, knowing your own values and affirming them, when it is hardest to affirm these things, all of this will stand you well. . . .

JUNE 10, 2007

. . . . I would like also to extend a special salute to all of you who are receiving graduate and professional degrees. We celebrate your accomplishments, and we are enriched by your contributions to this community of learning. We have full confidence in you and all that you will accomplish.

Members of the Class of 2007, at your convocation I welcomed you to the world of the liberal arts. The liberal arts provide us with a context, with a means of reflecting on who we are and what we value, how we understand our world and relate to our time and place in the human experience. But this journey is not confined to four years. You are now prepared for a lifetime of learning. Knowledge is never static. . . . Acknowledging our limits does not mean accepting them. Take with you an insatiable curiosity, an absence of stubborn certainty, and a capacity to adapt to change. At the opening ceremony of Winter Carnival this year, I reminded you of Alice's discovery in Wonderland: "Alice had begun to think that very few things indeed were really impossible." Continue to extend the possible and dream big dreams.

You have learned that the world can sometimes be a scary place. You have seen individuals guided by the dark voices within them or led by demagogues of hate from without. You grew up with scenes of Columbine, were stunned by 9/11, and now you reflect on images of Virginia Tech.

But as Dartmouth graduates, you know neither to accept pessimism or fatalism nor to hunker down in fear. There are in this world vastly more people who care than there are those who hate. Love and respect and caring can stand up to evil and hatred. They can do so if those who embrace those values will stand.

One of the problems of our time may be the growth of a culture of fear, where our children grow up afraid of strangers and wary of the strange. Walls and gates of security come with some costs. Liberty, freedom of thought, of speech, of belief, and of association; a culture that welcomes the different and a society that assumes responsibility for the less fortunate; openness, generosity, curiosity—these explain American society at its best. They are not abstract sentiments to be traded for a false sense of security.

You are here today through hard work and discipline and accomplishment. But you are also here by the accident of history, rather than through a history predetermined to entitle you. You are part of a privileged company and with that privilege comes responsibility. The agenda of your time will surely include fundamental changes in the global economy, in international security, in energy availability, in the earth's temperatures, in the tensions of nationalism, of religion, of race, of difference. Remember that in a world of change there are those who are left behind. But the difference between the social contract of human society and the natural world of selective survival is the existence of a common responsibility for the weak and the vulnerable and for each other. Education is not enough to assure wise or good or responsible citizens. These need draw on their moral and spiritual energy, forces that I hope and trust have been sharpened here.

What are the shared truths and values of your generation? It is okay not to be sure of the answers; but I do hope you have pondered that question. To be uncertain about shared values, faith, conviction, and purpose is not to be cynically indifferent to them.

The Class of 1957 joins us today. Fifty years ago they left here to live lives, to meet goals, to make a difference. Their college welcomes them back with great pride. So many have done so much. But if you were to ask them to reflect on lives well led, I suspect few of them would mention quantifiable markers and even fewer would measure by currency or tangible possessions.

There is of course nothing at all wrong with you seeking to accomplish measurable things and nothing wrong with material success. You will, I expect, do well. But along the way you will recognize that material accomplishments do not alone make a satisfying life.

At the 1957 Commencement, President John Dickey said: "Caring is a precious thing. Its intensity is personal to all creatures. . . . The quality of your caring is what Dartmouth is all about. Remembering this you will fail neither her nor yourself, and you will grow in grace." Your legacy here of service and of generosity attests that you have already grown in grace.

Never stop. Carry with you images of this special place—and take one more with you in your mental album: the Inuit sculpture standing in front of McNutt Hall. It reminds us of Dartmouth's historic ties and ongoing commitment to Native American education. And it whispers, "welcome," as you always will be here.

. . . . As one who has been at Dartmouth for many commencements over many years, I still admit to the bittersweet ambivalence of this occasion. We say farewell this morning, too soon, to those who have inspired and energized us, as well as one another, and who leave a good place the better. But if we have done our job well here, this is not necessarily and inevitably the final step. It is the next step. It is not too soon, but it is just right. So it is with pride that today we witness your ceremonial transition from student to graduate, and we salute you as you now go on to make the world the better. Leave your doubts behind because you are more than ready for this challenge.

For all of your shared experiences and memories, each and every one of you harbors your own hopes and your own expectations. It is critical for you to have ambitions and dreams. However, it is also essential to know that lives are to be lived—and that the most interesting ones resist planning. As Gwendolyn Brooks wrote, "Live not for the end-of-the-song. Live in the along."

Some will tell you—and somewhat condescendingly they will tell you—that you are now joining the "real world." But I will not allow this assertion to go unchallenged. Places such as Dartmouth, which are fundamentally concerned with ideas and ideals—places that explore the unknown; that value independence, creativity, and a sense of true community where all are welcome and all are included—such places are very much part of the real world. Dartmouth is a place where individuals can make a difference, where learning is a lifetime commitment, where those of us who have been privileged by the randomness of fate now assume a responsibility for those who have not shared in our good fortune, and where our real world is a true world, a global place, where the parochial and the narrow have ever-decreasing consequence.

The worlds of commerce and health care, of law and diplomacy, of public service and military service, of teaching and research, and of artistic creativity, these are each rooted in Dartmouth's real world—the world of learning, of grappling with the fundamental questions about the human condition, of breathtaking moments of human creativity. They are rooted in this place that encourages teamwork, responsibility, and leadership. They are rooted in a world here that encourages students and faculty to engage always in discovery. Those who will lead in the world beyond, stand here in this world today—you. And they are ready; you are ready— ready intellectually, morally, and personally—to lead.

Ellen Johnson-Sirleaf, who has spoken to us today, used her education to challenge the powerful military and political authorities in her home- land of Liberia, and she used her knowledge to transform her country. Some of you may lead nations—perhaps this nation. Most of you will not. But each of you can make a difference, a difference as leaders in your lives and your communities.

Speak to members of the fifty-year class who join us here today. Their memories of half a century have been both complicated and enriched by twists of history that none of them could possibly have predicted back in 1958 when they stood in front of Baker Library to celebrate their singular moment. They went on to make a difference, and we are proud of their embrace of John Sloan Dickey's challenge to them that "the world's prob- lems are your problems."

Most immediately you of the Class of 2008 can make a difference by participating in the forthcoming national election. Four years ago, in Sep- tember of 2004, I greeted you at convocation as we were entering then the last six weeks of a presidential election campaign. I told you then that it was your future that was being debated. I acknowledged that it was not being debated very well—that the well-being of our political system is de- pendent upon the engagement of the young—upon you—and that you should not allow the process to be distorted by anything that was less than real debate over real issues. Personal attacks, cynical manipulation, and game-board strategy about red and blue states are not debates, and they do not engage the issues. Paul Simon and Art Garfunkel described it well over forty years ago:

> People talking without speaking,
> People hearing without listening,
> People writing songs that voices never share.

The problems of our time are serious and the possible solutions are likely to be complicated. You have learned here the value of debate and the importance of testing ideas, the importance of standing for values that you believe in, even as you listen to and learn from those who differ with you. The wider world needs you now, and we are confident that you are ready to take on this, your next assignment. . . .

JUNE 14, 2009

. . . . So here we are at commencement, by definition and design a beginning, not an end—hard though it is for some of us to get our arms around
that distinction today. But we shall. My approach to this ceremony has
been to encourage graduates, on a day filled with memories, to embrace
the future.

We acknowledge that this is a beginning in a world that is different
from the one you likely imagined when you came to Dartmouth. And that
fact alone should provide all the rationale you need for the value of a Dartmouth education.

The liberal arts provide you with the intellectual capacity to deal with
the unexpected. And the best advice I can give is that you should always
expect the unexpected. The Class of 1959, whom we welcome today in
celebration of the fiftieth anniversary of their commencement, can affirm
that the world in which lives are lived and dreams are pursued is an un-
predictable place. Despite this, they accomplished much, and we salute
them with pride and welcome them back with affection.

But you also know about unpredictability. Your class matriculated during the same year as the tragedy of Katrina; you saw war in Iraq reach its
most violent depths; you were horrified by acts of genocide; you spent
your senior year facing the headwinds of the greatest economic downturn since the 1930s. But you also shared in the excitement of the historic
inauguration of an African American as president of the United States,
bore witness to the first Olympic games hosted in China. You experienced
firsthand the power of social networking sites like Facebook and Twitter,
which will change the ways in which we interact with one another.

In your time here, you have engaged the forces of change, the twists of
fate and the turns of history. Some of you volunteered to support Katrina's
victims; others joined the political campaigns. You advocated for the
people of Darfur; you decided to enlist in the military or to join the Peace
Corps or to teach or to participate in service groups. And all of you are
imbued with a commitment to make a difference and the confidence to

believe that you can, whether you seek to do that on the world's stage, in your profession, or in your local community.

Over the years I have shared with graduates some of my observations about the potential they have in a world of change. I would summarize them:

> It is fine to seek fame and fortune. You never need to be defensive about pursuing material dreams, which many of you will succeed in achieving. But the best things in life cannot be counted or owned. Rather, they can be enjoyed—and they can be most fully enjoyed with those whom you care about and those who care about you.
>
> A corollary is that each of us associated with Dartmouth is privileged, regardless of the degree of privilege with which we arrived here.
>
> With privilege comes responsibility, a responsibility to those who do not share our good luck. No personal accomplishment is as rewarding as watching those whom you have encouraged, mentored, taught, and supported accomplish their dreams.
>
> Be independent and self-sufficient, but be those things without also being selfish or lonely. Reach out to help others or to seek a helping hand when you need it.
>
> And, finally, even though many of you think you know what you will do with your lives and when you will do it, you are due for some surprises. Embrace the surprises and pursue the unplanned. Lives are things to be lived; they are not agendas to be followed.

My approach to this ceremony has been to encourage graduates, on a day filled with emotion, to embrace the future. I still do that even as I grapple with the same bittersweet feelings of not being quite sure about letting go of the present. Each of our lives is energized by our dreams and aspirations and is anchored by experiences that fill our memories. Memories are wonderful, but for the young it is dreams that must dominate. You can all be forgiven for allowing memories of friends and experiences, of the sights and sounds of this place, to fill your thoughts today. So they do with me. But we all need to resist surrendering to memory in ways that suggest that the best parts of our lives are done. Dartmouth encourages our aspirations and our confidence; let us not relegate this place of optimism and hope to the fixed frame of memory.

As I told you four years ago, we have work to do, you and I. And so now we each move on to another phase of that life assignment. As we do, Susan and I will follow your accomplishments even while we pursue our own new adventures and dreams. If the memories of my life enrich it immensely, I am not yet ready to allow them to crowd out the dreams. But I surely shall cherish those dreams and those memories. But now, now it is time for leave taking. And this takes on a new and more personal meaning for me today. As Dr. Seuss asked, "My goodness how the time has flewn. How did it get so late, so soon?"

Finally, this day is about you, and surely it is for you. We know that you go forth from Dartmouth in good and capable hands—your own. Near the end of the nineteenth century Walt Whitman wrote, "The strongest and sweetest songs yet remain to be sung." We leave them, still, for your voices. But know too as you leave today that the door here is always open. The Inuit sculpture standing in front of McNutt Hall reminds us of Dartmouth's historic ties and ongoing commitment to Native American education. But that is more than a reminder of our history. It also whispers to each of us, "welcome," welcome as you always will be here. You are ever a part of Dartmouth undying, as Dartmouth is forever a part of you. President John Sloan Dickey always concluded his annual commencement address by saying, "And now the word is 'so long' because in the Dartmouth fellowship there is no parting."

So, good and sustaining friends, congratulations. I am so very proud of you. Good luck.

And, so long.

5

FAREWELL

LETTER TO THE DARTMOUTH COMMUNITY, JUNE 29, 2009

Dear Dartmouth Friends,

Susan and I have finished a period of several weeks marked by generous farewells and "last time" occasions. I have been engaged in the work of our spring academic calendar, even as I prepare for a time of transition in the history of Dartmouth as well as a major change in our personal lives. Commencement and class reunions beautifully completed a very full year. As I suggested to the graduates two weeks ago it is a bittersweet time. It is also a time that we will always treasure. Susan and I would like to thank all of you who have made our time at Dartmouth so special.

We have now moved into our home overlooking Lake Sunapee and the mountains. I will have an office in one of the college buildings in downtown Hanover, where I will work on sorting some of my papers, participating in the Dartmouth oral history project, pulling together some of my addresses and papers for publication, and serving the college in any way that I can. I have taken on a few non-Dartmouth speaking and conference engagements, and I will also continue my work on behalf of veterans. I am excited by these prospects.

Even as we move on, I am also excited about the future of Dartmouth. President Jim Yong Kim was an inspired choice, and he has demonstrated that he will be an inspiring president. He already understands so well Dartmouth's mission, values, and legacy even as he seeks to expand our ambitions. We enthusiastically join in welcoming him and his family, Dr. Younsook Lim, Thomas, and Nicolas. How lucky we are to have this family in residence in Hanover. How lucky Dartmouth is to have this first family!

I do take satisfaction in all of the things that the college accomplished during my administration. I know full well that any accomplishments are due to the generosity of the many friends of the college, to the commitment and strength of the faculty, to the tremendous hard work of my colleagues in the administration, and to the incredible talents of our stu-

James Wright and Susan DeBevoise Wright on Baker Tower, October 2008. Photo by Joe Mehling.

dents. Anytime I needed to be reminded of the importance of our work, I simply joined students for lunch, went to hear their academic presentations, watched them compete in athletic contests representing their college so well, or joined in applauding their performances and exhibitions. They energize us all, and they affirm our purpose.

Surely there are things that I wish we could have completed. I say this knowing the good task we are engaged in is always unfinished. I told graduating seniors and some alumni/ae this spring that the task of administering Dartmouth is really quite simple and that there are two fundamental goals: First, to provide an educational experience for each class, for each generation of Dartmouth students, that is so special, that meets their needs so fully, that they graduate from Dartmouth convinced it surely could not be improved upon—and so no one better change it! And then even as they graduate we need to begin the work to make certain that we initiate whatever changes are required to meet the needs of the incoming class and to respond to the changing expectations of our world. Doing these two things well is what assures the finest educational experience and what makes for an enduring institution—and one that deserves to endure!

The downturn in the economy derailed a number of final projects and of course caused some difficult reductions in our budget. Dartmouth handled these well. Early on we worked with the board on setting our goals, we sought significant community input into ways in which we might proceed, we made clear that financial aid and faculty positions would not be reduced, and we consulted on the details. We worked through it early and did all reductions at once, except for the Medical School. It was difficult. We had hoped to avoid layoffs but finally some were inevitable. This was the hardest part; we lost some very good people.

I visited with the twelve classes who returned for their reunions this year; I was pleased to see so many women and men whom Susan and I knew as students. And I was humbled by their fundraising accomplishments on behalf of the college despite the state of the economy. I am reminded that at times like this, Dartmouth graduates have always stepped up to make certain that the current generation of students continues to have the finest educational experience available anywhere. Thanks to all of you who have remembered and have personally affirmed your support of this wonderful story.

James and Susan Wright as they left the platform at President Wright's last commencement in 2009. Each of them had just been awarded an honorary Dartmouth doctorate. Photo by Joe Mehling.

Summit of Moosilauke in 2009. Photo by unidentified hiker using Joe Mehling's camera.

Wright passing the Wentworth bowl to President Jim Yong Kim at his inauguration as Dartmouth's seventeenth president, September 2009. Photo by Joe Mehling.

Over Memorial Day weekend, Susan joined me in doing something I wanted to accomplish before I stepped down. We asked several students to join us in a climb of Mt. Moosilauke to honor the hundred-year anniversary of the founding of the Dartmouth Outing Club. Although I thought I was in pretty good physical condition, I realized early on that I had taken on a more difficult assignment than anticipated. The students allowed me to set the pace—a steady one, but very slow!—and they were incredibly supportive and helpful. Anytime I would stumble a bit I felt a hand steady my arm.

Two of the students whom I had invited to be part of our small group were Marines who are now enrolled at Dartmouth. I reminded them that Marines don't leave Marines along the trail! They didn't—in fact they kept asking if they could carry my backpack. My pride overruled my instinct only for a time, and then I happily handed it over. At the end of the trip, down at the Ravine Lodge, I said to the Dartmouth Marine who handed me back my pack, "Did you ever think when we first met, you recovering from serious wounds at Bethesda hospital, that we would climb a mountain together, and that you would carry my backpack along with your own?" He said, "No, sir, I didn't!"

Nor did I. But life takes some remarkable turns. I have now completed forty years serving Dartmouth, the last eleven as president, and I am filled with gratitude for all of the members of this community, literally 'round the girdled earth, who have reached to steady me and who have carried my backpack. We have climbed quite a mountain together. Susan and I will not forget you.

So long,

Jim Wright

A WELCOME TO THE WHEELOCK SUCCESSION, SEPTEMBER 22, 2009

It is my honor to join today in welcoming to the Wheelock Succession Jim Yong Kim, a man who will make a strong tradition the stronger. One of the sustaining qualities of Dartmouth's Presidency derives from the legacy of its founder, the Reverend Eleazar Wheelock. It was he who left a stern and unequivocal bequest to each of his successors. Nearly two hundred and forty years ago, Dr. Wheelock charged those who were to follow him with these words: "And it is my purpose, by the grace of God, to leave nothing undone within my power, which is suitable to be done; that this school of prophets may be and long continue to be a pure fountain. And I do with my whole heart will this my purpose to all my successors in the presidency of this seminary to the latest posterity, and it is my last will, never to be revoked. . . ." If we no longer define this college as a seminary and if modern humility inhibits us from describing ourselves as prophets, the fundamental task is constant. We are reminded of the continuity of this succession by the handsome silver monteith, known as the Wentworth Bowl, a gift from New Hampshire's Royal Governor, who, acting on behalf of the British Crown, granted Dartmouth's charter in December 1769. The bowl's inscription reads:

> His Excellency John Wentworth Esquire
> *Governor of the Province of New Hampshire,*
> *And those Friends who accompanied him*
> *To Dartmouth College the first Commencement 1771.*
> *In testimony of their Gratitude and good wishes*
> *Present this to the*
> *Reverend Eleazar Wheelock D.D. President*
> *and his Successors in that Office.*

President Kim, the sixteenth president of Dartmouth salutes the seventeenth president of this college. I enthusiastically celebrate your place in the Wheelock Succession. Susan and I are certain that your presidency will be one of fulfillment for you and Younsook and one of great accomplishment for Dartmouth. We have every confidence that the goodness and generosity of the members of this community will sustain you in the years to come.

And I now affirm and personally pledge that the bond of the Wheelock Succession will support you as you lead this noble institution so that it will always be a "pure fountain" of knowledge and a place that continues to encourage and to enable students who will assume the responsibility and the leadership of their generation. My warmest congratulations to you, sir.

And now if you will join me, President Kim, I am privileged to hand over to you a historic treasure that symbolizes the office you hold.

244